# Praise for *Minding Her Own Business*

"*Minding Her Own Business* is a great addition to anyone's business library. Zobel has the ability to explain financial issues in a clear and understandable manner."
  —Jane Applegate, nationally syndicated small business columnist;
  author, *201 Great Ideas for Your Small Business*

"One of the best I've seen."
  —Paul Tulenko, *Atlanta Business Chronicle*

"Essential reading for anyone thinking about, or already engaged in, having their own business."
  —*The Bookwatch*

"*Minding Her Own Business* is right on target. It addresses all those frequently asked questions that people who are starting and running their own business have. It is written in a clear, concise, understandable manner that makes the information easy to use. I will highly recommend it to all my clients."
  —Beth Wickham, Counselor, Business Development Center,
  *Central Oregon Community College*

"An excellent starting point for learning how to keep records effectively and becoming informed about the latest tax regulations."
  —*Library Journal*

"Whether handling the paperwork herself or contracting out for tax preparation services, every woman entrepreneur should read *Minding Her Own Business*—and keep it handy for future reference as well."
  —*The Midwest Book Review*

"*Minding Her Own Business* gives you the necessary tools to take control of your finances and run a successful small business. Highly recommended."
  —Salli Rasberry, coauthor of *Running a One-Person Business*

"A step-by-step guide that explains everything from reconciling a bank statement to filling out complicated tax forms."
  —Patricia Holt, *San Francisco Chronicle*

# MINDING HER OWN BUSINESS

The Self-Employed Woman's Essential Guide
to Taxes and Financial Records

By Jan Zobel
*Enrolled Agent*

SPHINX® PUBLISHING
AN IMPRINT OF SOURCEBOOKS, INC.®
NAPERVILLE, ILLINOIS
www.SphinxLegal.com

Fourth Edition: 2005

Published by: **Sphinx® Publishing, An Imprint of Sourcebooks, Inc.®**

<u>Naperville Office</u>
P.O. Box 4410
Naperville, Illinois 60567-4410
630-961-3900
Fax: 630-961-2168
www.sourcebooks.com
www.SphinxLegal.com

This publication is designed to provide accurate and authoritative information in regard to the subject matter covered. It is sold with the understanding that the publisher is not engaged in rendering legal, accounting, or other professional service. If legal advice or other expert assistance is required, the services of a competent professional person should be sought.

*From a Declaration of Principles Jointly Adopted by a Committee of the
American Bar Association and a Committee of Publishers and Associations*
**This product is not a substitute for legal advice.**
*Disclaimer required by Texas statutes.*

**Library of Congress Cataloging-in-Publication Data**
Zobel, Jan.
  Minding her own business : The Self-Employed Woman's Essential Guide to Taxes and Financial Records/ by Jan Zobel.-- 4th ed.
     p. cm.
  Includes index.
  ISBN 1-57248-455-1 (pbk. : alk. paper)
  1. Income tax--Law and legislation--United States--Popular works. 2. Self-employed women--Taxation--United States. I. Title.

KF6369.6.Z63 2004
343.7305'2--dc22
                                              2005022883

Printed and bound in Canada.
TR — 10 9 8 7 6 5 4 3 2 1

# Contents

## Section 7: Getting Help

*Over and over again courts have said that there is nothing sinister in so arranging one's affairs as to keep taxes as low as possible.*

—Judge Learned Hand

# Introduction

Once upon a time someone decided that financial matters were a man's domain. A woman's money and financial affairs were handled by her father, and after she married, they were handled by her husband. Many women overtly, or more subtly, received messages about money, such as *You don't need to worry about that; It's not polite to talk about money*; or, *You don't really need a career—just something to fall back on until you get married.*

Times have changed. Fortunately, most women are being more fully exposed to money principles. However, I still hear statements from many of the women I work with, like, "I've never understood anything about taxes;" "My father (or husband) has always handled my (our) finances;" or, "You'll probably think I'm dumb, but...."

Despite confusion and ambivalence about money and taxes, millions of women are starting their own businesses. According to the Center for Women's Business Research (Center), the number of women-owned businesses is growing at almost twice the rate of all businesses. The Center reports that in 2004, there were 10.6 million women-owned businesses representing 48% of all businesses, employing 19.1 million people, and generating $2.46 trillion in sales annually.

If you've picked up this book, it probably means you're thinking about joining or have already joined the ranks of the self-employed. Congratulations! As head of your own business, you're in charge. You're the one who gets to make all the decisions—what type of clients and customers you want to attract, how much to charge, where to locate the business, what hours you want to work, and much more.

You're also the one who has the responsibilities of being self-employed. And high on that list is your responsibility for keeping good financial records and meeting your tax obligations. You may choose to get help with part or all of this. Ultimately, however, the buck stops with you, so it is important that you understand what's needed.

> **EXAMPLE**
>
> *Elizabeth didn't realize that becoming self-employed meant her taxes would be different from what they were when she was an employee. It wasn't until she had her tax return prepared in March that she learned she could deduct all the business-related books and supplies she'd bought during the previous year. Unfortunately, by that time, she'd thrown away the receipts. As for all those miles she drove for her business last year, she had no idea she should have been keeping track of them. She tried to reconstruct what she could, but Elizabeth's taxes were higher than they would have been if she'd known how to keep track of her business expenses. Elizabeth owed so much on April 15th that the IRS penalized her for not having made tax deposits on a quarterly basis during the year.*

You've probably picked up this book because you want to avoid mistakes like Elizabeth's. Maybe you're frightened of the IRS and fear that a misstep could land you in jail. As you go through the pages of this book, I hope you will feel empowered by what you learn and use the information not only to avoid paying more than your fair share of taxes, but also to create an ongoing financial picture of your business.

Section 1 tells you why this book was written specifically for women. Although taxes have no gender bias, some women (and men) may be giving the IRS more than they need to. Section 1 also helps you get your business started correctly. The different entities under which you can operate your business, and the licenses and permits you need to have are discussed. Also, questions such as *Do I need to have a separate bank account for my business?* and *Should I have a separate credit card for my business?* are answered. This section also answers the perennial question *How do I know when I've really started my business?*

Section 2 provides the information you need to know about keeping records. You will learn easy methods to keep track of the money coming into and going out of your business. Chapter 7 tells you what the IRS expects to see when they call a taxpayer in for an audit. Chapter 11 gives tips and warnings about using a computer to do the recordkeeping for your business.

The often confusing topic of employees versus independent contractors is the focus of Section 3. If you're currently working as an employee, as well as being self-employed, this section explains the differences in your taxes. If you've recently become an entrepreneur after leaving your employee job, you will be especially interested to learn about the benefits that were available to you as an employee that you may no longer have once you're self-employed. Taxes for independent contractors are also covered in this section. If hiring help is on your to-do list, pay special attention to Chapter 15, as well as the chapters on payroll withholding and issuing 1099 forms.

Section 4 of this book is the one that many readers turn to first—what can you deduct when you have your own business? Your car? Your travel? Your home office? The costs you had in getting your business started? Read the requirements carefully and be sure to hold onto the necessary receipts. If you've been thinking about starting a retirement plan, Chapter 32 tells you about the different plans that are available and helps you decide on the one that's best for you.

Section 5 is the central spoke of this book. It discusses and shows the tax forms used by self-employed people. Some of the concepts from earlier and later chapters become even clearer as you see how they relate to your income tax forms. The focus isn't to teach you how to prepare your own tax return (although you may now have enough information to feel comfortable in doing so), but rather to help you see how all the pieces fit together onto that piece of paper—the Form 1040.

One of the most confusing areas for self-employed people is introduced in the chapters of Section 6—calculating and making quarterly estimated tax payments. The late comedian Red Skelton was once quoted as saying, "I always send in my estimated tax payments anonymously. If the government expects me to guess how much I owe, they can guess who owes it." While you might not choose this tactic, you can avoid penalties by becoming familiar with our pay-as-you-go tax system. If, after reading this section, you need more information about quarterly payments, Appendix B provides a step-by-step calculation of estimated tax payments, along with an area for you to do your own figuring.

Section 7 wraps up this book by telling you where to get help. If you don't have enough money to pay your taxes, are looking for help with your business bookkeeping, are concerned about being audited, or are wondering how long to keep records, this section answers all your questions. The different types of tax preparers and the pros and cons of using a computer tax program are also discussed.

Appendix A walks you through the steps of reconciling a bank statement. If this is a skill you've never mastered, you can be assured that you are not alone. Running a business means that you need to be constantly in touch with your finances, so it may be time to learn how to make your checkbook match your bank statement.

As mentioned earlier, Appendix B provides detailed information about calculating estimated tax payments.

Appendices C and D contain lists of resources, such as small business organizations, helpful books and publications, and tax-related websites, that provide further help in running your business.

In many cases, round numbers are used for the examples in this book. This is not meant to imply that you should use round numbers in your recordkeeping or tax preparation. Rather, it's intended as a way to move the focus away from the numbers so that more emphasis can be placed on the concept being illustrated.

Great effort was made to include the most current tax information and forms available at the time this book went to press. In many cases, tax and deduction rates for the year 2005 were not yet available. Most of the tax rates and forms included in this edition are for 2004 and are applicable for returns being prepared and filed in 2005. The IRS's website (**www.irs.gov**) and annually updated publications are a good source of information about changes in tax law.

Running a business is an exciting adventure, as well as a lot of hard work. Spending a little time learning the basics of recordkeeping and taxes will lessen your anxiety level and your work load, allowing you to spend more time doing the activities that led you to start your business in the first place.

*—Jan Zobel*

**Publisher's Note:** *The final version of some of the forms found throughout this text may not have been available at the time this book went to press. If the final version was not available, the Internal Revenue Service's official draft version was used in its place. Check with the IRS at 800-TAX-FORM or go to **www.irs.gov** for the latest version of any form.*

# Why a Tax Book for Women?

Taxes don't differentiate between women and men—the complexity of the laws leaves *everyone* feeling confused! In my years as a tax preparer, however, I've found that many women (and some men, as well) have the added difficulty of number-phobia. This is usually the result of not having been adequately exposed to math and finances while growing up. With number-phobia, a numbing or spacy sensation occurs when encountering a tax form, a bank statement, or any other piece of paper that already contains figures or requires the filling-in of numbers. This state of mind results in statements such as, "Taxes are my greatest fear about starting a business" or "I've never been good with numbers."

Do number-phobic women pay more than their share of taxes? Maybe. Women as a group tend to be cautious about the business deductions they claim. Many women entrepreneurs profess that they would rather pay more taxes than be audited.

Fortunately, this anxiety about numbers and taxes hasn't kept women from starting businesses at a rapid pace. In 1960, only 3% of this country's businesses were owned by women. Today, nearly 50% of all businesses are woman-owned. This increase is due to women seeking out the information they need—financial and otherwise.

This book is designed to be another piece of that necessary information. It was written with the belief that anyone—no matter how unfamiliar with or afraid of numbers—can learn to take charge of her finances. Calculators and computers can deal with the numbers. Your job is to learn how the numbers are used and what records you need to keep to make sure they're used to your advantage. This approach is designed to let those who are afflicted with number-phobia push it out of the way long enough to learn the underlying concepts that make up the tax system. Armed with that knowledge, a fear of numbers is less likely to cause anyone to pay more than her share of taxes.

# Determining What Is a Business

**2**

The IRS defines a business as being an activity you participate in regularly and continuously with the intent of making a profit. For tax purposes, the terms *self-employed, business owner* (if a sole proprietorship), and *independent contractor* all mean the same thing. (See the next chapter for information on sole proprietorships.)

Often, people who own a one-person service business (*e.g.*, consultants, graphic artists, psychotherapists, house cleaners) may think of themselves as being self-employed without realizing that they've created a business of which they're the owner. And while independent contractors may not think of themselves as business owners, the tax implications for them are the same as for any other small business. Look at these four women. They are business owners, although they may not think of themselves that way.

- Anne is a technical writer for Cyberspace Company. Her job is to put together a manual to accompany Cyberspace's new software program. Anne was hired as an *independent contractor* (that is, no taxes are withheld from her paycheck), not as an employee.
- Maria opened a needlepoint shop last year. She has an employee who works part-time in the store.
- Lenore sells skin care products at home parties. She also recruits new people to sell the products. This type of business is called *network* or *multilevel marketing*, which means that when Lenore's recruits make their own sales, Lenore gets a percentage of the sales price.
- LaToya is a psychotherapist who is an employee at a counseling center. She also has a small private practice and sees clients in her home office.

## Determining When a Business Starts

The IRS says once you are set up and ready (open) for business, you're considered to be in business. *Ready for business* means:

- you have obtained all necessary licenses and permits;
- you have rented store or office space (if you're planning to do that); and,
- you have told the public that your services or products are available.

(Chapter 4 discusses the licenses and permits you might need.)

Although the IRS expects you to be aware of your tax obligations from the start, if you plan to operate as a sole proprietor without employees, there is no need to let the IRS know you've opened a business. The IRS will be able to see that you are self-employed when you file your first income tax return after starting the business.

On the other hand, owners of partnerships, corporations, or limited liability companies (LLCs) *do* need to let the IRS know when they start a business, because these entities are required to have a *federal employer identification number* (FEIN). This number is necessary because partnerships and corporations exist separately from the individuals who own them, whereas a sole proprietorship is intimately connected to its owner so can usually use the owner's Social Security number. The differences between sole proprietorships, partnerships, corporations, and LLCs are discussed further in the next chapter.

# Choosing Your Business Structure | 3

Choosing the entity for your business is an important decision. There are often both tax and nontax reasons for choosing one entity over another.

## Sole Proprietorship

A *sole proprietorship* is a business owned by one person. The IRS usually allows a married couple to operate as a sole proprietorship, but this is the only exception to the one-person-only rule. Any other two (or more) people wanting to be in business together must choose an entity other than a sole proprietorship.

In a sole proprietorship, your business and you are one. You cannot borrow money from your business because you would be borrowing money from yourself. You cannot have the business buy a car because it's really you buying the car. As the owner, you cannot be treated as an employee of your business.

According to the IRS, nearly 80% of U.S. businesses are operated as sole proprietorships. That is because a sole proprietorship is the easiest, fastest, and cheapest way to set up and run a business. There are no government regulations that determine how the sole proprietorship is operated. Financial records are relatively easy to keep and tax returns are simpler than for other entities. As a sole proprietor, you don't need to account to anyone else. You can run the business in whatever way you choose.

One disadvantage to operating as a sole proprietorship is that it's hard to borrow money in the name of the business. Often, sole proprietors are forced to use a personal asset (such as a home) as collateral when applying for a loan for the business. Another disadvantage is that the owner of the business is responsible for all financial risks. She has unlimited liability, which means that her personal assets are at risk if someone sues the business. Sole proprietors also aren't able to have fringe benefits—

such as child care or health care costs—paid by the business, although they may offer these to any employees they have.

# Partnership

A *partnership* is two or more people in business together. As with a sole proprietorship, the partners cannot be treated as employees of their business. There are different types of partnerships. Sometimes all the partners are actively involved in the business. In other situations, one or more of the partners are investors or limited partners, while the other partners run the business. In either case, the partnership is a separate entity from the partners.

A partnership needs to have a federal identification number issued by the IRS. Your home state may also require an identification number for the partnership. The partnership files a tax return, but no taxes are paid with the return. Partners pay tax on the profits earned by the business. Each partner includes her share of the partnership income on her individual tax return. The profits (and losses) can be allocated unevenly, which may be helpful in reducing taxes for a high income partner.

Like a sole proprietorship, a partnership is relatively free of government interference. However, the partnership tax return is more complex than the Schedule C used by sole proprietors, and the recordkeeping system needs to be more sophisticated.

A partnership allows you to work with one or more partners. This means that the responsibility of running the business is shared with others. Being able to work well with the partners you select is crucial to the success of the partnership.

There are also disadvantages to operating as a partnership. The major one is that each partner is responsible for all the liabilities (*e.g.*, loans) of the business. All partners are bound by any business contracts signed by any other partner and are liable for any partner's negligence. It also can be hard to sell or dispose of a partnership interest. Many attorneys believe that the risks and possible problems of a business partnership make this an undesirable entity to choose. This is particularly true because an S corporation or limited liability company (LLC) can provide many of the advantages of a partnership without the problems.

# Corporation

Like a partnership, a *corporation* is an entity that is separate from those who own it. A corporation must be registered with the IRS and the state in which it operates. As part of the registration process, the corporation will be given identification numbers by these agencies. The incorporation process is done at the state level. Many states charge corporations an annual fee for the privilege of doing business in their state.

For example, California's fee is $800 a year, whether the corporation makes any money during the year or not.

In addition to the expense and time involved in becoming incorporated, the shareholders (owners) must adopt bylaws, elect officers, and conduct and keep records of regularly scheduled meetings. Financial recordkeeping and tax returns for a corporation can also require significant time and expense.

Some people choose this way of operating a business because they feel that incorporating gives the business a sense of legitimacy. Another major nontax reason for incorporating is that the shareholders are protected from personal liability if someone sues the corporation. If you own a home and operate your business as a sole proprietor or partnership, you could lose this asset if the business is sued. If you are incorporated, you are not likely to lose a personal asset unless the person suing you is able to prove that you didn't treat the corporation as a separate entity, but instead commingled personal and business funds.

Other advantages of incorporating include the ease in which the business can be transferred to a new owner, the continuity of the business (it does not end if a shareholder dies or leaves), and the ability to sell shares of stock to raise money for the business.

Owners who work in the business are treated as employees of the corporation. This means that taxes are withheld from the owners' paychecks, just as if they were working for someone else. An incorporated business may or may not pay less tax than one operating as a sole proprietorship or partnership. This calculation is different for each business, since the tax benefits of incorporating will depend somewhat on the needs of the shareholders. This is explained further in the descriptions of the different types of corporations—C *corporations*, S *corporations*, and *personal service corporations*.

## C CORPORATION

When a tax return is filed for a C *corporation*, the corporation pays taxes on the net profit of the business. One tax benefit of a C corporation is that income splitting can be used. Shareholder salaries and dividends can be adjusted in such a way that taxes on the corporation's profits are split between the corporation and the shareholders. This strategy may reduce the total tax liability because the corporate tax rate is only 15% on the first $50,000 of profit. This may be less than an individual shareholder would pay on wages of $50,000.

A major disadvantage of a C corporation is double taxation of earnings. The corporation pays income tax on its earnings. Then the company distributes those earnings to owners as dividends, and the owners pay tax on the dividends.

Since employee/owners of a C corporation are treated like other employees, they are covered by whatever fringe benefits the business offers. These benefits could include health insurance; medical, child care, or tuition reimbursement plans; life, long-term care, and disability insurance; and, retirement plans. The cost savings of being covered by these nontaxable fringe benefits may be enough of an incentive that incorporating will look inviting. Of course, these benefits reduce the profit of the corporation and they must be available to all employees of the business.

A new business that expects to show a loss (have more expenses than income) for one or more years will probably not want to become a C corporation. Any losses remain with the corporation and can only be deducted when the business begins to make a profit. This is unlike other entities in which losses from the business flow through to the owner's individual tax return, offsetting other types of income (*e.g.*, wages or interest income) by the amount of the business loss.

## S CORPORATION

An *S corporation* is somewhat of a hybrid between a partnership and a C corporation. While it files a corporate tax return, the profit (or loss) from the business is reported on the shareholders' (owners') individual tax returns. It is the shareholders—not the corporation—who pay tax on the profit. This avoids the C corporation problem of double taxation. If the business has a loss, the shareholder can reduce other income (such as wages from another job) by deducting the loss. Some states impose a tax on the S corporation even though the profits are being taxed to the shareholders.

An S corporation differs from a partnership in that the profit is calculated after the salaries of the employee/owners have been deducted. Some S corporations pay salaries based on actual profits so that by the time salaries have been deducted, there is no profit to be reported on the shareholder's individual return.

Some S corporation employee/owners try to avoid paying the Social Security tax imposed on wages by taking money for themselves out of the business, not withholding taxes, and calling the distribution a dividend. The IRS is aware of this and expects owners to take a reasonable salary before taking dividend distributions.

Children or grandchildren (or other family members) can be shareholders of an S corporation and income from the business can be split with them. This will be advantageous if you want to keep income from being taxed in your high tax bracket, and instead want it taxed at their (usually) lower tax rate.

Unlike a C corporation, fringe benefits are not available to employee/shareholders who own more than 2% of an S corporation—although they can be available for any other employees of the business. As with a C corporation, S corporation shareholders are protected from personal liability for business errors and debts.

This entity must make an election to operate as an S corporation; otherwise, the IRS will treat the business as a C corporation. There are restrictions on who can be shareholders of an S corporation. For example, there must be fewer than seventy-five shareholders and all stock must be owned by U.S. citizens or U.S. residents. If you have foreign investors, you cannot be an S corporation.

## PERSONAL SERVICE CORPORATION

Professionals in the fields of health, law, engineering, accounting, performing arts, and consulting usually must be *personal service corporations* (PSCs) if they want to incorporate. Personal service corporations are taxed at a higher tax rate than other corporations. However, as with other corporations, a personal service corporation can adjust the shareholders' salaries so there is no profit for the corporation, and thus, the higher corporate rate isn't paid. Instead, salaries are taxed at the lower individual tax rate.

PSCs don't offer the same degree of protection from liability as other corporations. Individuals who are PSCs are usually still personally liable for their own negligence. Shareholders of PSCs are able to take advantage of some of the fringe benefits available to C corporations. However, some of the benefits are only allowed if the corporation has more than one shareholder.

# Limited Liability Companies

*Limited liability companies* (LLCs) are a fairly new entity that combines the advantages of a partnership with the advantages of a corporation. Creating an LLC requires registering with a state agency (usually the secretary of state).

There is not actually an LLC entity for federal tax purposes. Unless the LLC chooses to be taxed as a corporation, single-member LLCs will be taxed as sole proprietors and multi-member LLCs will file taxes as a partnership. Like partnerships and sole proprietors, the profit from an LLC flows through to the owners who pay tax on it via their individual tax returns. The advantage of an LLC over a partnership or sole proprietor is that, like corporation shareholders, all the owners of an LLC have limited personal liability for the business.

One of the advantages of an LLC over an S corporation is that profit and losses from the business can be allocated to members disproportionately, whereas S corporation income must be allocated to members based on their ownership percentage. Another advantage is that an LLC has none of the S corporation restrictions on who can be investors. LLCs are generally easier and may be cheaper to form than corporations in some states, and there are no requirements for formal meetings or minutes.

Some states have a special tax on LLC income. Other states tax LLCs in the same way they tax corporations. As you review your entity choices, make sure you're aware of all fees and taxes that apply to each.

**Note:** *Because the tax ramifications of single-member LLCs are identical to those of sole proprietors, and the taxes for multi-member LLCs are the same as those for partnerships, this book will not specifically mention LLCs when discussing tax matters.*

## Choosing the Best Entity for Your Business

There's no one right answer for which entity is best for you. However, following are some of the questions that need to be answered before making this important decision.

- Are you in a type of business in which lawsuits are common?
- Are you going into business with other people?
- Do you feel that you're not being taken seriously as a sole proprietor while your incorporated colleagues are getting all the business?
- Do you have large child care or medical expenses that could be covered by an employee benefit program if you were incorporated?
- Do you anticipate several years of losses before you start making a profit?

It's best to sit down with an accountant, tax practitioner, or attorney who is knowledgeable about the tax benefits, as well as the nontax implications (*e.g.*, protection from liability and ease of selling the business) of the various entities.

Do not rush into creating an entity. They may be more difficult, expensive, and painful to get out of than they were to get into. Make sure you understand why you're making the choice you make. Too many people spend thousands of dollars to become incorporated in the hopes it will give them legitimacy, without understanding the tax implications of this decision. Often, people move easily into a business partnership with lovers or friends. Sometimes working together causes strain on the personal relationship, and getting out of a business partnership is often messy. Don't go into business with anyone else, even your closest friend, without first discussing together the worst possible scenarios, such as what happens if one of you dies, wants out of the partnership, or is working more (or harder) than the other one. You will never regret taking the time and spending the money to prepare a written business agreement.

# Necessary Licenses and Permits

## 1

Now that you're a small business owner and you've chosen the entity to operate under, what's next? It's time to look into what licenses or permits you might need. If you are a professional (*e.g.*, chiropractor, attorney, psychotherapist, contractor, real estate broker), most likely you already know what licenses are required before you can see clients or do work. Opening a restaurant or other food service requires meeting city health department guidelines. Any business that operates from a public facility, such as a store or office building, needs to be in compliance with the guidelines of the *Americans with Disabilities Act* (ADA). It is important to be aware of the regulations that apply specifically to your type of business, as well as those that are applicable to all businesses in your city or state.

If you set up your new business as a partnership or sole proprietorship, and your business name doesn't include your last name, you need to file a fictitious name statement. This is true also if words such as *associates*, *group*, or *company* are included in your business name, since those words imply that there are additional owners.

A *fictitious name statement* is generally filed with the county clerk's office. You pay a fee to register the name, and then must run a public notice in the newspaper stating the business name and the names of those who own the business. The purpose of this is to protect consumers so that if they are cheated by a business, they can find out the names of the individuals who are responsible. Having a fictitious name means you are *doing business as* (DBA) a name other than your own.

Your city or county may require that you have a business license. Some cities require a license if you sell products or see clients in that city, even if it's not your principal work or residence location. The penalties can be substantial if you don't get a license when it's required. In California, for example, the state taxing agency provides local municipalities with a list of residents whose tax return reported self-employment income. The cities then contact those on the list who aren't registered and assess a stiff penalty for each year that the business owner operated without a license. In addition, some cities have zoning regulations and require a permit to operate a business out of your home. Be sure that you are operating within the regulations before giving your home office address to anyone.

If you live in one of the forty-five states with a sales or excise tax and are responsible for collecting tax on your products or services, you need to register with the sales or excise tax agency. Generally, that agency also issues resale permits that keep you from having to pay sales or excise tax on items you buy to resell to clients or customers. Some states require businesses to collect tax only on products sold, whereas others assess a sales or excise tax on all business transactions—including professional services. Since each state has different regulations regarding sales tax and resale permits, you need to investigate this further on your own.

If you have employees (including yourself, if you're incorporated), you need to get a federal and a state *employer identification number*. The IRS and the state employment department will be able to tell you what taxes you must pay as an employer and what taxes must be withheld from employee's paychecks. This will include some combination of federal and state income taxes, Social Security tax, unemployment insurance, and perhaps mandatory disability and health insurance. A workers' compensation policy may be a requirement also. (Chapter 17 provides more information about payroll responsibilities.) Remember, if you're a sole proprietor or a partner in a partnership, you are *not* considered an employee of your business, so these requirements apply to your business only if you hire employees.

To find your local agencies that deal with the permits and taxes, look in the government pages of your telephone book. The state section lists agencies that deal with employee and sales or excise taxes. The city or county section includes the departments that handle zoning and business licenses.

---

## Q & A

**Q: What is a federal employer identification number?**

A: A *federal employer identification number* (FEIN) is another name for an employer identification number (EIN). If you need an EIN, get it by applying to the IRS on Form SS-4. A sole proprietor is not required to have one unless she has employees, or a Keogh or self-employed 401(k) retirement plan. (see Chapter 32.) When you open a business bank account, you may be told that you need a federal ID number, but you can tell the bank that you don't fall under the IRS's requirements for having one. All other business entities must have an EIN whether they have employees or not.

# Bank Accounts and Credit Cards | 5

Most business books and classes advise that one of the first things to do when starting a business is to go to the bank and open a separate business checking account. Many business owners find it helpful to have a separate business account, but in many cases it is not a requirement. If not handled correctly, the extra account can cause extra work and confusion.

> **EXAMPLE**
>
> *Barbara says, "I have a separate business checkbook, but whenever I'm at the office supply store it seems like I always forget to take it with me, so I end up writing the check out of my personal account. When I'm at the grocery store, I always seem to have my business checkbook with me but not my personal one, so I end up writing checks to the grocery store out of my business checkbook."*
> *At the end of the month, Barbara has two checking accounts for which she has to pay fees and do reconciliations. Meanwhile, the expenses are all mixed up, with business purchases in the personal account and personal purchases in the business account.*

## Bank Accounts

If you are going to have a separate business account, be sure to deposit all money from the business into that account, even if you later transfer it to your personal account. As much as possible, write business checks out of the business account and personal checks out of the personal account.

There are certain circumstances when you must have a separate business account. One is when you operate as a corporation, a partnership, or an LLC. A separate entity requires a separate bank account. Also, if you're doing business under a name other than your own, you may not be able to cash or deposit checks from your clients if you don't have a bank account in that name.

> **Note:** *Unless your bank is willing to give you an account called Jane Smith, DBA (doing business as) Smith's Carpeting, you need an account for Smith's Carpeting. Clients will write checks to Smith's Carpeting, not to Jane Smith.*

It's also a good idea to have a business bank account if you share a personal account with someone who is not your legally married spouse—for example, your mother, your roommate, or your domestic partner. If audited, you'll be asked to bring the bank statements from all accounts—checking and savings. If you bring in statements from an account you share with someone else, you will involve the other person in your audit. To minimize that involvement, keep your business income and expenses in a separate account, even if the remainder of your finances are commingled. This is not an issue if you're married and have a joint account with your spouse—your spouse will already be part of your audit.

Another reason to consider having a separate checking account is that it will provide you with a clear picture of how your business is doing. For example, if your checkbook is your sole recordkeeping system and you run out of money in this account, you can easily tell that your business expenses exceed your business income.

If your business name is the same as your personal name, consider simply opening another personal account as your business account. Fees for personal accounts are much lower than those for business accounts. Order checks for the second account in a different color so you can easily tell which checks go with which account.

## Credit Cards

Whether or not you have a business bank account, you may find it helpful to have a separate business credit card. The card does not need to be in the business' name—just pick one of your cards as your business credit card. Many people find it easier to keep track of business costs by using one credit card just for those expenses.

Also, while personal credit card interest is not deductible, business credit card interest is 100% deductible. By using one credit card exclusively for business, it will be much easier to determine how much interest you've paid on the business expenses you've charged. If you use a credit card for both personal and business expenses, you need to figure a way to prorate the interest, as it is deductible only to the extent that you can prove it's attributable to business expenses.

# Balancing Your Checkbook | 6

Do you call your bank on a regular basis to find out the balance in your account? Have you ever closed your current account and opened a new one because your account balance was so muddled that you gave up on ever reconciling it?

*Balancing your checkbook* (adding the deposits and subtracting the checks and withdrawals from the beginning balance) and *reconciling your bank statement* to your checkbook (making sure both have the same ending balance) are important steps in keeping track of your finances. By knowing your correct current bank balance, you avoid the embarrassment of not having enough in the account to cover checks you write, which can result in bounced checks. Also, you save yourself a substantial amount in bank charges, since each bounced check will incur an *insufficient funds* charge. In some states, the payee can sue you for three times the amount of a check that bounces. Most important, knowing the amount of money you have at any given time gets you out of the fog about money and is one more step in your money empowerment plan.

Each month you receive a bank statement from the institution where you have your account. Normally the bank statement lists all checks that have cleared (usually in numerical order), all withdrawals, and all deposits made during the prior thirty-day period. Somewhere on the bank statement is the date of the last statement and the cutoff date for the current statement. The time between those two dates is the period covered by the statement. If you would find it easier to have a bank statement that ends on the last day of each month, ask the bank to change the statement ending date for your account.

Since the bank statement has an ending date, you need to look at the balance in your checkbook as of the same date. The checkbook balance should match your account balance as indicated by the bank statement. Chances are the two will not match. Reconciling your bank account is the process of finding out why the balances don't match. The following are some of the reasons they may be different.

■ Not all the checks you wrote have been cashed yet. Those that have not been cashed and returned to your bank are called *outstanding checks*. Outstanding checks have been recorded in your check register, but won't appear on the bank statement.

■ You may have deposited some money in your account after the statement's cut-off date. Although you recorded the deposit amounts in your check register, they are not included on your bank statement. These are called *outstanding deposits*.

■ Your bank may charge a monthly service fee or pay monthly interest on your account. These amounts will be reflected on the bank statement, but probably have not yet been entered in your check register.

■ Automatic monthly payments may have been deducted from your account, but may not have been recorded in your check register. This might also be the case with a regularly scheduled transfer made from one account to another. Also, you may have neglected to make note of ATM withdrawals (and any related fees).

■ The amount of a check may have been entered differently in your check register than it was on the check itself. Typically, this is a transposition error (*e.g.*, writing a check for $6.41 and entering it in your register as $6.14).

■ The addition or subtraction in your check register may be incorrect.

You need to decide for yourself how much of a discrepancy you can live with. While it is always possible to get the balances to match to the penny, you may decide that it is not worth the time involved, and instead you'll accept the bank's balance if it's within, for example, $3.00 of your own checkbook balance.

If you want further help in getting the two balances to match, refer to the detailed instructions on bank statement reconciliations in Appendix A.

# The Records the IRS Expects You to Have

If you're like most people, you have an innate dread of hearing from the IRS. Possibly one of your worst fears is receiving a letter that starts out, "Your return has been selected...." It's helpful to know what you would be expected to bring to an audit so that you can be sure to keep adequate records throughout the year.

If you should get called in for an IRS (or a state) audit, you will be asked to bring a number of items. In most cases, the audit will focus on only one year. You will be asked to bring all bank statements for that year from all accounts, both business and personal. (If you have only one account, you'll obviously bring only the bank statements from that account.) The auditor will compare the deposits made to all your accounts with the amounts shown as income on your tax return. The IRS wants to make sure that no income from the business was deposited to personal accounts without having been included on your tax return.

Typically, an audit letter will ask you to bring all records of your business income and all canceled checks and receipts that verify the expenses you claimed for that year.

It isn't a problem if the bank doesn't return your canceled checks, as long as the checks you use have carbon copies or your bank statement lists all the checks you wrote during the month. The statement must indicate payee name, amount of check, and date of payment. Most banks make available (generally, for a fee) a microfiche of your canceled checks should you need them.

The auditor wants to see both your canceled checks and your receipts, because the check shows that an item was paid for, while the receipt specifies what was bought.

*Lynn Ann paid Betsy, a handyperson, to do some repairs around her office. In the memo section of the check to Betsy, Lynn Ann wrote "office repairs," but she did not keep the receipt Betsy gave her. How will she be able to prove that the check she wrote Betsy wasn't just a check to a friend? Will she be able to remember, if she is audited two years later, exactly what work Betsy did?*

*Lauren, a psychotherapist, was once audited. She had bought a lot of office furniture at a large department store, paying for it in installments. She had the canceled checks, on which she had written in the memo section, "office furniture." Unfortunately, she had no receipts indicating what she'd bought. Who's to say she didn't buy an expensive stereo system or a new wardrobe rather than office furniture?*

In addition to canceled checks and receipts, you also should have the original charge card receipts from any business expenses you charge. The monthly statement is acceptable if nothing else is available, but it gives no information about what was purchased. Also, the name shown as the payee on the monthly statement is sometimes different from the name of the business where you made the purchase.

Even the original charge card slip may not be sufficient when expenses for travel lodging are involved. The IRS wants to see a detailed receipt from the hotel so that they can be sure that the amount paid doesn't include personal items, such as gifts.

You may have heard that you don't need to keep receipts if the amount of the expense is less than $75. This is true. However, you still need to record all information about the expense—how much it was, to whom payment was made, what type of expense it was, the date paid, and so on. It is usually easier to just keep the receipt.

Receipts should be properly documented. For example, if you buy some paper clips for your business, the receipt may not indicate what was purchased. If it doesn't, you need to write "paper clips" on it. Otherwise, at the end of the year you'll have a pile of receipts showing the amounts of purchases but having no indication of what was bought. The IRS will accept the receipt with your notation so long as the amount and type of purchase are consistent with the kind of expense you need to have for your business.

What the IRS looks for in an audit is consistency. Does everything fit together? You cannot always get receipts for money you spend, but if everything else seems to fit together, you shouldn't have any problems proving the expenses for which you don't have receipts. For example, you cannot get a receipt for money you put in a parking meter, but if it's clear that you use your car in your work, the auditor will realize that you need to park somewhere, so this expense shouldn't be questioned. It's best, of course, if you enter parking meter costs in your car log (see Chapter 25) or appointment book.

Your appointment book or calendar is an important part of your tax materials and should be kept with them from year to year. If you have a PDA (personal digital assistant) or other electronic calendar, it might be helpful to print out a paper copy of each year's appointments at the end of the year. Notations on appropriate dates can provide backup information for things such as business mileage, meal expenses, parking meters, and business trips. In fact, if you're traveling at all for business, it's a good idea to record in your appointment book what activities you did each day you were away. This can be helpful should you ever need to prove that it was really a business trip.

Receipts, canceled checks, charge card slips, and appointment books can all be used to prove the expenses you had for your business. If you haven't been keeping all of these in the past, there's no sense worrying about it at this point, but make plans to hold on to them in the future. That way, if necessary, you'll be able to show the IRS how you spent your money, and you won't miss out on the deductible expenses discussed in later chapters.

In addition to canceled checks, receipts, and appointment books, the IRS will ask to see all other records related to your business in an audit. These include:

- payroll records if you have employees;
- copies of leases you have for store or office space, a car, or office equipment;
- your tax return for the year before and the year after the one being audited;
- copies of client or customer invoices;
- dimensions of your home if you claim office-in-home; and,
- anything else related to the tax return being examined.

(This list is standardized and some items may not apply to your business.)

What the taxpayer perceives as records and what the IRS interprets as records can be very different. Being aware of what you'd be expected to bring if selected for an audit will enable you to keep ongoing records in such a way that you have those items the IRS would want to see. The format in which you're keeping your business records may not exactly fit into the list of items the IRS wants to see in an audit, but if you're able to provide the backup documentation *in some form*, you (or your representative) can go to an audit with your head held high.

# Keeping Track of Business Expenses

If you have just started your business, you may have little or no idea how to begin keeping the records the IRS requires. If you have been in business for a while, you may find that you are not happy with the recordkeeping system you've set up.

The IRS does not require sole proprietors to have a formal bookkeeping system. As long as you have the necessary backup materials, the method you use to record or store them is up to you. If you are comfortable keeping a sophisticated set of books, that's great. However, your situation may be more like those in the following examples.

> **EXAMPLE**
> *Rachael met with an accountant several months before she came to see me. Hearing that she'd just started a new business, the accountant set up a comprehensive, double-entry bookkeeping system for Rachael to use. When she was in the accountant's office, she understood what she was supposed to do, but by the time she got home, she couldn't remember any of it. As a result, she hadn't been keeping any records for her business.*

> **EXAMPLE**
> *Katy had been advised by a colleague to purchase Quickbooks®, a business accounting program. She bought the software but, because she didn't know how to proceed next, it remains unopened on her bookshelf while Katy worries that she isn't doing any business recordkeeping.*

You probably didn't choose to go into business in order to learn bookkeeping. If you have figured out some way of keeping records for your business and that system is working for you, continue with it—no matter how unsophisticated it might seem.

If you're currently using your checkbook as your record of expenses, that's fine. If you keep receipts filed by month or by type of expense or all collected together in a shoebox, that's fine too. What's not okay is to have some receipts in the kitchen drawer, some in the glove compartment of the car, and some on top of the TV.

This chapter provides an example of a simple but effective way of keeping track of your business expenses. If your business is a partnership, a corporation, or a multiperson LLC, you will need a somewhat more sophisticated recordkeeping system than the one described here. The principles are the same, but additional information is needed on an ongoing basis. Since you will probably consult a tax or accounting professional when establishing one of these entities, you will be able to get that person's suggestions for setting up an appropriate recordkeeping system.

Whether you keep records by hand or on a computer, it's helpful to know how the process works, even if your computer program is doing the recording. The method shown in this chapter provides you with additional information in a more accessible format than you have if a checkbook is the only record of your expenses. This system uses a disbursement sheet to record all money paid out. *Disbursement* is just another word for *expense.* A disbursement sheet done on a computer is usually called a spreadsheet. Important tax information is imparted in the discussion on how to use a disbursement sheet.

Look at the sample disbursement sheet. (see page 24.) One advantage of using this method to keep track of expenses is that you can see at a glance all of your business expenses to date, and whether they were paid by cash, check, or credit card. One of the potential problems in using only a checkbook as a record of expenses is that it's easy to forget to report the business purchases you paid for with a credit card or cash. If they're for your business, those expenses are just as deductible as the ones paid for by check.

Additionally, a disbursement sheet provides information that is helpful in making business decisions. At a glance you can see how much you've spent on advertising or postage. You can determine which months tend to bring in the most money and which months have the most expenses. With this information you can do some planning and answer questions like *Could I go on vacation next year during one of the months in which business seemed slow this year?* and *Will I have enough income to cover the months that have extra expenses?*

The disbursement sheet is made up of a series of columns. The first column is for the date the payment is made. The second column indicates the name of the person or company to whom payment was made. The next four columns are for the check number and amount for those things paid by check, the cash amount if paid in cash, and the charge amount if paid by credit card.

To the right of the double line are columns for some potential expenses. You already know or will determine the most common expenses in your business. Each of the most frequently occurring expenses should be given its own column. If you sell a product, you'll need a column called "Inventory" or "Merchandise Purchases" to record the amount of money spent in purchasing the product (or its components) before reselling it. Most businesses will have advertising or marketing expenses and office or computer supply costs. You may also pay for things such as professional dues, publications,

## Q & A

Q: Is it good to break down the expense categories into those shown on Schedule C?

A: Schedule C is the tax form used by sole proprietors to show business income and expenses. Many people think they need to use the same expense categories as are on Schedule C. However, Schedule C categories are not necessarily applicable to your business. Fortunately, the form has some blank lines to write in expense categories that are more appropriate for your business. If you break down your expense categories, you lessen your chance of being audited. Rather than listing, for example, $5,000 in supplies, divide the total amount into office supplies, computer supplies, small furnishings, and whatever other categories might apply.

2

and insurance. If you have employees, payroll will be a frequently used column, as will the columns for each type of tax withheld from the employees' paychecks.

If you use a manual bookkeeping system and you try to have a column for each possible business expense, you will need such a wide disbursement sheet that it will be totally unmanageable. This is not a problem with a computerized disbursement sheet, since you can have an unlimited number of columns. Computerized accounting programs also provide a generous (and sometimes unlimited) number of expense categories. With a manual system, however, you need to pick those expenses that occur most often and give them each a column. The remainder of the expenses go in the last two columns, which are called "Miscellaneous" and "Description of Miscellaneous."

These columns, however, are just a temporary place to put infrequently occurring expenses. On a tax return, you would never report that you had $1,577.42 worth of miscellaneous expenses (unless you're anxious to be audited). At the end of each month or at the end of the year, you will need to review the expenses listed in the "Miscellaneous" column and sort them into appropriate categories. The "Description of Miscellaneous" column will help you to do this.

## DISBURSEMENTS—MARGIE LEONG, COMPUTER CONSULTANT

June 2004

| Date | To: | Check # | Amount of Check | Paid In Cash | Paid In Credit Card | Office Supplies | Client Expenses | Inventory Purchases | Draw | Misc. | Description of Misc. |
|---|---|---|---|---|---|---|---|---|---|---|---|
| 6/3/04 | Minneapolis Paper | 101 | 40.09 | | | 40.09 | | | | | |
| 6/5/04 | Janet Jones | 102 | 400.00 | | | | | | | 400.00 | Office Rent |
| 6/7/04 | Margie Leong | 103 | 250.40 | | | 50.40 | | | | 200.00 | Travel |
| 6/23/04 | North Airlines | 104 | 116.18 | | | | 116.18 | | | | |
| 6/24/04 | Computer Shoppe | 105 | 78.95 | | | | | 78.95 | | | |
| 6/25/04 | Third City Bank | 106 | 560.72 | | | | | | | 500.00 / 60.72 | Principal / Interest |
| 6/26/04 | Margie Leong | 107 | 500.00 | | | | | | 500.00 | | |
| 6/26/04 | Petty Cash Reimbursement | 108 | 45.03 | | | | | | 8.93 | 20.00 / 13.20 / 2.90 | Book / Faxing / Telephone |
| 6/27/04 | VISA Credit Card | 109 | 73.10 | | | | | | | 73.10 | Entertainment |
| 6/28/04 | Ace Furniture | 110 | | | 300.00 | | | | | 300.00 | Desk |
| 6/30/04 | Third City Bank | | 7.50 | | | | | | | 7.50 | Bank Charges |
| 6/30/04 | The Office Store | | | 30.19 | | 30.19 | | | | | |
| 6/30/04 | Computer Shoppe | | | 11.56 | | | | 11.56 | | | |
| TOTAL | | | 2,071.97 | 41.75 | 300.00 | 120.68 | 116.18 | 90.51 | 508.93 | 1,577.42 | |

# How a Disbursement Sheet Works

The disbursement sheet on page 24 is for one month of Margie Leong's computer consulting business. Margie's is primarily a service business; but occasionally, when setting up a computer system for a client, Margie sells disks, software, or computer cables.

On the first line of Margie's disbursement sheet is a check for $40.09 to Minneapolis Paper Company for office supplies. The $40.09 is noted in the column labeled "Amount of Check," indicating how Margie paid for the expense. The same amount is also noted in the "Office Supplies" column, indicating what was purchased. Each expense is listed in two places—how it was paid and what was bought.

Next is a check to Janet Jones for $400. Margie pays office rent to Janet. This is not an in-home office, but an office outside the home. This expense has been entered in the "Miscellaneous" column. Since $400 is a large amount, you might wonder why rent doesn't have its own column. The reason is, in most cases, office rent is due only once a month, so it isn't paid as frequently as many other types of expenses. Since her disbursement sheet has a limited number of expense columns, Margie allocates them to the expense categories for which she writes the most checks. It will be fairly easy at the end of the year to go through the "Miscellaneous" column and total the amounts for the twelve times office rent was paid. (Chapter 23 explains how office-in-home expenses are handled.)

## REIMBURSEMENTS

The next line on the disbursement sheet is a check made out to Margie Leong. This check for $250.40 is reimbursement for $50.40 of office supplies and $200 of travel. Margie was at the office supply store and at the travel agency, and both times she had only her personal checkbook with her. She wrote the checks out of her personal checkbook and then went back to the office and reimbursed herself out of the business checkbook.

Even if Margie had not reimbursed herself, the expenses would still be deductible. It doesn't matter how you pay for something. If it's a deductible expense, it's deductible. Margie reimbursed herself to maintain a clear picture of her business and to be able to see at a glance what expenses she's had. Otherwise, she might forget about the expenses paid from her personal checkbook and think that her business has had fewer expenses than is really the case. Also, when it comes time to do her tax return, if Margie has reimbursed herself, she won't need to go back through her personal checkbook to see if there were business expenses paid out of her personal account.

If you're just starting your business, you may not have enough money in your business account to reimburse yourself for expenses paid from your personal account. Again, these business expenses are just as deductible, no matter which account was used to pay them. If you don't have a separate business account, you won't reimburse yourself. If you did, you'd be writing a check from your account and then depositing it right back into the same account.

The next line on the disbursement sheet shows another type of reimbursement. Margie paid for a plane ticket while doing work for one of her clients and will submit the bill to the client for reimbursement. Because she often has reimbursable client expenses, Margie has labeled one of her columns "Client Expenses." In Chapter 9, which covers money coming into the business, you'll see that Margie includes in her record-keeping a column called "Client Reimbursement." The two columns will cancel each other out (assuming that Margie gets reimbursed for all her client expenses) and there will be no tax ramifications. If Margie is not fully reimbursed for client expenses, she will deduct them on her tax return as if they were her own business expenses.

## INVENTORY

Next on the disbursement sheet is the purchase of some computer cables from the Computer Shoppe. These are cables that Margie will resell to clients when she sets up their computer systems. When something is bought to be resold, it becomes part of inventory. (see Chapter 13.) The $78.95 spent on cables is entered in the column called "Inventory Purchases."

## LOANS

The next line on the disbursement sheet is a check to Third City Bank. Margie borrowed $7,000 from Third City Bank to buy a computer. The $7,000 loan is not considered income and is not reported on Margie's tax return. Every month Margie makes a loan payment of $560.72 to Third City Bank. Although she has a monthly expense of $560.72, $500 of this amount is the principal payment, repayment of a portion of the amount she borrowed. The amount that goes towards principal is not a deductible expense, whereas the $60.72 interest portion is deductible.

The difference between how the principal is handled and how the interest is deducted is important to understand. When it's time to calculate

---

### Q & A

Q: Are you saying that the cost of the computer is not deductible?

A: No. The portion of the loan that is principal repayment is not deductible, but the computer is fully deductible. This is a separate issue from the deductibility of the loan that was used to purchase it.

her quarterly estimated tax payments (see Chapter 36), if Margie thinks her deductible loan expenses are $560.72 a month, her calculations will be incorrect. All she can deduct of the loan payment is the $60.72 monthly interest, not the entire $560.72 payment. Margie may or may not know during the year how much interest she's paying. Although her tax professional or a computerized financial program can create a loan payment schedule for her (which shows the interest paid each month), Margie may not have the exact figure until the end of the year when Third City Bank sends her a statement of interest paid.

## DRAW

Looking again at the disbursement sheet, you see that the next line lists a check to Margie Leong, the owner of the business. She has given herself $500 from her business. It is recorded in the column labeled "Draw." As a sole proprietor or a partner in a partnership, what you pay yourself is called a draw. *Money you take out of your business that is for anything other than business expenses is called a draw.*

If you're at the grocery store and you have your business checkbook with you, the check you write from that account for groceries is a draw. If you give yourself $500 every week out of the business, that's a draw.

If your business operates as a corporation, you are paid as an employee—just as you would be if you were working for someone else. But if you operate as a sole proprietorship or partnership, you cannot be an employee of your business and you do not withhold taxes when you take money for yourself from the business. If you use only one bank account, anything for which you write a check is either a business expense or a draw.

Draw is discussed further in Chapter 14, where you'll see that it is not a deductible expense. For that reason, you can choose whether or not to keep track of it. The main reason to record the draw checks is so that you can see how much you take out of your business during the year. By keeping track of your draw, you'll be able to see where the profit goes.

## PETTY CASH

Next on the disbursement sheet is a line for *petty cash* reimbursement. If you have a business that has frequent small purchases (*e.g.*, a carpenter purchasing supplies or an editor making frequent trips to a nearby copy center), it may be helpful to have a petty cash account. It can be difficult to keep track of the money spent via a petty cash account, so you need to keep careful records.

Begin a petty cash account by putting a specified amount of money—for example, $50—into a petty cash box or envelope. Whenever money is taken out, replace it with a receipt or slip of paper, indicating how the money was spent. At any time, you should be able to add up the receipts and the remaining cash and have them equal the amount that was originally put in the box. When you run low on cash in the box, remove and total the receipts, and replace the cash that has been spent.

In this example, a check for $45.03 is being written to restock the petty cash fund. By looking at the expense columns you can see that $20 was spent on a book, $13.20 was spent on faxing at the local copy center, $8.93 was a draw (Margie took money out of petty cash one day to buy lunch), and $2.90 was spent on pay telephone calls. What's entered on the disbursement sheet is the breakdown of how the $45.03 was spent. When Margie adds the amount of this check to what remains in the petty cash box, the total cash will again equal $50.

**Note:** *There is no such expense as petty cash—the money was spent on something.*

## CREDIT CARD PURCHASES

The next line on the disbursement sheet is a payment to VISA® Credit Card. When Margie's credit card bill came, the total due was $73.10, which had been spent on business entertainment. Margie pays the credit card bill and enters the amount of the check under business entertainment. Unfortunately, most credit card bills aren't so simple. What if the credit card bill had been for $573.10, of which $73.10 was for business entertainment and $500 was for something personal? Margie would have several choices about how to pay that bill.

### Q & A

**Q: What about the credit card interest?**

A: Interest on credit cards used for business expenses is 100% deductible. You can either record the interest monthly or wait until you get the statement from the credit card company at the end of the year telling you how much interest you paid during the previous year. Remember, interest paid on a credit card used for both personal and business expenses can be deducted only if you can prove how much interest was incurred on the business purchases.

- Since she has separate business and personal accounts, she could write two checks: $73.10 from the business account and $500 from her personal account. She would then send both checks in payment of her bill.
- She could write one check from her personal account for $573.10, then reimburse herself from the business account for the $73.10.
- She could write one check from her business account for $573.10, of which

$73.10 is for business entertainment and $500 is a draw. (Remember, paying for something personal from the business is a draw.)

What if Margie pays off her credit card bill by sending $50 or $100 a month? How does she know whether that amount is paying for the business entertainment or the personal item or for some other expense? The next line on the disbursement sheet demonstrates a way to handle this.

That line indicates a $300 purchase from Ace Furniture that was paid by credit card. Margie bought a desk for her office and the date listed is the date she charged it. As far as the IRS is concerned, the date you charge something is the date it's considered paid for. If you charge something before December 31, you can deduct it on that year's tax return, even though you won't be paying the credit card bill until the following year. If you pay off your credit cards in monthly payments, record the full amount of the purchase at the time you charge the item so you can deduct the expense in the current year. Don't worry about the fact that you're not actually going to be paying it off until sometime next year. If you record your credit card purchases this way, the checks you write each month to make payments on your credit card bill should be listed under "Draw" to avoid recording the expense twice.

> ## Q & A
>
> **Q: If I pay off my credit cards on time, there is no interest to deduct. Is it better for a business not to pay them off in full each month?**
>
> A: It's never better to spend money in order to save money. If you spend $23 on interest, that doesn't equal a $23 tax savings. Don't get into the trap of thinking that you should spend some money in order to have a deduction. Just remember, you don't save $1 in tax when you spend $1 on a deductible expense.

## ASSETS

Look again at the Ace Furniture line on the disbursement sheet. Margie's purchase of a desk is listed in the "Miscellaneous" column. A desk, a computer, a fax machine, and similar items are called *assets*. A business asset is something of value that you use in your business. When you buy an asset for your business and the asset is expected to last for more than a year, the IRS says you must *depreciate* the item over a period of years.

Depreciate means that instead of deducting the full cost of the item in one year, you deduct the cost over a period of years. Chapter 22 explains depreciation more thoroughly, but what you should note here is that when you file your tax return, you need to list the assets purchased during the year. By recording the asset in the "Miscellaneous" column rather than including it under, for example, office supplies, it will be easy at the end of the year to compile a list of the assets purchased for your business in that year.

## BANK CHARGES

In keeping track of your expenses, don't forget bank charges. If your checking account is for business only, deduct 100% of the service charge. If it's part business, part personal, you need to prorate the amount in some equitable manner. Margie has listed her bank charges on the next line of the disbursement sheet.

## CASH EXPENDITURES

The last two lines of the disbursement sheet are expenses that Margie paid for in cash. Each purchase has also been listed in one of the expense categories.

## TOTALING THE DISBURSEMENT SHEET

When Margie adds together columns 4, 5, and 6 (which indicate the amount spent and the method used to pay for the expense), they should equal the total of the columns on the right side of the double line (which indicate what was purchased). This confirms that every transaction has been correctly entered in two places on the disbursement sheet.

# Keeping Track of the Money Coming into Your Business

The opposite of disbursements (money out) is *receipts* (money in). Although you may think of receipts as things you get when you pay for groceries, receipts is also a technical term used by bookkeepers, accountants, and the IRS to refer to money that comes into a business. If the word *receipts* confuses you, just think of it when used in this context, as *money in*.

As with your disbursements, if you already have a system of keeping track of the money coming into your business, that's great—keep it up. If you haven't yet set up a system, this chapter helps you get started.

The most important thing you should know about receipts is that you need a record of every single deposit made to all bank accounts. At the least there should be a notation in your checkbook summarizing the source of each deposit. Some people keep a duplicate deposit slip and write the source on that. You can also use a receipts spreadsheet (discussed later in this chapter).

Whichever method you use, it is important to record all money coming in, whether it is taxable or not. This record is necessary for your personal and your business account. If, besides being self-employed, you also work as an employee, when you deposit your paycheck you should make a

> ## Q & A
>
> **Q: Is the birthday gift I received from my mother taxable?**
>
> A: No. Any person can give any other person up to $11,000 per year, and the money is neither taxable nor shown on either person's tax return. That doesn't mean, however, that you shouldn't keep track of any monetary gifts—you wouldn't want the IRS to think it was income from your business that you failed to report.

notation that the paycheck was the source of the deposit. Make note also of which deposits are from client fees, which is a birthday gift from mom, which is reimbursement from a colleague for a dinner you paid for, and so on. *Wherever it came from and whichever bank account it's deposited into, every single dollar should be recorded.*

Sole proprietorships file a Schedule C with their tax return, showing their business income and expenses. For this reason, the IRS calls sole proprietors *Schedule C filers*. Schedule C filers are audited more often than other people because the IRS thinks they may not be reporting all their income. There is less focus on businesses that don't have a lot of cash transactions than there is on businesses, such as restaurants and hair salons, where much of the business is done in cash. Nevertheless, all businesses need to keep good records.

The IRS also expects you to keep track of and report any bartering you do. If you are an auto mechanic and you fix Paige's car in exchange for a dress from her dress shop, you have taxable income. The value of the dress is the amount that needs to be included with your income. If, instead of giving you a dress, Paige does some bookkeeping for your business, you must report the value of the bookkeeping as income. Since the work was done for your business, you can deduct as a business expense the value of the car repair you did. This is because you could have deducted the bookkeeping if you had paid money for it. Although most people don't think about recording their *barter income*, you can be assured that one question asked at every audit is, "Did you participate in barter transactions?"

In an audit, the IRS looks at the monthly statements from all bank accounts. They add up the deposits made to all the accounts and compare the total to the income reported on your tax return. If more money went through your bank account than shows up as income on your tax return, you need to have a good explanation for the difference. Neither the gift from mom nor the computer loan from Third City Bank are taxable, but unless you keep a record indicating the source of that money when you deposit it, the assumption will be that it was income you didn't report. *Keeping track of your money coming in is at least as important as, if not more important than, keeping track of your expenses.*

If you have a separate business bank account, all business income should be deposited into that account and then transferred, if you wish, to other accounts. Similarly, the paycheck from your work as an employee and the birthday gift from mom should be deposited into your personal account.

## RECEIPTS (MONEY IN)—MARGIE LEONG, COMPUTER CONSULTANT

July 2004

| Date | From: | Total Amount of Deposit | Retail Sales | Sales Tax Collected | Client Fees | Client Reimbursements | Transfer from Savings | Misc. | Description of Misc. |
|------|-------|------------------------|--------------|---------------------|-------------|----------------------|----------------------|-------|---------------------|
| 7/3/04 | North Airlines reimbursement | 116.18 | | | | 116.18 | | | |
| 7/5/04 | Computer supply sales | 200.90 | 190.00 | 10.90 | | | | | |
| 7/7/04 | Transfer from Third City Bank | 850.00 | | | | | 850.00 | | |
| 7/10/04 | Client fees | 600.00 | | | 600.00 | | | | |
| 7/24/04 | Bounced check | (70.00) | | | (70.00) | | | | |
| 7/25/04 | Client fees | 80.00 | | | 70.00 | | | 10.00 | Bank Charges |
| TOTAL | | 1,777.08 | 190.00 | 10.90 | 600.00 | 116.18 | 850.00 | 10.00 | |

2

# Using a Receipts Sheet

A *receipts sheet*, like a disbursement sheet, allows you to see at a glance what business activity has occurred. Like the disbursement sheet, the receipts sheet is made up of columns. The total amount of each deposit is noted, and then, to the right of the double lines, the amount is noted again in the appropriate column to indicate the source of the money.

As with the disbursement sheet, choose column headings that most accurately reflect the sources from which you get money. In Margie's business, "Client Reimbursements" is one column heading and "Retail Sales" is another.

If clients reimburse you for expenses as Margie's do, you may have a column labeled "Client Reimbursements." Theoretically, these reimbursements should equal the "Client Expenses" column on your disbursement sheet, which is where you would record those expenses for which you expect to be reimbursed. Sometimes the end of the year comes before you've received a reimbursement for something you paid for late in the year, so the two column totals may not always be identical. The first line in the receipts sheet on page 33 shows the reimbursement Margie received for the $116.18 North Airlines ticket.

If you sell a retail product (that is, you are selling something directly to the person who will use the product), you may, like Margie, have a column labeled "Retail Sales" or "Store Sales." The second line in the example shows a deposit of $200.90 from computer supply sales. Of that total, $190 is the amount received for the items that were sold, and $10.90 is the sales tax collected. (In your state, the sales tax may be called excise tax, or you may live in a state where no sales or excise tax is paid.) The sales tax collected is not your money. You collect the tax when you make a sale, but you are serving as the intermediary who will pass it on to the state or city agency that is actually assessing the tax. The reason for listing the sales amount separately from the tax collected is so that you don't make the mistake of thinking you made $200.90 today, when in reality you made $190.

Next on the receipts sheet you'll see a line indicating a transfer from Margie's savings account. Transferring money from one account to another is not a taxable transaction. It's already your money and you're simply transferring it from one place to another. If you don't keep track of the transfer of money, however, an IRS auditor could assume it was income you didn't report, so it's best to record it in some way.

The next line on Margie's receipt sheet shows client fees received. Client, patient, or customer fees are the amounts received by service businesses such as plumbers, consultants, doctors, and artists. Margie received $600 in client fees and deposited them that day. A few days later she received a notice from her bank telling her that one of those checks, in the amount of $70, had bounced. On the next line Margie records the bounced check by entering the $70 amount in parentheses to indicate, in bookkeeping language, that the amount is to be subtracted out. Margie subtracts the $70 as if she'd never received the check. After the amount has been subtracted, the total of the deposits is $70 less, and the "Client Fees" column now totals $530 instead of $600.

Margie then contacts the client and requests a new payment of the $70, plus a reimbursement for the $10 bank charge she incurred. She collects the $80, of which $70 is recorded in the "Client Fees" column and $10 goes in the "Miscellaneous" column as bank service charge reimbursement.

When you total the deposits column (column 3), it should equal the total of all the columns to the right of the double line. This confirms that each deposit has been entered correctly in two columns.

2

# Ledger Books and Recordkeeping Systems | 10

In an office supply store, you will find different types of ledger books available for use in recording disbursements. Some of the books will have preprinted expense column headings. If you're a very small business, you may find that the categories of expenses listed are not pertinent to your business. For example, unless you have employees, an expense column labeled "Employee Pension Plan" won't be useful for you. For that reason, you may find it easier to use a book with blank column headings so that you can enter your own expense categories.

One option is to use a *columnar pad*. Columnar pads come in many different widths—2-column, 6-column, 13-column, and so forth—and are readily available. Typically, these pads are light green. The width most commonly used to record disbursements is a 13-column pad with address space, which is an especially wide column on each page. This wide column can be used to record to whom payment is made or from whom payment is received. The narrow columns next to the address space can be used to record the date and check number, if payment is made by check. The remaining columns can be labeled with your business's most frequently occurring expenses.

A columnar pad with fewer columns is often sufficient for keeping track of money in (receipts). List money in and money out on separate sheets of paper. You'll confuse yourself if you try to include them both on one sheet. The individual sheets on a columnar pad can be torn out easily. By putting them in a three ring binder, you'll have a very adequate set of business books.

# One-Write Systems

Another way of keeping manual records is to use a *one-write system*. Safeguard® and McBee® are two brand names of one-write systems. Other brands are available through office supply dealers, mail order companies, and your bank. You cannot go into an office supply store and buy a one-write system off the shelf because the checks need to be coded to your bank account. The checks in a one-write system have a strip of carbon on the back of them so the date, the payee's name, the check number, and the amount of the check is entered automatically on the disbursement sheet as you write the check. All you need to do to complete your expense records is to label the columns of expenses on your disbursement sheet and enter each expense amount in its appropriate column.

A one-write system is a big time-saver, since all of the information about each check is entered only once (when the check is written). People who write a lot of checks will find this very helpful. One-write systems also avoid the situation of writing a check for $58.90 and entering it in your check register as $59.80.

One disadvantage of using a one-write system is that it's considerably more expensive than buying a box of checks. Also, some people find it inconvenient to carry around because the one-write checkbook is generally quite large and won't easily fit into your purse or pocket. Another potential problem is that you may find it hard to remember to record expenses paid by cash or credit card, since the one-write system focuses primarily on expenses paid by check.

# Doing Your Recordkeeping on a Computer    11

More and more people are doing their recordkeeping on a computer. While it may not be appropriate to buy a computer just to run a bookkeeping program, if you already have one, you will probably find that your financial chores can be handled more quickly and easily with the use of technology.

If you are planning to computerize your recordkeeping, you have several choices of how to do it. The first option is to use a spreadsheet program such as *Lotus 1-2-3*® or *Microsoft Excel*®. Even though some of the programs come with appropriate templates, you will need to set up the spreadsheet yourself. It will probably look similar to the disbursement sheet shown in Chapter 8. After you insert the appropriate formulas, the columns will automatically total themselves each time you make an entry.

Another option is to use a personal finance or basic accounting program. *Quicken*®, *Microsoft Money*®, and *Peachtree Accounting*® are among the programs in this category. *Quicken*® even has a version called *Quicken Home and Business*® that includes extra features helpful for small businesses. These programs are designed for easy use by nonaccountants and are quite adequate for many small businesses.

If, however, you have inventory, need complex reports, have employees, or do business internationally, you may need a more sophisticated finance program. *QuickBooks*®, *Peachtree Complete Accounting*®, or *M.Y.O.B.*® (Mind Your Own Business) are designed for these purposes. You'll also want to use one of these more sophisticated programs if you need to keep track of the costs for each job you do.

If at all possible, before buying a financial program, try out a friend's copy or a trial copy if offered by the manufacturer. That way you'll see whether the program organizes records in the way you intuitively expect them to be organized. You'll also be able to see whether it has all the features you need without overwhelming you with those you don't need. If one program doesn't meet your needs, try another.

One of the major advantages of most financial programs is that you're able to use the computer to write and print your checks. Although you need to order special checks, the time savings is great when you use this feature. As you write and print the check, the information on that check (payee, date, etc.) is entered automatically into the appropriate expense category of the program. This is especially helpful for those checks you write month after month, such as rent and utilities. Once you've written a check to a particular payee, as soon as you begin the first few letters of that payee's name for a later check, the program will finish the remainder of the name and also fill in the amount of the check. At any time you can print out a summary of your business income and expenses and a variety of other reports. These reports can help you tremendously in running your business. You'll easily be able to see how your expenses compare to your income and how, for example, this year's sales compare to last year's.

However, there's one major caution to remember when using computer programs to do your recordkeeping. The old adage, *Garbage in, garbage out*, means that if you don't understand the information you're entering into the program, what comes out may or may not be correct.

| | |
|---|---|
| **EXAMPLE** | *When Donna had her tax return prepared, she was shocked to discover she owed more taxes. She was sure that the number reported for her business income was too high. Upon reviewing her computer printout, she discovered that she had somehow included her beginning business bank balance of several thousand dollars as business income.* |

It's tempting to conclude that a computer printout must be correct. Just remember that this won't be the case if the data entered is faulty.

# Financial Statements | 12

At some point you may be asked to provide someone with a financial statement. This might happen when you ask a supplier for credit.

*Audrey owns a hair salon and uses a linen service to provide her with clean towels each week. She is expected to pay for the towels as they are delivered. As this payment arrangement becomes more inconvenient, Audrey asks the linen service to bill her and allow her to pay at the end of the month (which is called "extending credit"). The service says it will consider it, if Audrey will provide a financial statement of her business.*

You may also be asked to provide a business financial statement if you apply for a loan to buy a car, computer, house, or any other large purchase. When the lender learns you are self-employed, he or she will often ask for two or three years of tax returns and a current financial statement.

There are two parts to a *financial statement*. The first is the *balance sheet*. This is a listing of business assets (things of value that your business owns) and liabilities (what the business owes to others) as of a particular date. The difference between your assets and liabilities is your *equity*, or ownership in the business. A balance sheet is like a photograph of your business finances as of the date of the report. Although not required of sole proprietors, a balance sheet must be included on the annual tax return of corporations and most partnerships.

**Barbara's Import Jewelry Company**
**Balance Sheet**
**December 31, 2004**

**Assets**

| | |
|---|---|
| Computer | $1,550 |
| Work Table | 130 |
| Inventory | 1,093 |
| TOTAL ASSETS | $2,773 |

**Liabilities**

| | |
|---|---|
| Computer Loan Balance | $976 |
| TOTAL LIABILITIES | $976 |

**Owner's Equity** $1,797

The second part of a financial statement is the income and expense statement, also called a *profit and loss statement*. It covers a specific period of time, usually from the beginning of one month to the end of another month, for the quarter, or for the entire year.

Barbara sells and repairs jewelry. Her profit and loss statement (P&L) shows the amount of income that came from customer fees and from sales. Barbara doesn't report here any income she received from her job as an employee (where taxes are taken out of her paycheck) or from any other source. This statement represents solely her business income.

After income, Barbara lists her expenses. Again, these are only business expenses. One line indicates the business rent she paid. This is not for an office-in-home, but rent for an office outside her home. She also lists employee salaries. This is not what she paid herself because, as a sole proprietor, she's not an employee of her business. This is the amount she paid the employees who work for her. (If Barbara were incorporated, her salary would be listed here, along with those of any other employees.) Barbara lists the amounts she spent on office supplies, education expenses, business entertainment, interest on loans (not the full payment amount—just the interest), books and subscriptions, dues, and so forth. She also includes depreciation (an expense discussed in depth in Chapter 22).

**Barbara's Import Jewelry Company**
**Income and Expenses**
**December 31, 2004**

### Income

| | |
|---|---|
| Jewelry Sales | $29,976 |
| Repair Fees | 2,643 |
| TOTAL INCOME | $32,619 |

### Expenses

| | |
|---|---|
| Rent | $4,000 |
| Employee Salaries | 2,611 |
| Office Supplies | 700 |
| Education Expenses | 325 |
| Depreciation | 411 |
| Entertainment | 56 |
| Interest on Loans | 280 |
| Books and Subscriptions | 54 |
| Dues | 75 |
| Cost of Goods Sold | 9,907 |
| TOTAL EXPENSES | $18,419 |

| | |
|---|---|
| **NET PROFIT** | **$14,200** |
| *(Income minus Expenses)* | |

2

Barbara's P&L also includes something called *cost of goods sold*. Cost of goods sold is an expense incurred by businesses that sell products and have an inventory. Inventory and cost of goods sold will be described more fully in the next chapter. Here, the P&L was prepared in the most easily understood format. Normally, the cost of goods sold figure is subtracted directly from the income and the resulting figure is called the gross profit. The operating expenses are then subtracted from the gross profit.

After Barbara adds up all her expenses, she subtracts the total from her income. The result is her *net profit*, sometimes referred to as the *bottom line*.

What Barbara (and every owner) pays tax on is the net profit from the business.

# Cash-Flow Projections

There is another type of report that needs to be mentioned because of its importance in the health of your business. That report is a *cash-flow projection*. A cash-flow projection shows whether your anticipated income will be sufficient to take care of your expected (projected) expenses. This report is prepared for your benefit, not because someone else is asking to see it. You can do a cash-flow projection for the next week, month, quarter, or year of your business. The report will show whether you can expect enough income to cover your business expenses and which time periods you need to be especially aware of (either because you expect less income or will have higher than normal expenses). Projecting in this way will lead to better control of your cash flow and will give you adequate time to plan and prepare for the growth of your business.

It's best if you have enough cash on hand each month to pay the bills for the following month. A monthly cash-flow projection helps to identify deficiencies or surpluses in cash and to compare actual figures to past months. If you discover that you will not have enough income to cover your projected expenses, you may be able to take some of the following steps.

- Collect money that's due to you. Too many business owners complain about poor cash flow and neglect to send out bills for services already provided or items sold. It's important to send bills to your clients on a timely basis. It not only helps your cash flow, but you're less likely to end up with uncollectible bills.
- Review your policy for extending credit. If you are very loose about when you expect clients to pay, they will be very loose about paying you.
- Consider raising your prices. This is an area you should review on a regular basis.
- Take out a short-term loan. If you have a business or personal line of credit, use it to cover the time periods in which your expenses exceed your income. However, this should not be a permanent arrangement. While it's fine to use a line of credit or a credit card to buy a major piece of equipment or to pay for start-up expenses, your goal needs to be to earn enough income to cover your expenses.
- Make more sales or get more customers. While this is easier to say than to do, running your business at a profit requires that you be aware of how much income you need to generate.
- Review your expenses. While you should be regularly trying to cut unnecessary business expenses, this becomes even more important when you are projecting a negative cash flow.

- Borrow money from friends or family. Although, those closest to you may be your greatest supporters, money can change relationships. If you temporarily need to borrow money from a friend or family member, approach this loan in a business-like manner. Decide exactly what you need the money for, how much you need, when you realistically can expect to pay it back, and what rate of interest you'll pay. Borrow only from someone who will not need the money before you've made all the payments. Have a written agreement and consider this loan at the top of your *must pay on time* list.
- Consider bringing on an investor or silent partner to give you a cash infusion. As with the family and friends, it's very important that this be handled in a business-like way and that all expectations be in writing. An investor is making an investment in your company, not giving you a loan. She will expect to reap some of the benefit of her investment (*e.g.*, a portion of profits). It's best to set up this kind of arrangement with the help of an attorney.
- Contact your local small business development center (SBDC) for help in reviewing the financials (including cash flow projection) for your business. (See Appendix C for information about SBDCs.) Many of them have small loans available for businesses. If you need a larger amount, they can provide information about what's available through the Small Business Administration (SBA).

2

# Inventory and Cost of Goods Sold

*Inventory* is what you have on hand to sell to others. This does not include office supplies or office equipment, unless you're in the business of selling offices supplies or office equipment to others. Service businesses will generally not have inventories. Because Barbara sells jewelry, she does have an inventory. On January 1, her beginning inventory was zero—she had no jewelry on hand to sell to others. During the year she bought $11,000 worth of jewelry. She bought 3,500 bracelets at $2 each, and 4,000 pairs of earrings at $1 per pair. The per-item cost is an important figure for her to know. Barbara's inventory is now worth $11,000.

> **Note:** *This isn't the price at which she will sell the jewelry to others. It's her cost of purchasing the inventory.*

### Barbara's Import Jewelry Company
### Inventory

| | | |
|---|---|---|
| Jan. 1 | | no inventory |
| Jan. 6 | Purchase: 3500 bracelets @ $2 | = $7,000 |
| May 23 | Purchase: 4,000 pairs of earrings @ $1 | = $4,000 |

As Barbara sells each item of jewelry, she keeps in mind the original amount she paid for it so she can reduce her inventory figure accordingly. At the end of the year, Barbara will need to count what's left of her inventory. The total dollar value of the physical inventory should match closely the inventory tally Barbara has kept throughout the year as she sold her jewelry.

No doubt you've noticed stores that are closed temporarily for inventory. Once a year, at least, every business that sells goods needs to do a physical inventory. This means they need to do a hands-on count of what is left of the items they bought to resell to others.

At the end of the year, when Barbara counts what's left of her jewelry, she has 500 bracelets and 93 pairs of earrings. She knows that each bracelet cost her $2, and each pair of earrings cost her $1. This means her ending inventory is $1,093. She subtracts her ending inventory from the earlier $11,000 inventory and finds that her cost of goods sold is $9,907. This figure represents the cost of the goods that were sold—in other words, the cost of the jewelry she sold during the year.

**Barbara's Import Jewelry Company**
**Cost of Goods Sold Calculation**

| | |
|---|---|
| Beginning of year inventory | 0 |
| + Inventory purchases | $11,000 |
| - End of year inventory | - $1,093 |
| **Cost of Goods Sold** | **$9,907** |

*To check figures:*

| | |
|---|---|
| Bought 3,500 bracelets @ $2 | |
| 500 are left, so 3,000 must have sold | 3,000 x $2 = $6,000 |
| Bought 4,000 pairs of earrings @ $1 | |
| 93 pairs are left, so 3,907 must have sold | 3,907 x $1 = $3,907 |
| **Cost of Goods Sold** | **$9,907** |

Since Barbara originally had 3,500 bracelets and has 500 left, she must have sold 3,000. Since she had 4,000 pairs of earrings and now has 93 pairs left, she must have sold 3,907 pairs. When Barbara multiplies the number of bracelets and pairs of earrings she has sold by the amount they cost her, she should again come out with the $9,907 cost of goods sold figure. What Barbara can deduct on her tax return is the $9,907 cost of the items that sold, not the $11,000 she spent to buy all the bracelets and earrings originally.

If Barbara had bought all her jewelry inventory on December 31 and not sold any of it, she would not be able to deduct any of the $11,000 purchase cost for that year because none had been sold. In that case, the $11,000 becomes the beginning inventory figure for the following year. In this example, the $1,093 worth of remaining bracelets and earrings becomes Barbara's beginning inventory for next year. As she sells them during that year, she will then be able to deduct their purchase cost.

In addition to keeping track of the cost of each item and the number left at the end of the year, anyone who has inventory needs to keep a record of any inventory removed for personal use. For example, if you sell cosmetics and you keep a supply on hand to sell to customers, you cannot deduct as a business expense (cost of goods sold) any cosmetics you use personally. Anything personal taken out of the business is a *draw*, a concept discussed more fully in the next chapter.

2

# Taking a Draw | 14

When we looked at Barbara's profit and loss statement on page 43, you may have noticed that draw (the amount of personal money taken from the business) is not listed at all. Remember, if you pay yourself $500 a week from your business or if you pay for groceries from your business checking account, that is a draw. Anything personal paid by the business is a draw. Draw is not a deductible expense. It is not included as income. In fact, for sole proprietors, a *draw is not recorded anywhere on a tax return.*

Partnerships report on their tax returns the amount of a draw taken by each partner. However, this is for information only and isn't part of calculating the net profit. Owners of corporations do not take a draw because they are paid as employees.

In Barbara's case, she is taxed on $14,179, which is her net profit after paying business expenses. You cannot take out as a draw all the income you bring in, because if you did, you wouldn't be able to pay your business expenses. The amount of the net profit (in this case, $14,179) is the most you can take out for yourself and still be able to cover your business expenses.

The IRS doesn't care what you do with the net profit—whether you take it out as a draw or leave it in the business bank account. That's why there

---

### Q & A

**Q: Could I try to make my net profit zero by taking more of a draw?**

A: No, a draw is not a deductible expense, so it doesn't affect your net profit at all. The only way you can reduce your net profit is to have more deductible expenses or less income. If you take all your profit out as a draw, you may not have any money left in your bank account, but you will still have a net profit to report and pay taxes on.

is no place on the tax return for you to indicate whether you took out the whole amount, took part of it, or kept it all in the bank account. It doesn't matter. The net profit is what you pay tax on, but the IRS doesn't care how you spend it.

People sometimes have trouble understanding how you can take money out of your business and not report it. But if you report the draw as you take it out, you will be paying tax on the same money twice. You're already paying tax on it as your net profit. What you do with it is no one's business but yours.

# Employees vs. Independent Contractors | 15

*Employees* are individuals who work for someone else and have Social Security and income taxes withheld from each paycheck. *Independent contractors* are people who work for someone else and do not have taxes withheld from the money they are paid.

Chapter 17 explains which taxes and benefits an employer needs to pay when she has employees. For most states, this includes workers' compensation insurance, unemployment insurance, and the employer's share of Social Security (and in Hawaii, health insurance).

Rather than taking on the extra cost of having employees, many employers have chosen to hire workers as independent contractors or freelancers. The IRS and state taxing agencies are very aware of this and are unwilling to let it continue. As a result, *misclassified employees* is a hot audit focus.

## Classifying an Independent Contractor

Many people think that if they hire a student or someone who works only occasionally or part-time, it is appropriate to classify that person as an independent contractor. In reality, student status or number of hours worked is not the factor that determines whether it's correct for the worker to be treated as an independent contractor. There are two key questions in determining whether someone is an employee or an independent contractor—*Who has control over the working arrangement?* and *How independent is the person performing the services?*

For many years, the IRS relied on a guide they called "Twenty Common-Law Rules" in determining whether an individual had been correctly classified as an independent contractor. More recently, the IRS has boiled the rules down to three major categories:

3

- behavioral control;
- financial control; and,
- type of relationship.

*Behavioral control* covers such issues as whether the worker already has the skills necessary to do the job or whether he or she is provided with instructions and/or training. The IRS also looks at whether the worker has control over when and where to do the work, what tools or equipment to use, what workers to hire, where to purchase supplies and services, and what work must be performed by a specified individual. The most important factor in determining behavioral control is whether the worker is told how to do the work or only what end result is desired. The more control you exert over a worker's behavior the more likely he or she will be classified an employee and not an independent contractor.

*Financial control* includes such factors as the extent of the worker's investment in the work. Question to ask include the following.

- Could the worker have a loss from the work that she is doing or will she always make a profit?
- Whose tools and equipment are used?
- Are the worker's expenses reimbursed?

Also looked at is whether the worker makes her services available to the general public or works only for this company. The more freedom a worker has over the work, the tools used, and the greater the risk of financial loss, the more likely she will be classified as an independent contractor.

*Type of relationship* covers factors such as whether the business provides the worker with employee-type benefits, such as insurance, a pension plan, vacation pay, or sick pay. Also looked at is how temporary or permanent the work is and whether there is a written contract between the business and the worker. Employee status is also determined by examining the extent to which services performed by the worker are a key aspect of the regular business of the company. If the work is integral to the business, the assumption is that the worker has less control over how it is performed and will more likely be classified an employee.

Generally, no single factor indicates who should be classified as an employee and who is classified as an independent contractor—the determination is made by looking at the total work arrangement.

Some companies require independent contractors to have an employer ID number. They're hoping that by having this number, independent contractors will be considered an entity separate from them and there will be less of a question about whether they're truly independent contractors. But just having that number isn't enough to make someone an independent contractor if other factors point to her being an employee.

Written agreements are not always sufficient to prove independent contractor status either. If an independent contractor should have been hired as an employee, an agreement won't be sufficient to keep her from being reclassified if the IRS investigates. However, if you hire someone who really does qualify for independent contractor status, be sure to have her sign a written agreement that includes a statement specifying that she is responsible for paying all of her own taxes.

The penalties are severe for an employer who is caught hiring someone as an independent contractor when that person should have been hired as an employee. The additional taxes owed, plus penalties, equal about 50% of the amount the employee was paid. An employer will be provided with a *safe harbor* (will not be penalized) in classifying an individual as an independent contractor if the following requirements are met.

- The employer has always treated the worker as an independent contractor.
- The employer has filed all required 1099 forms for this worker.
- The employer has a reasonable basis for treating the worker as an independent contractor.

*Reasonable basis* applies if the employer relied on a past audit in which the employment status of the worker was allowed to remain as that of an independent contractor. It also applies if a significant segment (at least 25%) of the employer's industry treats workers in a similar way.

# Form SS-8

Form SS-8 is used to ask the IRS to determine whether a worker should be classified as an employee or an independent contractor. Although workers may be tempted, they should not submit this form unless they believe they've been incorrectly classified as independent contractors and don't care whether they lose their jobs. In almost all cases in which the IRS makes an SS-8 determination, independent contractors will be reclassified as employees. Being under the scrutiny of the IRS will not make your employer happy, which is why you should be ready to look for another job if you file a Form SS-8.

## Seeking Help

This whole area is one in which you need to be very careful if you're planning to have people help you in your business. If you aren't sure whether the person you're hiring should be considered an independent contractor or an employee, consult with an accountant or attorney who specializes in small business tax issues. The fee you pay for that information may save you a great deal in penalties later.

# Differences Between Employees and Self-Employed People | 16

As mentioned in Chapter 15, employees work for someone else and have taxes withheld from their paychecks. Independent contractors work for someone else and don't have taxes withheld from the money they're paid. Self-employed people are business owners who work for themselves and generally offer their services and/or products to more than one customer.

When the term *self-employed* is used in this book, it refers to sole proprietor, non-corporation LLC owners, partnership business owners, and independent contractors. The tax implications for these four groups are identical. On the other hand, as discussed in Chapter 3, corporation shareholder/employees are taxed in the same way as are all other employees.

This chapter discusses some of the differences between employees and self-employed people. Because each state has different employer and employee responsibilities, this book covers these regulations in generalities only.

## Insurance

In some states, the premium for disability insurance is paid by the employee. In other states, the premium is paid by the employer. In many states, disability insurance is not an offered benefit. When disability insurance coverage is offered, an employee who is unable to work because of a medical problem is eligible to collect disability benefits.

As a self-employed person (or independent contractor), you have no coverage for disability insurance unless you buy a policy yourself. You can buy a private policy through an insurance company, or in some states, you can get elective coverage through the State Human Resources or Employment Development Department. Private disability insurance can be quite costly and is not generally available (or has severe restrictions) to those with existing medical conditions. If you don't have disability insurance, however, an illness or injury that keeps you from working could be catastrophic.

Workers' compensation is another type of insurance available to employees, but generally not to self-employed people. Most states require employers to purchase this insurance policy. It provides benefits to any employee injured on the job. Rates for coverage vary according to the risk involved in the job responsibilities. In some states, the business owner who has a workers' compensation policy for employees can include herself in the coverage. Self-employed people with no employees or residing in states that don't allow the business owner to be included will have no coverage if they are injured while working.

Employees are also eligible for unemployment insurance. The employee and/or her employer (depending on state requirements) pay somewhere between 1% and 6% of the employee's gross wages (depending on the state and the employer's experience rating) into the unemployment insurance fund for the employee. If the job ends, she is eligible to collect unemployment. On the other hand, if a self-employed person has a slow period or closes her business, she will not be eligible for unemployment insurance benefits.

## Taxes

Another difference between employees and self-employed people is Social Security tax (also called FICA). When you're an employee, 7.65% of your wages is withheld from your paycheck and deposited into your Social Security account. Your employer adds another 7.65% to your Social Security account, for a total contribution of 15.3% of your wages.

When you're self-employed, no one else is contributing for you, so you are responsible for the entire 15.3%. For self-employed people, Social Security tax is called *self-employment tax*. All of the self-employment tax you pay is credited to your Social Security account. Self-employment tax is owed any time net self-employment income for the year reaches $400.

Because self-employed people are required to pay such a large amount into Social Security, a calculation is done to reduce the amount on which the Social Security tax is calculated. An example of how this tax is calculated for a self-employed person follows.

First, the net income from self-employment is calculated. Remember, net income is the amount left after business expenses have been deducted.

In an effort to partially equalize the Social Security liability of employees and self-employed people, Congress has exempted the first 7.65% of a self-employed person's net income from Social Security tax—so the next step is to multiply your net income by 7.65%. In the example, you can see that multiplying your net income by 7.65% and then subtracting that amount from your net income is the same as multiplying your net income by 92.35%. Self-employed people pay Social Security tax on 92.35% of their net earnings from self-employment.

### Calculating Social Security (Self-Employment) Tax

| | |
|---|---|
| Net self-employment income | $12,000 |
| Percentage of income exempt from self-employment tax | x 7.65% |
| Amount not subject to self-employment tax | $918 |

| | | |
|---|---|---|
| $12,000 | | $12,000 |
| - 918 | *is the same as* | x 92.35% |
| $11,082 | | $11,082 |

| | |
|---|---|
| Amount subject to self-employment tax | $11,082 |
| Self-employment tax rate | x 15.3% |
| Self-employment tax on $12,000 net profit | $1,696 |

The Social Security tax rate for self-employed people is 15.3%. The next step is to multiply the 92.35% of your net self-employment income by the 15.3% Social Security tax rate. The result is the Social Security tax you will owe on your self-employment income. In this example, the amount owed is $1,696. This is separate from and in addition to the federal and state (where applicable) income tax that is paid whether you are an employee or self-employed.

Later in this book, when tax forms are discussed, you will see that there is a line on the front page of Form 1040. (see page 141.) on which a self-employed person is able to deduct from her total income one-half of the self-employment tax she pays.

There is a limit to the amount of annual income on which Social Security or self-employment tax must be paid. The maximum amount is increased each year. For 2005, the maximum income on which you have to pay Social Security or self-employment tax is $89,700.

The following example is Heidi, who had a job as an employee where she earned $60,000 and also had net self-employment income of $36,700. Combined, her two sources of income exceed the maximum income subject to Social Security or self-employment tax. She calculates the amount of income she must pay self-employment tax on as follows.

| | |
|---|---:|
| Wages with Social Security tax already withheld | $60,000 |
| Net self-employment income | + 36,750 |
| Total earned income | $96,750 |
| Maximum Social Security income amount | - 89,700 |
| Excess earnings | $7,050 |
| | |
| Net self-employment income | $36,750 |
| Excess earnings | - 7,050 |
| **Amount of self-employment income** | **$29,700** |
| **Subject to self-employment tax** | |

Heidi has already had Social Security tax withheld on the paychecks from her job as an employee, so the adjustment is made on her self-employment income. She needs to pay self-employment tax on only $29,700 of her self-employment income, rather than on the whole $36,750.

## THE SOCIAL SECURITY TAX VS. MEDICARE

The 7.65% that an employee has withheld from her paycheck for Social Security and the 7.65% that an employer pays into Social Security on behalf of the employee are actually made up of two taxes—6.20% for Social Security and 1.45% for Medicare. The 15.3% self-employment tax paid by self-employed people is actually 12.4% Social Security and 2.9% Medicare. Social Security tax is paid on the first $89,700 of income. Medicare tax is paid on all earned income, no matter how much it totals. In Heidi's case, she will pay the Social Security portion of self-employment tax on $29,700 of her self-employment income and the Medicare portion on all $36,750 of her net self-employment income.

Social Security and Medicare taxes must be paid by employees and self-employed people of all ages. Even those who are collecting Social Security benefits are required to pay into these two funds if they are earning wages or have a business net profit of $400 or more.

## Evaluate Your Alternatives

Although you won't often have the choice, if you take a job in which you are not certain whether it would be more beneficial to be an employee or an independent contractor, you need to calculate the advantages of one over the other. For example, figure how much Social Security tax you would pay as an employee. Also, bear in mind that as an employee, you are covered for unemployment compensation, workers' compensation, and possibly other benefits (such as health insurance or retirement plans). Then, calculate how much self-employment tax you would pay as an independent contractor. Remember that you won't be covered for unemployment compensation and workers' compensation, but you will be able to deduct expenses that may not be deductible for an employee.

To make up for the benefits and taxes you'll be paying on your own, your payment as an independent contractor should be more than what you typically would be paid as an employee. Don't forget to consider the nontax benefits of one status over another (e.g., having a regular paycheck as an employee versus being able to choose which hours to work as an independent contractor).

3

# Employee Payroll and Withholding

# 17

Hiring workers as independent contractors may save a business money. Additionally, employers prefer hiring people as independent contractors because they're able to avoid the paperwork and hassles of having employees. However, as pointed out in Chapter 15, the desire to avoid becoming an employer is not sufficient justification for hiring workers as independent contractors.

If you have employees working for you or you are an employee of your incorporated business, it is important that you be fully aware of the requirements for withholding and remitting payroll taxes. Each employee must fill out Form W-4, indicating how many exemptions she wishes to claim. As the employer, you use that information to withhold from each paycheck the proper amount of federal and state (if applicable) income tax, along with the employee's share of Social Security and Medicare tax. You need a copy of IRS Circular E to help you do this correctly. Depending on your state's regulations, unemployment, disability, or health insurance deductions may also need to be taken from each paycheck.

Once these taxes have been withheld from the employee's paycheck, they must be turned over to the federal and state taxing authorities. Depending on the total amount withheld, the IRS requires that deposits of federal payroll taxes be made quarterly, monthly, or twice a week. IRS payroll deposit coupons are used to deposit this money. State taxing agencies have their own deposit requirements.

At the end of each quarter, employers need to fill out federal and state quarterly payroll tax reports, showing the amount of payroll tax owed and the amount already deposited during the quarter. The federal form is Form 941.

After the year ends, Form W-2 must be sent to each employee reporting how much she earned during the previous year and the amount of taxes that were withheld from her wages.

Employers also are responsible for filing a Form 940, the Federal Unemployment Tax (FUTA) report. The FUTA tax is .8% of the first $7,000 earned by each employee. This amount is reduced by the amount of state unemployment tax paid during the year.

The IRS has no tolerance for incorrectly withheld and remitted payroll taxes. One of the worst tax mistakes you can make is to withhold payroll taxes and then not send them to the IRS in a timely manner. Since the amount you've withheld belongs to the employee, you are treated as though you had stolen the money if it is not remitted to the IRS as required.

You can expect large penalties for not making payroll tax deposits as required. While it may be tempting to use withheld tax monies to pay rent or other necessary business expenses, don't do it. If you cannot keep your hands off the withheld tax, keep it in a separate bank account until it's time to send the money to the IRS and the state.

The outline of your responsibilities as an employer is purposely brief. This is to ensure that you will seek proper guidance once you're ready to hire employees. Some suggestions for avoiding problems in this area follow.

- Attend IRS classes on how to withhold and deposit taxes.
- Meet with a knowledgeable bookkeeper, accountant, or tax preparer. Have that person either handle the payroll responsibilities or provide you with the information you need to do the job yourself.
- Hire a payroll service to handle all the withholding, deposits, and paperwork. It may be well worth the cost, even if you have only one or two employees. Banks provide payroll services, as do private payroll companies. There also are online companies that prepare employee paychecks and payroll tax returns. Be sure to get references before having an outside service take over your payroll duties. You are the one who's ultimately responsible if forms don't get filed or withheld taxes don't get deposited.
- Buy and use the payroll module for your financial software. Make sure you use an updated version each year.
- Consider leasing employees. Some temporary agencies have arrangements whereby you can lease employees and the agency handles all the payroll requirements. You may be able to lease an employee or independent contractor who is already working for you, and thereby reduce your administrative headaches.

Whether you choose to have someone else compute your payroll or you do it yourself, you should be aware of two employment-related state programs. The first is the *New Hire Reporting* program. Within twenty days of hiring a new employee, all employers are required to submit information about the employee to the designated agency for the state in which the business is located. The New Hire Reporting program is an effort to locate workers who are not paying court-ordered child support.

The other state program employers should be aware of is the *Enterprise Zone program*. Enterprise zones are economically depressed areas of a city. In an effort to stimulate development and employment in these areas, employers are being offered tax incentives to operate their businesses in those locations. The largest incentive is provided to enterprise zone-located employers who hire certain categories of employees. Those categories include workers who are:

- economically disadvantaged;
- receiving unemployment;
- dislocated;
- disabled;
- receiving subsidized training; or,
- recently discharged veterans.

The employer receives a credit of 50% of the wages paid to qualified new employees in the first year of their employment. In the second year, the employer receives a credit of 40% of the employees' wages. The credit is 30% for the third year, 20% for the fourth year, and 10% for the fifth year. Check with your city's or state's economic development agency for more information about the Enterprise Zone credits.

3

# 1099 Forms | 18

Each January, as an employee, you are given a W-2 form by your employer. This form indicates the amount earned during the previous year and the taxes withheld from your wages. As a self-employed person or independent contractor, by January 31 you should receive a 1099 form from those who, in the course of their business, paid you $600 or more for your services during the previous year. 1099 forms are slightly smaller in size than W-2 forms.

## Receiving 1099 Forms

The purpose of 1099 forms is to help the taxing authorities find the underground economy—people who aren't reporting and paying taxes on the money they earn. The payer who issues the 1099 form will send the IRS (and possibly the state) a copy of the form they send to you. When you file your tax return, the IRS will check to see whether you've included the reported income.

Because no taxes have been withheld from the income reported on a 1099 form, the only figure listed will be the amount you were paid during the year. You will be given only one or two copies of the 1099 form because, unlike W-2s, the 1099 form doesn't get attached to the income tax return you send to the IRS. (Some states require that you attach a copy of your 1099 forms to your state return.)

As mentioned earlier, you should receive a 1099 form from any person or company who, *in the course of their business*, paid you $600 or more for your services during the year. If you are a painter and you painted someone's house, you won't receive a 1099 form for that work—even if you were paid more than $600—because the money wasn't paid as a business expense. But if you paint someone's office, it's an expense that person had in running her business, so she should send you a 1099 form.

Will you get a 1099 form from everyone who should give you one? No. A lot of people don't know they're supposed to give them. It's not your responsibility to chase after the 1099 forms. Since you don't need to attach the form to your tax return, if you don't get one, it's not your problem. *However, you still must report the income on your tax return whether or not you receive a 1099 form.* This is also true if you don't receive a 1099 form because the amount you were paid was less than $600. Some people mistakenly believe that you are not required to report income unless it's over a certain amount. That is not true. All earned income should be included on your tax return.

It's important to keep accurate records of your income so that you're not dependent on the 1099 forms to show your income. Occasionally, you will receive a 1099 form with an amount on it that differs from your records. This can happen for a number of reasons. Maybe the business wrote you a check on December 29 that you didn't get until January 2, but the check amount was included on your 1099 form for the year in which the check was written. Or perhaps you were reimbursed for expenses during the year and the business included on the 1099 form the amount you were reimbursed, along with the amount you were paid for services. If you don't keep your own records of income earned, you may not know whether the amount reported on the 1099 form is accurate and whether it includes amounts paid as reimbursements.

If you receive 1099 forms that include reimbursements for travel or other expenses, you need to include on your tax return the total amount of income shown on the 1099 forms. Then, in order to make your net income accurate, deduct the travel or other expenses as if they were your own business costs.

**Note:** *Some of your clients will include the reimbursement amount on the 1099 form and some will not. It won't be consistent.*

You may get one or more 1099 forms late. You are supposed to receive them by January 31, but sometimes the person who should send out the form is not aware of this requirement. When she has her taxes done in March and her accountant realizes the 1099 forms were never issued, you may be sent one at that time. Meanwhile, you may have already prepared your tax return. This is another reason to keep complete records of your income, rather than depending on the 1099 forms to tell you how much you've been paid.

As you receive the 1099 forms, make sure they're accurate. If you do receive an incorrect form, contact the person who gave it to you and ask her to send you a corrected copy. Most important, insist that a corrected copy be sent to the IRS.

It's critical that you make sure that the amount of self-employment income you report on your tax return is equal to or greater than the total of your 1099 forms. The IRS can easily check whether you have reported all the income for which you received a 1099 form. If you don't earn much of your income from other businesses and won't be receiving many 1099 forms, it is not as important that the forms you receive be correct down to the penny. In that situation, you will be including on your tax return much more income than is reported on the 1099 forms, so each separate 1099 form won't be distinguishable.

> **EXAMPLE**
>
> *Leslie is a divorce attorney with her own practice. She also teaches a class for which she is paid as an independent contractor. Since Leslie's clients are not paying her in the course of their business, she will not receive 1099 forms from them, even if they pay her $600 or more during the year. Leslie will receive a 1099 form for teaching the class.*

## ISSUING 1099 FORMS

You need to issue a 1099 form to anyone to whom you paid $600 or more for services in the course of your business. This does not include wages paid to employees, since you'll be giving them W-2 forms. The 1099 forms are for people who are not your employees. This might include subcontractors, a bookkeeper, or a colleague who handled part of a job for you. Also, you need to give a 1099 form to anyone to whom you paid rent in the course of your business. This includes subletting or renting an office or studio outside your home. It does not apply to rent you pay for your personal home or for your home office.

You do not give a 1099 form to vendors, such as the telephone company or the office supply store. This is because you don't need to issue 1099 forms to corporations. However, unless a business name ends with *Inc.*, there is no way to know whether the subcontractor you hired or the person to whom you pay your business rent is incorporated—the only way to know for sure is to ask.

Form 1099 cannot be downloaded from the IRS website because the top copy must be printed with pink ink. You can ask the IRS to send you paper copies or you can buy a package of 1099 forms at an office supply store. Alternately, some online services prepare 1099 forms for a modest fee. As of this writing, **www.FileYourTaxes.com** will prepare up to five 1099 forms per business at no charge.

If you are preparing your own 1099 forms, you'll notice that the forms come three to a page. The IRS asks that you not separate the top copy, which is the one you'll be sending to them.

## Q & A

**Q: What if the person I paid refuses to give me her Social Security number?**

A: You can issue the 1099 form anyway with her name and address, and in the area where her Social Security number should be listed, put "refused to give." You can avoid this situation in the future by getting the necessary information when the person begins working for you. At that time, you can require her to fill out Form W-9 (available from the IRS), which asks for her Social Security number. If she doesn't return the form to you, you must withhold 20% federal tax from each payment you make to her. To avoid having this tax withheld, most people will give you their Social Security number.

If you look at the Form 1099 on page 71, you can see what information is needed to fill it out. You are asked for your name, address, and Social Security number, as well as the name, address, and Social Security number of the person you paid. That information should be gathered when you hire the person or rent the office, not at the end of January when you're trying to get the forms out. If you wait to get this information until the forms are due, you may find that the person is on vacation, has left the country, is otherwise unavailable, or is uncooperative.

Box 7 of Form 1099 says, "nonemployee compensation." Generally, it is here that you indicate the amount you paid the person or company. If applicable, Box 1 is where you report the amount of rent you paid in the course of your business.

Form 1099 is a five-part form. In the bottom corner it tells you where to send that copy. The first part goes to the IRS. The next copy goes to the state if your state requires it (many don't). The next two copies go to the recipient (the person you paid). Recipients are given two copies because some states require them to attach a copy to their tax return. The final copy is for your records.

The copies sent to the IRS need to be accompanied by Form 1096. It acts as a cover sheet, telling the IRS how many 1099 forms you're sending them.

The 1099 form must be sent to the recipient by January 31. Form 1096, along with the federal copy of Form 1099, must be sent to the IRS by February 28.

There are penalties for not issuing the 1099 forms and for issuing them incorrectly or late. The penalty for not sending a 1099 form to the payee and a copy to the IRS is $50 per 1099 form, for a total of $100 per recipient. Reduced penalties apply if you don't send out the forms on time but do issue them before August of the year in which the forms are due.

9595 ☐ VOID ☐ CORRECTED

| PAYER'S name, street address, city, state, ZIP code, and telephone no. | | 1 Rents <br> $ | OMB No. 1545-0115 <br><br> 2004 <br><br> Form **1099-MISC** | **Miscellaneous Income** |
|---|---|---|---|---|
| | | 2 Royalties <br> $ | | |
| | | 3 Other income <br> $ | 4 Federal income tax withheld <br> $ | **Copy A** <br> **For** <br> **Internal Revenue Service Center** <br><br> File with Form 1096. |
| PAYER'S Federal identification number | RECIPIENT'S identification number | 5 Fishing boat proceeds <br> $ | 6 Medical and health care payments <br> $ | |
| RECIPIENT'S name | | 7 Nonemployee compensation <br> $ | 8 Substitute payments in lieu of dividends or interest <br> $ | For Privacy Act and Paperwork Reduction Act Notice, see the **2004 General Instructions for Forms 1099, 1098, 5498, and W-2G.** |
| Street address (including apt. no.) | | 9 Payer made direct sales of $5,000 or more of consumer products to a buyer (recipient) for resale ▶ ☐ | 10 Crop insurance proceeds <br> $ | |
| City, state, and ZIP code | | 11 | 12 | |
| Account number (optional) | 2nd TIN not. ☐ | 13 Excess golden parachute payments | 14 Gross proceeds paid to an attorney <br> $ | |
| 15 | | 16 State tax withheld <br> $ <br> $ | 17 State/Payer's state no. | 18 State income <br> $ <br> $ |

Form **1099-MISC**  Cat. No. 14425J  Department of the Treasury - Internal Revenue Service

**Do Not Cut or Separate Forms on This Page — Do Not Cut or Separate Forms on This Page**

3

# Hiring Family Members | 19

Hiring family members and domestic partners to work in your business can be an effective way of transferring income from one person to another. Transferring this income is perfectly legal and can result in some significant tax savings for you.

**EXAMPLE**

*Inez hires her 14-year-old daughter Corinne to clean up around her home office. She pays Corinne a salary that is comparable to what she would pay any other person or service to clean the office. She is also giving Corinne the added benefit of gaining experience by having a job. Inez benefits from the arrangement by paying less tax because she can deduct the amount she pays Corinne.*

**EXAMPLE**

*Lisa owns a pet grooming business. Her life partner, Joan, has just been laid off from her job. Until Joan finds a new job, Lisa will need to pay all the household bills. Paying Joan's share of the bills is not a deductible expense for Lisa. However, by hiring Joan to work temporarily in her business, Lisa is able to deduct 100% of the wages she pays Joan (which Joan can use to pay her share of the bills).*

In general, the family member or domestic partner must be paid as an employee rather than an independent contractor, unless he or she already has her own business doing the type of work you're hiring him or her to do. This means you need to issue W-2 forms, register as an employer, withhold taxes, pay into Social Security, and so on. (See Chapter 17 for information about your tax and withholding responsibilities as an employer.)

# Hiring Your Children

A special rule applies if you hire your child. You don't need to withhold Social Security tax as long as he or she is under age 18. Your child won't owe any income tax until his or her total income for the year is over approximately $4,900 (the exact amount increases each year). Although you do need to issue a W-2 form, if he or she will have less than $4,900 total income, you don't need to withhold income tax from his or her paycheck.

Inez, from the previous example, pays Corinne $3,600 during the year. Corinne also has $100 in interest income from a bank account. Her income is under $4,900, so Corinne doesn't owe any tax. Meanwhile, Inez deducts as a business expense the $3,600 she paid Corinne, saving approximately $500 in self-employment tax and $1,000 in federal income tax.

> **Note:** *Corinne could have a total income of $7,900 and not owe any tax if she contributes (or Inez contributes for her) $3,000 to a traditional IRA retirement account. While it may be hard to imagine a 14-year-old contributing toward retirement, those who begin saving for retirement at a young age will need to contribute far less and will have more retirement money than those who start contributing later in life.*

Hiring your child is a wonderful way to be able to deduct your children's allowances or college funds. However, the child (or other family member) must actually perform the work he or she is being paid to do. His or her pay must also be commensurate with the work he or she is doing and with his or her age and abilities.

# Hiring Your Spouse

Hiring your spouse to work in your business can provide benefits to both of you.

**EXAMPLE** *Susan hires her husband, Daniel, as a sales rep for her office equipment sales company. Susan provides health insurance for all her employees, including Daniel. Daniel's policy covers his spouse (Susan) and their children. Susan is able to deduct the full cost of the health insurance policy as a business expense.*

Normally, a self-employed person can deduct 100% of the health insurance premiums she pays, but not as a business expense. (see Chapter 28.) In other words, the cost of a business owner's health insurance provides an income tax deduction but doesn't reduce her self-employment tax. However, in this example, Susan is able to deduct 100% of her health insurance cost as a business expense since it's part of the policy she provides for Daniel.

Other benefits, such as reimbursement for child care expenses, can be offered to employees of your business. If your spouse is an employee, he can take advantage of the benefits, saving you both money.

**Note:** *Any benefits you offer must be available to all employees. If your spouse is currently the only employee but you anticipate hiring additional workers in the future, consider carefully before setting up an employee benefit program.*

If your business is incorporated, you are treated as an employee of the business and will be eligible for most employee benefits offered by the corporation. As a sole proprietor, however, you are not an employee of your business. This means you can take advantage of such benefits as child care or medical reimbursement programs only if you offer them to your employees and hire your spouse as an employee of your business.

Obviously, there are more than tax ramifications to be considered in deciding whether to hire a family member. You will want to seriously think and talk about the potential personal effect of being in business together. However, with proper planning, hiring family members can be an effective tax savings move.

3

# Making Expenses Deductible | 20

The key to reducing your net profit (and thus, your tax liability) is not to have more expenses, but rather to make existing expenses legitimately tax deductible. Get into the mindset of being a self-employed person. Always ask yourself, *Is there any way I could deduct this expense as a business expense?* or *If I change the time or the way I do this, can I make this expense deductible?* If yes, get a receipt, keep canceled checks, and follow the other recordkeeping suggestions presented in Section 2 of this book.

Deductible expenses are those that are *ordinary* and *necessary*. *Ordinary* means that someone else in the same line of work would have a similar expense. *Necessary* means that in order to operate your business, it was necessary for you to have this expense. In an audit, the IRS may not ask you these specific questions, but this is what the auditor is looking at when reviewing the expenses you deducted.

- Is the expense helpful to your pursuit of profit?
- Is the expense needed in order for you to make money?
- Is the expense appropriate to your pursuit of business?
- Would you have had this expense if you didn't have the business?

In other words, in an audit, the IRS is not only interested in seeing that you have backup materials (*e.g.*, canceled checks and receipts) for expenses you claim, but also that there is a legitimate business reason for claiming each expense.

Knowing what the IRS looks for and making some (usually) small adjustments in your thinking can make many expenses deductible.

> **EXAMPLE**
>
> *Nancy is a workplace consultant. She sees an article about workplace stress in a magazine. She buys a copy of the magazine, but doesn't think of it as a business expense and fails to get a receipt. However, the magazine can be a deductible expense and she should get a receipt to prove her expense.*

# Business Start-Up Expenses 21

As part of preparing to go into business, you'll probably buy supplies, such as stationery and business cards. In addition, you may have other start-up expenses, such as advertising, telephone, rent, website creation, and leasehold improvements.

Purchasing inventory and other assets, such as equipment and furnishings, may also be part of your pre-business preparation. Inventory (as discussed in Chapter 13) can be deducted only as you sell it. Other types of assets are depreciated over a period of years, beginning with the year you start your business. (See Chapter 22 for information about depreciation.)

If you purchase an existing business, your costs may include items such as franchise fees and customer lists. Most of the purchase costs, other than inventory and equipment, are amortized (deducted) over sixty months beginning with the month the business starts.

As mentioned in Chapter 2, you are considered to be in business when you have gathered together everything necessary to be in business—licenses, inventory, and store/office rental (if appropriate)—and have let others know that your services or products are available for purchase.

If you have start-up expenses in the year before you open your business, you won't be able to deduct those expenses until your business

4

---

## Q & A

**Q:** What if I don't have any income my first year in business? Where do I deduct the expenses?

**A:** Although tax preparers differ in how they feel about this, many will not fill out a Schedule C for someone who has only business expenses and no business income, as it may call attention to the entire tax return.

actually begins. At that time, you can start depreciating any equipment you bought and begin amortizing over sixty months (or more, if you choose) the other pre-business expenses you've incurred. This means that $\frac{1}{60}$ of the start-up costs are deducted each month after your business begins.

# Depreciation | 22

*Depreciation* can be a hard concept to understand. It means the loss in value of an asset over the time that item is being used in your business. An *asset* is a thing of value—such as a computer, a desk, or a building—that will last for more than a year. When you buy an asset for your business, the IRS says the cost must be deducted over a period of years, since the item's useful life is longer than one tax year. Each year, you deduct a portion of the cost of these items. That deduction is called depreciation.

In order to be eligible for depreciation, the property must:

- be owned by you;
- have a useful life of one year or more;
- be tangible (something you can touch); and,
- be used in your business.

MACRS is the name of the method of depreciation currently in use. Prior to 1987, other methods such as ACRS and straight-line depreciation were used. Under any of the depreciation methods, if you own an item, such as a car, that is used both for business and personal purposes, you can depreciate only the business-use portion. It's your responsibility to keep adequate records in order to be able to prove the business-use portion of *mixed-use* property.

Cars, computers, trucks, copiers, cell phones, and electronic equipment are among the assets considered to be five-year property. This means they are depreciated over five years. Since the first year is calculated as if you bought the property in the middle of the year, it actually takes six years to fully deduct five-year property. If you look at the first column of the chart that follows, you will see that in the first year you begin depreciating five-year property, you deduct 20% of its cost. In the second year, you deduct 32% of its cost, and by the end of the sixth year, you will have deducted the full cost.

**Depreciation Using MACRS**
**(Modified Accelerated Cost Recovery System)**
**Depreciation**

| Year | 5-year property (cars, computers, trucks, copiers, and cell phones) | 7-year property (office furniture and other business equipment) | Cars and other 5-year property used less than 51% for business |
|------|------|------|------|
| 1 | 20% | 14.29% | 10% |
| 2 | 32% | 24.49% | 20% |
| 3 | 19.20% | 17.49% | 20% |
| 4 | 11.52% | 12.49% | 20% |
| 5 | 11.52% | 8.93% | 20% |
| 6 | 5.76% | 8.93% | 10% |
| 7 | | 8.93% | |
| 8 | | 4.46% | |

Other business equipment and office furniture is considered seven-year property. It gets depreciated, as you can see in the second column of the chart, over a period of eight years. At the end of eight years, the total cost of the item will have been deducted.

A different depreciation schedule is used for buildings. Depending on when you begin using the building in your business, it will generally be depreciated over thirty-nine years. Buildings *placed in service* after December 31, 1986 and before May 13, 1993 are depreciated over 31½ years.

(Land can never be depreciated because it doesn't wear out. Also, inventory is never depreciated.)

# Calculating Depreciation

The amount of depreciation allowed depends on the *basis* of the asset. The basis is generally the original cost of the item including sales tax, shipping, and installation (if applicable). The cost of any improvements made to the property is added to the basis. If the asset is used less than 100% for business, the basis for depreciation is the cost plus improvements multiplied by the percentage the item is used for business. The basis for real estate (buildings) used in business always excludes the value of the land.

The date you *place an item into service* is the date you begin using it in your business. When you stop using an asset in your business, you stop depreciating it. If you sell the item, you may have a taxable gain due to the depreciation you took on that item. (See Marisa's example on page 86.)

If you bought an item and used it in your business in a previous year and didn't deduct the depreciation on it, you're considered to have taken the depreciation anyway. If you begin claiming depreciation on the item this year, you use the percentage that applies to the number of years since the item was placed into service. For example, if you began using the item in your business three years ago, even if you have never depreciated it before, count this as year three in calculating the depreciation for the current year.

## ASSETS OWNED BEFORE YOU WENT INTO BUSINESS

If you owned an asset before you went into business and you're a sole proprietor, you cannot sell the item to your business when you begin using it for business. However, you can begin depreciating it as of the date you place it into service. The year you place it into service is year one on the depreciation chart, and you continue to depreciate the property over five, seven, or thirty-nine years, just as you would if it were an item bought originally for business use. However, the basis used for depreciation is not the original cost of the item, but rather its value as of the date it was placed into service. You can check newspaper want ads, stores that sell used items, or online sales venues—such as eBay—to learn what your item is worth now.

### Q & A

**Q: Does everything have to be depreciated?**

A: IRS regulations say that if an item will last more than a year, it needs to be depreciated. However, most tax preparers have a depreciation minimum (such as $250). If an individual item cost less than that amount, it will be deducted as a current expense—if more, it will be depreciated. For example, an electrician who buys screwdrivers and other small hand tools or a hair salon owner who buys scissors and magazine racks will find that most tax preparers won't depreciate these low-cost items, but instead will include them in expense categories such as small tools, office supplies, or small furnishings.

4

**EXAMPLE**

*Wendy bought a computer last year. She started her business this year and uses the computer in her work. When she placed her computer into service, Wendy looked at the classified ads in a newspaper and a computer magazine, and she contacted a used computer store. She learned that the computer she bought last year for $3,000 now has a fair market value of $2,000. Since she uses the computer exclusively for her business, $2,000 is the basis Wendy will use in depreciating it. The first year she's in business, Wendy's depreciation deduction is 20% of the basis of the computer ($400).*

If, for some reason, such as real estate increasing in value, the original cost is less than the value when you begin using a personal asset for business, the basis you use is the *lesser* of cost or fair market value.

# Listed Property

Certain types of property are called *listed property*. This means that there are further restrictions on how the property is depreciated. Listed property includes automobiles, cell phones, computers, and related equipment that is not used exclusively at a business establishment or qualified in-home office. Property used for entertainment or recreation, such as cameras, VCRs, and camcorders, is also considered listed property.

If you have listed property that is used less than 51% for business, you must use the depreciation schedule shown in the third column of the chart on page 82. As mentioned previously, it is your responsibility to keep records that prove what percentage the property is used for business. If listed property is used 100% for business and is kept at a business location (including a deductible home office), no records of business use need to be kept.

Cars, in addition to being considered listed property, have further restrictions on how they are depreciated. The annual depreciation limitation for cars is shown in the chart on page 82. As with all assets, only the business percentage of a car can be depreciated. (Calculating the business percentage of car use is discussed in Chapter 25.)

---

## Q & A

**Q: What if someone gave me something that I'm using in my business?**

A: You can depreciate it. Its basis (the amount you depreciate) is whatever the cost or basis was for the person who gave it to you.

---

# Section 179 Depreciation

The first part of this chapter discusses regular MACRS (Modified Accelerated Cost Recovery System) depreciation. Another method for depreciating property is to use the *Section 179* election. Section 179 refers to a section in the Internal Revenue Code that says when you buy something that normally would be depreciated over a period of years, you may choose instead to fully depreciate it in the year you purchase it.

**Note:** *Using Section 179 still means you are depreciating an asset; it doesn't mean you list the item as an expense on Schedule C.*

Up to $102,000 worth of assets you purchased in 2004 are eligible for the accelerated treatment. The maximum Section 179 deduction applies to both single persons and married couples, even if each spouse owns a business.

Section 179 is further limited by the total earned income reported on the tax return. The maximum Section 179 deduction that can be claimed is the lesser of total earned income (including wages), or $102,000 (for 2004).

> **EXAMPLE**
>
> Louise is married to Jerry. They each owned a business in 2004. Jerry had a profit of $30,000 in his business, while Louise had a loss of $3,000 in hers. Louise also earned $15,000 in wages this year. During the year, Jerry bought $35,000 worth of new equipment for his business, and Louise bought $12,000 for hers.
>
> The amount of Section 179 deduction Louise and Jerry can take is limited by their earned income, which totals $42,000 ($30,000 for Jerry, minus $3,000 for Louise's business, plus $15,000 in wages). Between them, they purchased $47,000 in assets in 2004. The remaining $5,000 ($47,000 in purchases minus $42,000 in earned income) can be carried over to next year and be deducted in full at that time.

As you can see, assuming your earned income is large enough, Section 179 allows you to buy, for example, a $5,000 computer system and $6,000 worth of office equipment and deduct the entire $11,000 in the year you make the purchase. It's important to understand that Section 179 is still a type of depreciation, and the depreciation form Form 4562 must still be included with your tax return—even though you're deducting the full cost of the items.

You cannot use Section 179 for property you've converted from personal to business use because Section 179 can be used only in the year you originally buy the asset. Also, you cannot use Section 179 for listed property used less than 51% for business. Real estate cannot be depreciated using Section 179. Cars remain limited to the figures shown in the chart on page 82, even if you use Section 179 to deduct the maximum allowed in the year you purchase the vehicle.

## DECIDING WHEN TO USE SECTION 179

As long as your wages (if any), plus your net self-employment income, exceed the amount of the Section 179 deduction you want to take, you're allowed to use Section 179. In most cases, when allowed, you will choose to use Section 179. However, there are a couple of situations when you might choose to use regular MACRS depreciation. One example is in a year in which you made very little money in your business. If you have only a small amount of business income, it may not be effective tax planning to depreciate using Section 179.

> **EXAMPLE**
>
> *Marisa bought a $2,000 computer to use exclusively in her business. Her wages were $20,000. Her gross self-employment income (before expenses) was $1,500. In addition to buying the computer, Marisa spent $200 on office supplies. If she deducts the computer in full (uses Section 179), her self-employment loss will be $700 ($1,500 minus $200 minus $2000). The $700 loss will offset $700 of her wages, so that her total taxed income will be $19,300. Deducting the computer in full will reduce Marisa's income tax. Since she's in the 15% tax bracket, the $2,000 she spent on the computer will save her $300 in federal income tax.*

If instead Marisa had taken regular MACRS depreciation on the computer this year, she would have been able to deduct 20% ($400) of the cost in the first year. Subtracting that amount, plus the office supplies, from her self-employment income, Marisa would have a net profit of $900 ($1,500 minus $200 minus $400). The $400 computer depreciation deduction saves Marisa $60 in federal income tax ($400 x 15%) and $57 in self-employment tax ($400 x 92.35% x 15.3%) in the first year. Assuming that she remains in the 15% federal tax bracket for the remaining five years she's depreciating the computer, Marisa will save a total of $226 in federal tax ($1,600 x 15%) and $245 in self-employment tax ($1,600 x 92.35% x 15.3%) over that period of time. Using regular MACRS depreciation saves Marisa a total of $583 in tax ($300 in federal income tax plus $283 in self-employment tax) over the six years versus the $300 she saves if she deducts the full cost of the computer in the year she buys it. This is because by depreciating the computer over a period of years, Marisa ends up with a net profit from her business—so the deduction saves her both income tax and self-employment tax.

On the other hand, by taking the Section 179 deduction for the full price in the year she buys the computer, Marisa gets a larger deduction the first year than she would if she used regular MACRS depreciation. If she needs the refund money or hasn't paid enough in estimated tax payments, she may choose the $300 tax savings she could get in one year over the $583 savings she would get over the six-year period. Also, Marisa needs to consider whether she'll still be in business and using the same computer in six years.

If Marisa takes Section 179 and deducts the full amount of the computer the year she buys it and then decides to sell it the next year, she may regret her depreciation decision. She bought the computer for $2,000. Using Section 179, she deducts the full

$2,000 in the first year. In year two, she sells the computer for $1,500. Because she took Section 179 (fully deducted the $2,000 cost) in year one, her basis in the computer when she sells it is considered to be zero. Therefore, the $1,500 she receives from selling it is fully taxable to her.

As you can see, there is no wrong or right answer about when to use Section 179. Before deciding which method of depreciation is best for you to use, tax planning is necessary to consider your taxes both for the year you purchase the item and for future years.

It needn't be an all-or-nothing choice. You can use Section 179 on some items bought in a year and use regular MACRS depreciation for other items. You can also use Section 179 for part of the cost of the item and regular depreciation for the remainder of the cost.

## Bonus First Year Depreciation

As if depreciation wasn't already complicated enough, an additional choice for calculating this deduction has been available for the last few years. The *bonus first year depreciation* was designed to encourage businesses to buy equipment after September 11, 2001 (9/11). An extra amount of first year deprecation has been allowed for assets placed in service after September 10, 2001 and before January 1, 2005. For property placed in service before May 6, 2003, the bonus is 30% of the asset's cost. For items placed in service after May 5, 2003, the bonus percentage is 50%.

This bonus is not extra depreciation. It's a greater-than-normal deduction allowed in the first year the asset is used in a business. This results in a lower-than-normal amount available to be claimed in the later years of the asset's use. Bonus depreciation can only be used on property for which you are the original owner. In other words, it's not available for used assets. It also cannot be used for listed property used less than 51% for business.

You might be wondering why you would choose to take bonus depreciation, which allows a deduction for 50% of the asset's cost in the first year, when you could instead use Section 179 and claim 100%. The answer is that, with one exception, you probably would choose to use Section 179. The bonus depreciation was really designed for companies who purchased more than $102,000 worth of assets during the year and who, after claiming 100% of the cost of those items under Section 179, needed a way to quickly deduct depreciation on the remainder of the items they bought.

The one advantageous use of bonus depreciation applicable to smaller businesses has to do with car purchases. As mentioned earlier in this chapter, there are limitations on the amount of depreciation that can be claimed on cars. Normally, $3,060

4

is the maximum depreciation that can be claimed on a car the first year it's placed in service. This is true whether regular MACRS or Section 179 depreciation is claimed. However, when using the 50% bonus depreciation for cars purchased between May 6, 2003 and December 31, 2004, the maximum first year depreciation increases to $10,710. (See Chapter 25 for more information about depreciation as it relates to cars.)

> **Note:** *Many states have not adopted the first year bonus depreciation. As a result, if you use it on your federal return, your federal and state depreciation amounts may differ, resulting in net profit amounts on the two returns that don't match. Some states have also not adopted Section 179 and/or the MACRS method of depreciation. Your state tax booklet should indicate what differences there are between depreciation methods allowed by your state and those that can be used on the federal return.*

# Form 4562

A copy of Form 4562, the form used to report the items you're depreciating, is found on page 89. Part I is where you list the items you want to depreciate using Section 179. If the items are considered listed property, you include them in Part V, then carry the total back to Part I. There are questions in Part V that ask whether you have sufficient records for the business use of your listed property. This section also provides a place for you to list your automobile's total mileage and business mileage for the year.

Part II of the form is where you include any bonus first year depreciation you are claiming.

In Part III, list the items you bought this year that you are depreciating using regular MACRS depreciation. All five-year items are combined, all seven-year items are combined, and so on. Line 17 of Part III is used to show this year's depreciation amount for items bought in previous years.

Part VI is used to list items to be amortized. *Amortization* is similar to depreciation, but is used for intangible items, such as franchise fees, trademarks, and closing costs on real estate purchases. This is the area in which you list the start-up costs you had before your business opened. They are amortized over sixty months, beginning with the month your business starts.

| Form **4562** | **Depreciation and Amortization** (Including Information on Listed Property) | OMB No. 1545-0172 |
|---|---|---|
| Department of the Treasury Internal Revenue Service | ▶ See separate instructions.  ▶ Attach to your tax return. | 20**04** Attachment Sequence No. **67** |

| Name(s) shown on return | Business or activity to which this form relates | Identifying number |
|---|---|---|

**Part I** Election To Expense Certain Property Under Section 179
**Note:** *If you have any listed property, complete Part V before you complete Part I.*

| | | | |
|---|---|---|---|
| 1 | Maximum amount. See page 2 of the instructions for a higher limit for certain businesses | **1** | $102,000 |
| 2 | Total cost of section 179 property placed in service (see page 3 of the instructions) | **2** | |
| 3 | Threshold cost of section 179 property before reduction in limitation | **3** | $410,000 |
| 4 | Reduction in limitation. Subtract line 3 from line 2. If zero or less, enter -0- | **4** | |
| 5 | Dollar limitation for tax year. Subtract line 4 from line 1. If zero or less, enter -0-. If married filing separately, see page 3 of the instructions. | **5** | |

| (a) Description of property | (b) Cost (business use only) | (c) Elected cost |
|---|---|---|
| **6** | | |

| | | | |
|---|---|---|---|
| 7 | Listed property. Enter the amount from line 29 | **7** | |
| 8 | Total elected cost of section 179 property. Add amounts in column (c), lines 6 and 7 | **8** | |
| 9 | Tentative deduction. Enter the **smaller** of line 5 or line 8 | **9** | |
| 10 | Carryover of disallowed deduction from line 13 of your 2003 Form 4562 | **10** | |
| 11 | Business income limitation. Enter the smaller of business income (not less than zero) or line 5 (see instructions) | **11** | |
| 12 | Section 179 expense deduction. Add lines 9 and 10, but do not enter more than line 11 | **12** | |
| 13 | Carryover of disallowed deduction to 2005. Add lines 9 and 10, less line 12 ▶ | **13** | |

**Note:** *Do not use Part II or Part III below for listed property. Instead, use Part V.*

**Part II** Special Depreciation Allowance and Other Depreciation (**Do not** include listed property.)

| | | | |
|---|---|---|---|
| 14 | Special depreciation allowance for qualified property (other than listed property) placed in service during the tax year (see page 3 of the instructions) | **14** | |
| 15 | Property subject to section 168(f)(1) election (see page 4 of the instructions) | **15** | |
| 16 | Other depreciation (including ACRS) (see page 4 of the instructions) | **16** | |

**Part III** MACRS Depreciation (**Do not** include listed property.) (See page 5 of the instructions.)

Section A

| | | | |
|---|---|---|---|
| 17 | MACRS deductions for assets placed in service in tax years beginning before 2004 | **17** | |
| 18 | If you are electing under section 168(i)(4) to group any assets placed in service during the tax year into one or more general asset accounts, check here ▶ ☐ | | |

Section B—Assets Placed in Service During 2004 Tax Year Using the General Depreciation System

| (a) Classification of property | (b) Month and year placed in service | (c) Basis for depreciation (business/investment use only—see instructions) | (d) Recovery period | (e) Convention | (f) Method | (g) Depreciation deduction |
|---|---|---|---|---|---|---|
| 19a 3-year property | | | | | | |
| b 5-year property | | | | | | |
| c 7-year property | | | | | | |
| d 10-year property | | | | | | |
| e 15-year property | | | | | | |
| f 20-year property | | | | | | |
| g 25-year property | | | 25 yrs. | | S/L | |
| h Residential rental property | | | 27.5 yrs. | MM | S/L | |
| | | | 27.5 yrs. | MM | S/L | |
| i Nonresidential real property | | | 39 yrs. | MM | S/L | |
| | | | | MM | S/L | |

Section C—Assets Placed in Service During 2004 Tax Year Using the Alternative Depreciation System

| | | | | | | |
|---|---|---|---|---|---|---|
| 20a Class life | | | | | S/L | |
| b 12-year | | | 12 yrs. | | S/L | |
| c 40-year | | | 40 yrs. | MM | S/L | |

**Part IV** Summary (see page 7 of the instructions)

| | | | |
|---|---|---|---|
| 21 | Listed property. Enter amount from line 28 | **21** | |
| 22 | **Total.** Add amounts from line 12, lines 14 through 17, lines 19 and 20 in column (g), and line 21. Enter here and on the appropriate lines of your return. Partnerships and S corporations—see instr. | **22** | |
| 23 | For assets shown above and placed in service during the current year, enter the portion of the basis attributable to section 263A costs | **23** | |

For Paperwork Reduction Act Notice, see separate instructions. | Cat. No. 12906N | Form **4562** (2004)

Form 4562 (2004)                                                         Page **2**

**Part V**   **Listed Property** (Include automobiles, certain other vehicles, cellular telephones, certain computers, and property used for entertainment, recreation, or amusement.)

**Note:** *For any vehicle for which you are using the standard mileage rate or deducting lease expense, complete **only** 24a, 24b, columns (a) through (c) of Section A, all of Section B, and Section C if applicable.*

**Section A—Depreciation and Other Information (Caution: *See page 8 of the instructions for limits for passenger automobiles.*)**

**24a** Do you have evidence to support the business/investment use claimed? ☐ Yes ☐ No    **24b** If "Yes," is the evidence written? ☐ Yes ☐ No

| (a) Type of property (list vehicles first) | (b) Date placed in service | (c) Business/ investment use percentage | (d) Cost or other basis | (e) Basis for depreciation (business/investment use only) | (f) Recovery period | (g) Method/ Convention | (h) Depreciation deduction | (i) Elected section 179 cost |
|---|---|---|---|---|---|---|---|---|
| **25** Special depreciation allowance for qualified listed property placed in service during the tax year and used more than 50% in a qualified business use (see page 8 of the instructions)   **25** | | | | | | | | |
| **26** Property used more than 50% in a qualified business use (see page 8 of the instructions): | | | | | | | | |
| | | % | | | | | | |
| | | % | | | | | | |
| | | % | | | | | | |
| **27** Property used 50% or less in a qualified business use (see page 8 of the instructions): | | | | | | | | |
| | | % | | | | S/L – | | |
| | | % | | | | S/L – | | |
| | | % | | | | S/L – | | |

**28** Add amounts in column (h), lines 25 through 27. Enter here and on line 21, page 1. . . **28**

**29** Add amounts in column (i), line 26. Enter here and on line 7, page 1. . . . . . . . . . . . . . **29**

**Section B—Information on Use of Vehicles**

Complete this section for vehicles used by a sole proprietor, partner, or other "more than 5% owner," or related person.

If you provided vehicles to your employees, first answer the questions in Section C to see if you meet an exception to completing this section for those vehicles.

| | (a) Vehicle 1 | | (b) Vehicle 2 | | (c) Vehicle 3 | | (d) Vehicle 4 | | (e) Vehicle 5 | | (f) Vehicle 6 | |
|---|---|---|---|---|---|---|---|---|---|---|---|---|
| **30** Total business/investment miles driven during the year (**do not** include commuting miles—See page 2 of the instructions) . | | | | | | | | | | | | |
| **31** Total commuting miles driven during the year | | | | | | | | | | | | |
| **32** Total other personal (noncommuting) miles driven . . . . . . . . | | | | | | | | | | | | |
| **33** Total miles driven during the year. Add lines 30 through 32 . . . . | | | | | | | | | | | | |
| | Yes | No | Yes | No | Yes | No | Yes | No | Yes | No | Yes | No |
| **34** Was the vehicle available for personal use during off-duty hours?. . . . . | | | | | | | | | | | | |
| **35** Was the vehicle used primarily by a more than 5% owner or related person? | | | | | | | | | | | | |
| **36** Is another vehicle available for personal use? . . . . . . . . . . . | | | | | | | | | | | | |

**Section C—Questions for Employers Who Provide Vehicles for Use by Their Employees**

Answer these questions to determine if you meet an exception to completing Section B for vehicles used by employees who **are not** more than 5% owners or related persons (see page 10 of the instructions).

| | Yes | No |
|---|---|---|
| **37** Do you maintain a written policy statement that prohibits all personal use of vehicles, including commuting, by your employees? . . . . . . . . . . . . . . . . . . . . . . . . . . . . . . . | | |
| **38** Do you maintain a written policy statement that prohibits personal use of vehicles, except commuting, by your employees? See page 10 of the instructions for vehicles used by corporate officers, directors, or 1% or more owners . . . . . | | |
| **39** Do you treat all use of vehicles by employees as personal use? . . . . . . . . . . . . . . | | |
| **40** Do you provide more than five vehicles to your employees, obtain information from your employees about the use of the vehicles, and retain the information received? . . . . . . . . . . . . . . . | | |
| **41** Do you meet the requirements concerning qualified automobile demonstration use? (See page 10 of the instructions.) . | | |

**Note:** *If your answer to 37, 38, 39, 40, or 41 is "Yes," do not complete Section B for the covered vehicles.*

**Part VI**   **Amortization**

| (a) Description of costs | (b) Date amortization begins | (c) Amortizable amount | (d) Code section | (e) Amortization period or percentage | (f) Amortization for this year |
|---|---|---|---|---|---|
| **42** Amortization of costs that begins during your 2004 tax year (see page 11 of the instructions): | | | | | |
| | | | | | |
| | | | | | |
| **43** Amortization of costs that began before your 2004 tax year. . . . . . . . . . . . . **43** | | | | | |
| **44** **Total.** Add amounts in column (f). See page 12 of the instructions for where to report. . . **44** | | | | | |

⊛ Printed on recycled paper                                     Form **4562** (2004)

# Deducting Your Home Office  23

In the past, strict rules for claiming a home office meant that many self-employed people didn't qualify for this deduction.

More recently, the rules have been liberalized, and you can deduct a home office if your work space is:

- a place where you met with clients or customers;
- a separate structure not connected to the house;
- the sole place business inventory or product samples are stored; or,
- the primary place of work for this business.

Your home office qualifies as your primary place of work if:

- it's where you spend the majority of your time while working on your business or
- you use it for administrative or management activities of your business and you have no other fixed location where you spend substantial time on these tasks.

> **EXAMPLE**
>
> *Lourdes is a management consultant who provides training to corporations. She spends most of each week either conducting training sessions or traveling for business. She prepares for her training sessions in her home office. She also does her invoicing for current clients and marketing for potential new clients there. Because it is the place she performs the administrative tasks for her business and she has nowhere else she does that, her home office can be deducted.*

Despite the present liberalized rules, not everyone will qualify to deduct a home office. As has always been the case, you can have a home office, but that doesn't necessarily mean you have a deductible office-in-home.

4

The basic rules for a deductible work space is that it must be used *regularly* and *exclusively* for your business. Exclusively used means that nothing else happens in that space. A home office does not need to be a separate room, but must be a clearly definable space. If you have a desk and computer in your bedroom and meet all the qualifications for a deductible home office, you can claim that portion of your bedroom as your office-in-home. If you work on the dining room table, you can claim a 3-by-6 (or whatever the size of your table) office-in-home. However, you cannot also use the dining room table as the place you serve Thanksgiving dinner (or any other meal). If you have a space that's used solely for your business, except that your child or spouse comes in occasionally to use your computer, you may want to relocate the computer, because the IRS won't consider your space to be exclusively used for business.

In addition to the regulations already mentioned, there is yet another hurdle to overcome in order to deduct your home office expense. You cannot deduct an office-in-home if you have a loss from your business or if the home office deduction would create a loss. The maximum expense you can deduct for your home office is the amount of net profit from your business, not including the office-in-home.

For example, if your net profit is $2,000, the most you can deduct for an office-in-home is $2,000. If your home office expenses are $2,000, your net profit will be zero. If your home office expenses are $3,000, you'll be able to deduct $2,000 of them and will still have a net profit of zero. Your net profit can be no lower than zero and still include a deduction for a home office.

If your business has a loss this year, you can't deduct your home office—even if it qualifies. However, you can carry the unused expense over to next year's return and deduct it then. The only exception to this is for expenses that would be deductible even without the business—that is, mortgage interest and real estate tax. These expenses can be deducted even if you have a business loss.

If you use space in your home on a regular basis to provide day care for children or for adults who are at least sixty-five years old or incapable of caring for themselves, you can take the deduction even though your business and personal space may be the same. To qualify for the home office deduction, you must have a license or certification as a day care center or group day care home.

## Calculating the Home Office Deduction

Once you've decided that you qualify for the home office deduction, you then need to calculate the percentage of your home used for business. The most accurate way to do this is to measure the total number of square feet in your home and the number of square feet used for business. If the rooms in your home are approximately the same size, you may base your office-in-home percentage on the number of rooms used for business versus the total number of rooms in the house. You can use either of these methods to determine what percentage of your home is used for business. (An example of the home office calculation is shown on page 94.) As you do the measuring, consider creating a diagram of your home office. This, along with photographs of the work space, can be extremely helpful if you're audited and questioned about your home office space (particularly if you've since moved to a new home).

If you operate a day care facility, calculating the percentage of your home office is done differently. Multiply the number of days you used your home for day care during the year by the number of hours used per day. Divide that figure by 8760 (365 days times 24 hours) to determine the percentage of your home to claim.

# Q & A

Q: **Since I can already deduct my mortgage interest and real estate taxes as a personal expense, what is the benefit of deducting a home office?**

A: There are three benefits. First, when you deduct those expenses as business expenses, they not only reduce your income tax, but also lessen your self-employment tax. Second, by deducting a home office, you're able to deduct utilities, insurance, and depreciation expenses that can't be taken as personal itemized deductions. The third benefit is that having a deductible home office allows you to deduct more of your car mileage expense (discussed in the next chapter).

After you've calculated the home office percentage, add together your total rent or mortgage interest, all your utilities, the amount of maintenance done on the entire home, and your total real estate taxes and insurance. Once you've combined these expenses, multiply the total by the percentage of the home that's used for business. To that figure, add maintenance on the part of your home that is used exclusively for business, such as painting your office room. The last figure to be added in is the depreciation on the business part of your home. (For more information on depreciation, see Chapter 22.) The portion of your home used for business is depreciated over thirty-nine years, so you get only a small deduction each year. Once all the figures are added together, you'll have your total allowable office-in-home expense.

Following is an example of how the office-in-home deduction is calculated.

First, divide the number of square feet in the office space by the number of square feet in the entire house to calculate the percentage of your home used for business. Then add together the expenses you had for the entire house—

rent or mortgage interest, real estate taxes and insurance, and utilities and maintenance for the entire home. Multiply the total of those expenses by the business percentage of home use. To that figure, add maintenance costs you had only for your home office space. If you own your home, add in depreciation. The end result is your total office-in-home expense. In this example, the net profit from the business is $5,000 so the most that can be claimed for home office expenses is the lesser of the actual expenses or $5,000.

### Calculating the Office-in-Home Expense

| | |
|---|---|
| Total # of square feet in home | 1000 square feet |
| Total # of square feet used for business | 200 square feet |
| Percentage of home used for business | 20% |
| Business net profit | $5,000 |
| *(not including deduction for office in home)* | |
| Total rent or mortgage interest | $8,000 |
| Total utilities | +500 |
| Total real estate taxes & insurance | +2,000 |
| Total household expenses | $10,500 |
| | x 20% business use |
| Office-in-home portion of expenses | $2,100 |
| Maintenance on part of home | +250 |
| used exclusively for business | |
| Depreciation on business part of home | +700 |
| (using MACRS 39 year method) | |
| **Total allowable office-in-home expense** | **$3,050** |

Where the office-in-home expense is listed on your tax return will depend on whether you're a sole proprietor, a partner, or a corporation shareholder/employee. A sole proprietor includes the expense on Schedule C. (see page 145.) If the office-in-home expense has not been reported on the partnership return, a partner will list it on Schedule E and use it to offset partnership income. A corporation shareholder/employee, like any other employee, includes the expense on Schedule A as a personal itemized deduction. If taken on Schedule A, the amount is deductible only if all work related expenses exceed 2% of her income. Sole proprietors must fill out Form 8829 in order to deduct the home office.

# Form 8829

Form 8829 is actually just a more official version of the home office calculation shown on page 95. It asks how much of your home is used regularly and exclusively for busi-

| Form **8829** | **Expenses for Business Use of Your Home** | OMB No. 1545-1266 |
|---|---|---|
| Department of the Treasury<br>Internal Revenue Service | ▶ File only with Schedule C (Form 1040). Use a separate Form 8829 for each<br>home you used for business during the year.<br>▶ See separate instructions. | 20**04**<br>Attachment<br>Sequence No. **66** |

Name(s) of proprietor(s)       Your social security number

### Part I   Part of Your Home Used for Business

| | | | |
|---|---|---|---|
| 1 | Area used regularly and exclusively for business, regularly for day care, or for storage of inventory or product samples (see instructions) . . . . . . . . . . . . . . . | **1** | |
| 2 | Total area of home . . . . . . . . . . . . . . . . . . . . | **2** | |
| 3 | Divide line 1 by line 2. Enter the result as a percentage . . . . . . . . . . | **3** | % |

● **For day-care facilities not used exclusively for business, also complete lines 4–6.**
● **All others, skip lines 4–6 and enter the amount from line 3 on line 7.**

| | | | | |
|---|---|---|---|---|
| 4 | Multiply days used for day care during year by hours used per day | **4** | | h r . |
| 5 | Total hours available for use during the year (366 days × 24 hours) (see instructions) | **5** | 8,784 | h r . |
| 6 | Divide line 4 by line 5. Enter the result as a decimal amount . . . | **6** | . | |
| 7 | Business percentage. For day-care facilities not used exclusively for business, multiply line 6 by line 3 (enter the result as a percentage). All others, enter the amount from line 3. . . . . ▶ | **7** | | % |

### Part II   Figure Your Allowable Deduction

| | | | | |
|---|---|---|---|---|
| 8 | Enter the amount from Schedule C, line 29, **plus** any net gain or (loss) derived from the business use of your home and shown on Schedule D or Form 4797. If more than one place of business, see instructions | | **8** | |

See instructions for columns (a) and (b) before completing lines 9–20.

| | | (a) Direct expenses | (b) Indirect expenses | | |
|---|---|---|---|---|---|
| 9 | Casualty losses (see instructions) . . . . . | **9** | | | |
| 10 | Deductible mortgage interest (see instructions) | **10** | | | |
| 11 | Real estate taxes (see instructions) . . . . . | **11** | | | |
| 12 | Add lines 9, 10, and 11 . . . . . . . . . | **12** | | | |
| 13 | Multiply line 12, column (b) by line 7 . . . | **13** | | | |
| 14 | Add line 12, column (a) and line 13 . . . . . | | | **14** | |
| 15 | Subtract line 14 from line 8. If zero or less, enter -0- | | | **15** | |
| 16 | Excess mortgage interest (see instructions) . . | **16** | | | |
| 17 | Insurance . . . . . . . . . . . . . | **17** | | | |
| 18 | Repairs and maintenance . . . . . . . . | **18** | | | |
| 19 | Utilities . . . . . . . . . . . . . . | **19** | | | |
| 20 | Other expenses (see instructions) . . . . . | **20** | | | |
| 21 | Add lines 16 through 20 . . . . . . . . | **21** | | | |
| 22 | Multiply line 21, column (b) by line 7 . . . . . . . . . . . . . | **22** | | | |
| 23 | Carryover of operating expenses from 2003 Form 8829, line 41 . . | **23** | | | |
| 24 | Add line 21 in column (a), line 22, and line 23 . . . . . . . . . . . . | | | **24** | |
| 25 | Allowable operating expenses. Enter the **smaller** of line 15 or line 24 . . . . . . | | | **25** | |
| 26 | Limit on excess casualty losses and depreciation. Subtract line 25 from line 15 . . . . | | | **26** | |
| 27 | Excess casualty losses (see instructions) . . . . . . . . . | **27** | | | |
| 28 | Depreciation of your home from Part III below . . . . . . . | **28** | | | |
| 29 | Carryover of excess casualty losses and depreciation from 2003 Form 8829, line 42 | **29** | | | |
| 30 | Add lines 27 through 29 . . . . . . . . . . . . . . . . . . . | | | **30** | |
| 31 | Allowable excess casualty losses and depreciation. Enter the **smaller** of line 26 or line 30 . . | | | **31** | |
| 32 | Add lines 14, 25, and 31 . . . . . . . . . . . . . . . . . . | | | **32** | |
| 33 | Casualty loss portion, if any, from lines 14 and 31. Carry amount to **Form 4684**, Section B . . | | | **33** | |
| 34 | Allowable expenses for business use of your home. Subtract line 33 from line 32. Enter here and on Schedule C, line 30. If your home was used for more than one business, see instructions ▶ | | | **34** | |

### Part III   Depreciation of Your Home

| | | | |
|---|---|---|---|
| 35 | Enter the **smaller** of your home's adjusted basis or its fair market value (see instructions) . . | **35** | |
| 36 | Value of land included on line 35 . . . . . . . . . . . . . . . . . | **36** | |
| 37 | Basis of building. Subtract line 36 from line 35 . . . . . . . . . . . . . . | **37** | |
| 38 | Business basis of building. Multiply line 37 by line 7 . . . . . . . . . . . . | **38** | |
| 39 | Depreciation percentage (see instructions) . . . . . . . . . . . . . . | **39** | % |
| 40 | Depreciation allowable (see instructions). Multiply line 38 by line 39. Enter here and on line 28 above | **40** | |

### Part IV   Carryover of Unallowed Expenses to 2005

| | | | |
|---|---|---|---|
| 41 | Operating expenses. Subtract line 25 from line 24. If less than zero, enter -0- . . . . . | **41** | |
| 42 | Excess casualty losses and depreciation. Subtract line 31 from line 30. If less than zero, enter -0- | **42** | |

**For Paperwork Reduction Act Notice, see page 4 of separate instructions.**     Cat. No. 13232M     Form **8829** (2004)

4

| Q & A |
| --- |

**Q:** I heard that if you claim an office-in-home, it has a negative effect when you sell your house.

**A:** This is only partially true. If you've lived in your home for two of the five years before you sell it and have a profit on the sale of less than $250,000 ($500,000 if married), you owe no tax on the gain. In calculating the profit from your home sale, you treat the home office room in the same way you treat the personal rooms. Thus, for this calculation, there is no negative effect from having claimed the home office. However, the depreciation you've claimed on your home office over the years must be recaptured, or paid back, at the time of your home sale. The chances are, however, that the tax savings you've had from claiming the home office will greatly exceed the recapture tax you owe.

ness and what the total area of your home is. Then it asks you to list your home office expenses as either direct or indirect. Indirect expenses include mortgage interest, real estate tax, rent, and other expenses you have for the whole house. Direct expenses are those that apply only to the space claimed as the home office. There is no line on the form for rent paid, so if you rent your home, list the rent amount under "other expenses" on *Line 20*. Write "rent" next to that figure.

Part III of the form is used to calculate the depreciation on your home. Only buildings can be depreciated, not the land on which the building sits. Although you can still deduct all the other expenses for your home office if you rent, you can claim depreciation on your home only if you own it.

At the bottom of Form 8829 is a section called "Carryover of Unallowed Expenses to [the next year]." This section is used when you otherwise qualify for the home office deduction, but are unable to claim it because you have a loss from your business or your business profit is less than your home office expense. The amount you aren't able to use on this year's return is carried over to next year and can be deducted then (assuming you have enough profit next year to deduct it). In order to carry the expense forward to the next year, you need to fill out Form 8829 and include it in this year's return.

# Audit Risk of Claiming a Home Office

As you can see, there are lots of hoops to jump through in claiming the office-in-home deduction. Many people don't claim this expense, even though they qualify for it, because they've heard that it increases the chance of an audit. While this may have been true at one time, current statistics don't show so. Don't take the office-in-home expense without making sure you qualify for it and that it's a wise move for your situation. However, it can be a valuable deduction for those who claim it.

# Telephone and Other Utility Expenses

If you qualify to deduct a home office, usually the same percentage used to calculate the deductible rent or mortgage interest is used to calculate the deductible utility expenses. Utilities include gas and electricity, as well as garbage, water, and sewer charges.

However, it will occasionally be appropriate to use a different calculation for one or more of the utilities rather than basing the deduction on the percentage of the house used for business.

> **EXAMPLE**
>
> *Rahmah provides therapeutic massages in her home. She has a room set aside for this business, and the space is 15% of Rahmah's total home. Although Rahmah deducts 15% of her rent, water, and garbage expense, she deducts 50% of her electricity cost as a business expense. Rahmah has found that since she's been doing massages at home, her electricity costs have greatly increased because she uses small electric heaters to keep the massage space warm. To calculate what percentage of the electricity to deduct for the business, Rahmah compared her utility bills before she began doing massages in her home to her current bills. She found that the electricity cost had doubled since she began her home business, so she's deducting 50% of the electricity cost as a business expense.*

Like Rahmah, your home business may use a disproportionate percentage of your home utilities. Computers, laser printers, and copy machines use large amounts of electricity. Photographers may use a lot of water in their darkrooms. Woodworkers usually fill more than the normal number of garbage cans. If your utility bills have increased since you began working in your home, be sure to include the increased amount when you calculate your home office deduction.

Unlike utilities, business telephone expenses can be deducted whether or not you claim a home office. Since there is not a separate line on Schedule C to list telephone expenses, some people include them with the utilities expense. With cell phones, faxes, and multiple phone lines common in many businesses, phone bills can be high. For that reason, it is a better idea to list the telephone expense on its own line in the "other expenses" section of Schedule C. (see page 145.)

If you have a deductible home office, your telephone expenses won't be deducted in the same proportion as other utilities. If you don't have a deductible home office, you can still deduct the business portion of your home phone. In either case, you cannot deduct the telephone base rate or monthly service charge if you have only one phone line going into your home. The IRS believes that you would have had that one line anyway. The deductible expenses are restricted to the additional costs incurred because you have a business.

Even if you have only one line in your home, you can still deduct any business-related long distance calls. Local business calls are also deductible, but only if there are extra charges for those calls. Also, a deduction can be taken for extra features, such as call waiting or call forwarding, that were added because of the business.

If you have a separate phone line that's used exclusively for your business, the costs for that line are 100% deductible. This is true even if it isn't registered with the phone company as a business line. If you have a second line coming into your home and it's used partially for business, you can deduct a portion of the monthly fees, plus the specific business calls.

Cell phone costs are deducted in the same way as other telephone expenses. Usually a cell phone is used less than 100% for business. This is true even if it's used only occasionally to tell your spouse or partner you're on the way home. If the phone is used 95% for business, 95% of the monthly charge can be deducted. In this case, 95% of the cost of the phone itself would be taken as a business expense.

# Using Your Car in Your Business | 25

In order to deduct car expenses, you need to know how much you used your car for business. In fact, the most crucial part of the automobile deduction is the record-keeping. If you are being audited for any other part of your Schedule C, the auditor will almost always examine any car expenses you've deducted. This is because auditors know that most people don't keep adequate records of car use. When they ask to see your log and you say, "What log?," the auditors are then able to quickly disallow what might have been a substantial deduction.

When asked how many miles their cars were used for business in the prior year, many taxpayers stare at the ceiling as if the answer's written up there. Some tax preparers call this the PFTA (Plucked from the Air) approach to recordkeeping. It will not stand up in an audit.

Business owners sometimes claim that they use their car 100% for business. If you have a deductible office-in-home, 100% business car use is possible if you have another car available for personal transportation. If you don't have a deductible office-in-home, your car generally won't be used 100% for business because you have at least some commuting miles. Often, the business car is also used for a vacation trip or to pick up groceries. True 100% business use is rare for a passenger vehicle.

In any case, you cannot just make a guess about your car mileage. You need to know how many total miles the car was driven this year and how many of those miles were for business.

A *business mile* is a mile from one business stop to another business stop. If you have a deductible office-in-home, deductible miles would include driving from your home office to see a client, going to lunch with a colleague, and picking up business supplies. If you do not have a deductible office-in-home, business mileage doesn't start until you get to your first stop of the day. From home to the first stop of the day and from the last stop of the day to home is considered commuting, just as if you were working for someone else.

If you don't have a deductible office-in-home, you may want to consider ways of reducing your commuting or nondeductible mileage. Would it be appropriate for you to have a post office box for your business? If so, open one near your home and use it as your primary business address. Can you buy from a supplier near your home? From home to the post office or supplier will still be commuting, but from that point on, you have deductible business miles. Of course, you might have a hard time explaining in an audit why you also stopped at the post office box or supplier on your way home. If this really isn't reasonable, your trip home will consist of nondeductible miles.

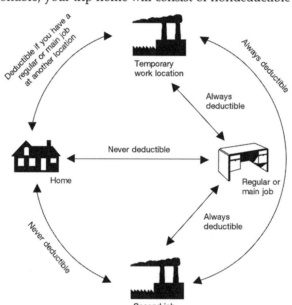

**Home:** The place where you reside. Transportation expenses between your home and your main or regular place of work are personal commuting expenses.

**Regular or main job:** Your principal place of business. If you have more than one job, you must determine which one is your regular or main job. Consider the time you spend at each, the activity you have at each, and the income you earn at each.

**Temporary work location:** A place where your work assignment is realistically expected to last (and does in fact last) one year or less. Unless you have a regular place of business, you can only deduct your transportation expenses to a temporary work location outside your metropolitan area.

**Second job:** If you regularly work at two or more places in one day, whether or not for the same employer, you can deduct your transportation expenses of getting from one workplace to another. You cannot deduct your transportation costs between your home and a second job on a day off from your main job.

If you travel to a business location outside your *tax home*, you can include the miles from your home and back to your home as business miles, even if you don't have a deductible home office. Your tax home is the approximately forty-mile perimeter around your main place of business. This exception to the general business mile rules will be helpful to those who travel great distances for their business, but don't have a deductible home office.

Another helpful exception is for those who have a regular place of business but commute to a temporary work location. You can deduct the round-trip from your home to the temporary location, even if you don't have a deductible office-in-home. To be considered temporary, the work at that location must be irregular or short-term.

## Keeping Records

The key to deducting business miles is having good records. Keeping track of the total miles you drive your car each year is easy—just write down the odometer reading each January 1. If you don't have that figure for this year, repair bills (which usually include the odometer reading) may help.

Keeping track of the business miles is harder. Ideally, you'll keep a log (available at any office supply store) or notebook in your car. Write down both the beginning and ending odometer reading for each business trip or note how many business miles you drive each day. In either case, also note what business locations you visited.

Although it's easy once you get into the habit, many people don't want to keep a car log. If you're one of those people, see if one of the following methods works better for you.

- Write down in your appointment book each day how many business miles you drove that day. The calendar notations will indicate what business locations you visited.
- If you go on the same route or to the same location regularly, measure the distance once and count the number of times you made the trip during the year.
- If you use your vehicle primarily for business, instead of keeping track of the business miles, keep track of the number of personal miles you drive.
- If your business driving is similar throughout the year, keep detailed records for only one month each quarter or for one week of each month. This will give you enough information that you can fairly accurately calculate your annual business mileage.
- Use a computer program, such as *MapQuest*®, to calculate the mileage from one business location to another.

4

# Calculating the Deduction

Whichever way you keep your records, once you know the total number of miles the car was driven for the year and how many of those were for business, there are two possible ways of deducting your car expenses.

## ACTUAL EXPENSE METHOD

The first is called the *actual expense method*. Using this method, you add together your expenses for gas, oil, repairs, insurance, auto club membership, car license, and loan interest or lease payments. Then multiply the total by the percentage you use the car for business. Add to this figure business parking, tolls, and your car's depreciation (which has already been calculated on just the business percentage).

Leased cars are handled similarly to owned cars except that lease payments, rather than depreciation and interest, are deducted when calculating the car expense. Also, a *lease inclusion* amount reduces the lease payment deduction for cars having a value of more than $17,500 (which the IRS defines as luxury cars). The lease inclusion amount is based on the value of the car when it was first leased and increases each year that the car is kept. (See IRS publication 463 for the lease inclusion tables.) These show how much must be included each year. The lease inclusion amount is designed to equalize the lease payment deduction for leased cars with the depreciation deduction for owned cars.

Depreciation is calculated differently for cars than it is for other assets. (See Chapter 22 for general depreciation rules.) There are yearly limitations on the amount of depreciation that can be claimed for vehicles. Although Section 179 depreciation allows business owners to deduct in full up to $102,000 worth of assets purchased during the year, this doesn't mean the full cost of a car can be claimed in one year. There are vehicle depreciation limitations that apply, whether or not Section 179 is used. However, the bonus first year depreciation mentioned in Chapter 22 does increase the limitation amount for cars and can be used advantageously here.

The table on page 103 shows the maximum depreciation that can be taken for a car each year. This figure assumes 100% business use, so it must be multiplied by the true business percentage before being included on your tax return. Note how much the allowable first year limitation figure increases for cars placed in service after 9/10/01. This assumes the bonus first year depreciation will be taken. If you elect not to claim this accelerated depreciation, the first year limitation for cars placed in service after 9/10/01 and before 1/1/04 is $3,060, with $2,960 being the limitation for cars purchased in 2004.

## Maximum Depreciation Limits for Cars

| Date Placed In Service | 1st Year | 2nd Year | 3rd Year | 4th & Later Years |
|---|---|---|---|---|
| 2004 | $10,610 | $4,800 | $2,850 | $1,675 |
| 5/6/2003– 12/31/2003 | $10,710 | $4,900 | $2,950 | $1,775 |
| 9/11/2001– 5/5/2003 | $7,660 | $4,900 | $2,950 | $1,775 |
| 1/1/2000– 9/10/2001 | $3,060 | $4,900 | $2,950 | $1,775 |
| 1999 | $3,060 | $5,000 | $2,950 | $1,775 |
| 1998 | $3,160 | $5,000 | $2,950 | $1,775 |
| 1997 | $3,160 | $5,000 | $3,050 | $1,775 |
| 1/1/1994– 12/31/1996 | $3,060 | $4,900 | $2,950 | $1,775 |

**EXAMPLE**

*Audrey bought a $30,000 car on June 20, 2003 and she uses it 80% for business. Since cars are considered five-year property and depreciated 20% in the first year they're used for business, Audrey can claim $4,800 in depreciation in year one ($30,000 x 80% business use x 20%). However, since Audrey purchased the car after May 6, 2003, she's able to take the bonus first-year depreciation. This adds an additional 50% of the car's cost to the depreciation she can claim. Instead of multiplying her business car use by 20%, Audrey multiplies it by 70%—or a total depreciation amount of $16,800. However, first-year depreciation is limited to $10,710, so $8,568 ($10,710 x 80% business use) is the maximum depreciation Audrey can claim in the first year she uses her car for business.*

4

The depreciation limitation table is applicable to passenger cars that typically weigh less than 6,000 pounds. A van or truck that weighs 6,000 pounds or less (including minivans and SUVs that are built on a truck chassis) have slightly higher limitations. If placed in service in 2004, the first-year depreciation limitation for these vehicles is $10,910 (assuming the bonus depreciation is taken). The second-year is limited to $5,300, the third-year is $3,150, and the limitation is $1,875 for the fourth and additional years.

Vehicles weighing more than 6,000 pounds or those weighing less than 6,000 pounds but designed for a purpose other than regular passenger transport (*e.g.,* ambulances, taxis, or vans with shelving installed on the inside) are not subject to the yearly limitations shown in the table. Your vehicle's weight can probably be found on a label inside the driver's side door. If your vehicle weighs more than 6,000 pounds, in the year you buy it, you can depreciate in full (take Section 179) the purchase price multiplied by the percentage of business use. The only limitation is a $25,000 maximum Section 179 deduction. Vehicles weighing more than 14,000 pounds may take up to the full $102,000 Section 179 deduction in the year of purchase. Some SUVs exceed 6,000 pounds in weight. In the previous example, if Audrey had bought an SUV that weighed more than 6,000 pounds and cost $30,000, she could take a depreciation deduction in year one of $24,000 ($30,000 cost x 80% business use).

**Note:** *All this information about depreciation assumes that your vehicle is used at least 51% for business. As shown in the chart on page 82, vehicles are considered to be listed property. If they are used 50% or less for business, a different rate of depreciation must be used. Instead of a 20% depreciation deduction in the first year, only 10% of the cost of the vehicle can be depreciated. Additionally, neither Section 179 nor the bonus first-year depreciation can be claimed for listed property used less than 51% for business.*

## MILEAGE METHOD

If all this talk about depreciation is making your head spin, you may prefer to use the second method of deducting your car expenses, which is called the *mileage rate* or *standard method.* This method doesn't require any depreciation calculations. To use the mileage method, simply multiply the number of business miles you drove during the year by a cents-per-mile figure. For 2004, the mileage rate figure is 37.5¢. The only expenses you can add to the 37.5¢ a mile is the business percentage of your car loan interest, the business percentage of your car registration, and your business parking and tolls (parking tickets are never deductible). All other expenses are considered to be covered by the 37.5¢-a-mile deduction.

A comparison of the two methods available for deducting vehicle expenses follows. In this example, the actual method provides a substantially larger deduction than the mileage rate method for this car this year. That doesn't mean the actual method will always be the more beneficial one to use. The deduction using the mileage rate method will often be greater when you drive a lot of business miles, while the actual expense method will usually be larger if a high percentage of your driving is for business. Which method comes out better will also depend in part on how much gas prices continue to go up and whether your vehicle weighs more or less than 6,000 pounds.

### Calculating the Business Car Deduction

| | |
|---|---:|
| Total miles car was driven this year | 20,000 |
| Number of business miles car was driven | 12,000 |
| Percentage of miles driven for business | 60% |

*Actual Expense Method*

| | |
|---|---:|
| Gas, oil, lube | $2,100 |
| Tires | +100 |
| Repairs | +400 |
| Insurance | +900 |
| AAA membership | +50 |
| Interest on car loan (or lease payment) | +424 |
| Car registration | +240 |
| | $4,214 |
| | x 60% |
| | $2,528 |
| Depreciation (on business part only) | + $4,440 |
| Business parking and tolls | +100 |
| **Total car expense** | **$7,068** |

*Mileage Rate (Standard) Method*

| | |
|---|---:|
| 12,000 miles @ 37.5¢ | $4,500 |
| Business % of car loan interest | +254 |
| Business % of car registration | +144 |
| Business parking and tolls | +100 |
| **Total car expense** | **$4,998** |

4

You can change methods from year to year as long as you use the mileage rate method the first year you buy the car or place it into service. If you use this method the first year, you can use whichever method is more advantageous in subsequent years. If you don't use the standard method the first year you begin using the car in your business, you'll have to continue to use the actual expense method for as long as you own this car.

# Leasing vs. Buying a Vehicle

Nearly one-third of all new vehicles (and up to 75% of all new luxury cars) are leased rather than purchased. In most cases, the decision whether to buy or lease a car is a personal and financial one rather than a tax decision. If you want to look at the tax consequences, many financial websites provide calculators to help figure whether it's better to lease or buy. To get an accurate answer, however, you'll need to have available all applicable information, such as proposed lease payment amount, current interest rates, number of miles you expect to drive annually, required down payment amount, and so on.

Some nontax factors to consider when assessing the pros and cons of leasing versus buying include the following.

*When you buy a car, you:*
- own it at the end of the loan term and can sell it to recoup some of your purchase price or use it as a trade-in on a new car;
- have lower insurance premiums than if you lease a car;
- have no restrictions on how many miles you can drive the car each year;
- will probably have a higher down payment and higher monthly payments than you would have for a leased car; and,
- will find that the car rapidly decreases in value, so the amount you are able to sell it for will probably be substantially less than the purchase price.

*When you lease a car, you:*
- will have lower upfront costs and lower monthly payments than if you buy;
- don't have to worry when the car decreases in value since you don't own it;
- can lease a more expensive car than you might have been able to buy;
- don't have to worry about disposing of the car when you want a new one; and,
- may be assessed unexpected fees at the end of the lease term because of excessive wear and tear or more miles driven than specified in your lease contract.

# Electric and Hybrid Cars

A credit equal to 7.5% of the cost of a qualified electric vehicle (to a maximum of $3,000) is allowed on *Line 54* of Form 1040. In calculating the credit, the cost of the vehicle must be reduced by any Section 179 deduction claimed. In addition to this credit, electric cars have higher depreciation limitations than what is available for gasoline-powered vehicles. IRS Publication 463 has tables showing the maximum depreciation amounts available for electric vehicles.

Hybrid cars (those powered by a combination of electricity and gas) are not entitled to the same tax credit and depreciation deduction available for electric vehicles. However, there is a deduction for clean-fuel vehicles on the bottom of the Form 1040 (see page 141), and hybrid vehicles qualify. This is not a business deduction (and you don't need to be self-employed to claim it), so it doesn't reduce your self-employment tax. It does, however, lessen your adjusted gross income, and thus, your federal income tax. For 2004, the clean air fuel deduction is $1,500. In calculating the depreciation on a car used for business, you must reduce the cost of the car by the amount of the clean air fuel deduction you've claimed.

**Note:** *Your state may also offer a clean-fuel vehicle deduction or credit.*

4

# Meals and Entertainment | 26

Meal and entertainment expenses are among the most highly audited expenses. As with car expenses, this is at least in part because many people don't keep adequate records and are unable to prove the deductibility of the receipts they have.

There are only two types of deductible meals. One is when you're away from home overnight. Those are the only meals you can deduct whether eating alone or with others.

The second type of deductible meals are those in which you meet with someone for a meal and have a reasonable expectation of receiving income or some other business benefit as a result. The *business benefit* might be getting a new client, a referral to a new client, or continuing business from an existing client. Meeting with a colleague to discuss better ways of running your business is another example of a meal with a business benefit. In some way, the discussion you have before, during, or after the meal must provide some immediate or expected benefit to your business. These meals are deductible whether you pay only for your own meal or you also pay for the meal of those with you.

Some meals that would seem to be deductible actually are not. For example, if you are working with a client and the client says, "I need you to work late tonight; go out and grab a bite to eat," that meal is not deductible. Even though you are at work before and after you eat, unless you eat with your client and discuss business, it is not a deductible meal.

In order to deduct a meal, it not only has to be one of the deductible types, but there also must be good records. For each meal, you need to record, preferably on the back of the receipt:

- the cost of the meal (don't forget tips);
- the time and date of the meal (your appointment book helps to verify this information);

4

---

**Q & A**

**Q: I thought that I didn't have to have receipts if the expense was less than $75. Most of my business meals are less than $75.**

A: You are right. Receipts aren't required for business expenses costing less than $75. However, you still need to record the amount spent, where and when it was spent, and what it was spent on. Additionally, for meal expenses, you need to list the business purpose and business relationship of the person with whom you ate.

---

- the location of the meeting, if not indicated on the receipt; and,
- the name of the person you ate with, her title, and your business relationship.

Most importantly, you also need to record the business purpose of the meal, including what was discussed. The deductibility is least likely to be questioned if you ate with a client or a prospective client.

Although this seems like a great deal of information to keep track of, one woman had thousands of dollars worth of meal expenses disallowed at an audit. Although she had included the other required information, she hadn't recorded the business purpose of the meal on each of her receipts. The auditor noted that the same names showed up over and over on the receipts and concluded she and her colleagues took turns picking up the check for their meals together (a tax no no).

Instead of keeping track of each meal, you can use a *per diem rate* of between $34 and $50 (depending on the city to which you're traveling) to deduct meal expenses for each day you're away from home overnight. IRS Publication 1542 lists the per diem rate allowed for individual cities within the U.S. If you choose the per diem rate, you must use it consistently for all trips taken during that year. Even if you use the per diem rate, you must have records showing the dates you were traveling (your appointment book is sufficient) and the cities to which you traveled.

---

**Q & A**

**Q: If I take a client to the theater or a ball game, can I deduct the cost of the tickets as business entertainment?**

A: In order to deduct meals or entertainment, a business discussion must take place before, during, or after the meal or entertainment. Also, the meal or entertainment must take place in a location that's conducive (*i.e.*, quiet enough) for a business discussion.

If you buy theater or ball game tickets and give them to a client but don't accompany her to the event, the tickets may be deductible as a business gift. (see Chapter 30.)

Whether you use the actual or per diem expense method, all meals—at home or out of town—are only 50% deductible. Keep track of the whole cost of the meal, including tips, but only 50% can be deducted.

## Day Care Meals

A standard allowance is available for children's meals provided by a day care center. As with using the per diem rate for regular business meals, day care operators must decide on an annual basis whether to claim the allowance or actual expense amounts for meals. The allowance for breakfast is $.99 per child per day. Lunch or supper is $1.83, and snacks (up to three per day) are $.54. For day care providers in Alaska and Hawaii, the rates are higher.

4

Travel is another highly audited expense. This means it requires good recordkeeping. Make calendar entries or keep a log for each day of a business trip so that you can prove the deductibility of your travel by showing what you did each day.

## Domestic Travel

Domestic travel is an either/or situation. Either it's primarily a business trip, in which case the airfare is 100% deductible, or it's primarily a personal trip, in which case the airfare is not deductible at all. The airfare is not prorated for domestic travel. Whether a trip is primarily for business is generally—but not always—measured by the amount of time you spend on business compared to the total amount of time you're away. For example, if you are gone for ten days and you spend eight of them on business, you are primarily on a business trip. You can deduct all your airfare and all of the expenses for the eight days you spent on business, and none of the expenses for the two days not spent on business.

If the trip is primarily a personal trip, you cannot deduct any of the airfare, but you can deduct the expenses, such as hotel and car rental, you had on the days you were doing business. Determining whether a trip is a primarily business trip is not necessarily based on the percentage of time spent doing certain activities.

**EXAMPLE**

*Emma, who lives in Chicago, is the keynote speaker at a conference for health professionals in Florida. She'll spend one day at the conference and then travel to North Carolina for three days to visit a childhood friend. Emma can deduct the cost of airfare from Chicago to Florida and back to Chicago. She also can deduct all of her expenses in Florida. She cannot deduct any of her expenses in*

*continued...*

> *North Carolina or her airfare from Florida to North Carolina. This is an example of an instance when a primarily business trip is not measured by the percentage of days spent on business. Emma would have had to pay for the trip to Florida to give the speech anyway, so that airfare is deductible no matter what she does during the remainder of her time away.*

Expenses you can deduct while traveling include airfare, airport shuttle, taxis, tips, laundry, bus, rental car, and so on. Travel is 100% deductible, but travel meals are only 50% deductible, so you need to record your meals separately from the other travel expenses.

## Foreign Travel

Foreign travel—travel outside North America—is handled a bit differently than domestic travel. For foreign travel, you can deduct a percentage of the entire trip based on the number of days you spend on business (travel days are counted as work days) versus the total number of days you're away. However, if you are outside North America for less than eight days, or if less than 25% of your trip is for personal purposes, no allocation needs to be made and the full cost can be deducted.

> **EXAMPLE**
>
> *JoAnn travels from New York to France to work with a client. While in France, she spends eight days with her client and five days relaxing in the French countryside. She spends two days in travel between New York and France, for a total of fifteen days away. JoAnn can deduct two-thirds (ten days out of fifteen days) of her total trip expenses.*

## Spouse Travel Expense

Travel expenses for your spouse are deductible only if your spouse is a *bona fide* employee of your business or if you co-own the business with him. This is true for both foreign and domestic travel. If one of your goals is to combine vacations with business trips and you want your spouse to accompany you, the potentially deductible travel should be considered in deciding whether you and your spouse or domestic partner should work together.

# Insurance Deductions | 28

Only some types of insurance are deductible. *Life insurance* premiums are not deductible anywhere on your tax return. *Disability insurance* premiums are not deductible either. However, if your state requires you to provide disability insurance for your employees, that amount is deductible. If you ever become disabled and begin collecting benefits, the money you receive is not taxable.

*Business insurance* of any type is deductible. This includes malpractice, business overhead, liability, and workers' compensation policies for your employees. If you have an office-in-home and buy a special policy to protect, for example, the business computers you have at home, those premiums are fully deductible.

*Car insurance* and *homeowners or renters insurance* are deductible to the extent that you use the car or home for business. A portion of the premiums are deductible along with other car and home expenses. (see Chapters 25 and 23, respectively.)

*Health insurance* premiums are 100% deductible on Form 1040 for sole proprietors, partners, and S corporation shareholders who own more than 2% of the corporation's stock. (*Long-term care insurance* premiums are deductible on the same line as health insurance premiums on Form 1040.) This deduction is *not* taken as a business expense (doesn't reduce your self-employment tax), except for the portion paid to buy insurance for any employees of the business.

Deductible health insurance premiums are those that the self-employed person paid for herself, her spouse (if married), and any dependents. If the self-employed person or her spouse is covered by a health insurance plan paid for by an employer, the health insurance deduction cannot be taken for any months in which either spouse was eligible for the employer-subsidized plan.

The health insurance deduction is limited to the net profit from the business. If your business has a loss, your health insurance premiums cannot be deducted this year. If it has, for example, a $450 profit, $450 of health insurance premiums can be claimed.

Another medical deduction opportunity is available through a *Health Savings Account (HSA)*. Self-employed people, as well as employees, can participate in this program. To be eligible, the individual must have a high-deductible health plan. This means that, before insurance starts paying towards medical expenses, the insured is responsible for at least the first $1,000 ($2,000 for a family).

At the same time that a high deductible health plan is selected, the insured opens up a savings account (called a *Health Savings Account*). The insured can contribute to this account money to pay for medical expenses that aren't covered by insurance, as well as expenses incurred before the insurance's deductible amount is met. As with contributions to an IRA, money put into an HSA is deductible and interest or dividends earned on the account are not taxable. If the money in the account is used for anything other than medical expenses, the distribution is taxable and there is a 10% penalty. Unlike most employee benefit plans, there is no *use it or lose it* provision. Money can continue to grow in the HSA until you're ready to spend it. You can consider this another retirement savings vehicle. Maximum annual contributions to the plan are the lesser of your health plan deductible amount or $2,600 for individuals ($5,150 for families). Those age 50 or over can contribute an additional $500 each year.

If interested in establishing an HSA, check first with your health insurance provider to see what's available. You will find that high deductible health plans generally have a lower monthly premium than other health plans. This can be ideal health insurance if you're mainly concerned about catastrophic health coverage. However, because of the potentially lower monthly premiums and the deductibility of the HSA contribution, these plans can be appropriate in a number of other situations as well. Once you've set up your high deductible health plan, contact a brokerage house or insurance company about setting up the Health Savings Account.

(For the IRS description and FAQs about HSAs, go to **www.treas.gov/offices/public-affairs/hsa**. Another helpful resource is **www.msainfo.net**. This website is full of information about HSAs. It also has a worksheet that helps you calculate what your tax savings will be if you contribute to an HSA.)

# Education Expenses | 29

Education expenses are not particularly prone to audit, but still must meet certain requirements. In order to deduct educational expenses, you need to be able to answer *no* to both of these questions.

- Did you need this education to meet the basic requirements of your profession? (In other words, were you unable to begin work in this field unless you took this class?)
- Will this study qualify you for a new business or profession?

The IRS does not allow you to deduct the costs of preparing to go into a new field of work. Once you're earning money in an occupation, you can deduct any classes that increase your skills and knowledge in that line of work. This includes all required continuing education classes.

Although education costs in preparation for a new career cannot be deducted as a business expense, they may be eligible for either the tuition and fees deduction or the lifetime learning credit. Neither the credit nor the deduction is related to being self-employed. Education expenses that can be claimed as a business expense cannot also be used for one of these tax-saving programs. The tuition and fees deduction allows you to subtract up to $4,000 worth of education expenses as an adjustment to income (*Line 27* of Form 1040).

The lifetime learning credit takes 20% of the first $10,000 you spend on tuition and fees and uses it as a credit on *Line 48* of Form 1040. Unlike a deduction, which is subtracted from your income before the tax is calculated, a credit is subtracted directly from your income tax, resulting in a greater tax savings. You can take either the deduction or the credit, not both, each year. Because the education credit and deduction each have income restrictions (they cannot be taken if your income is too high), you'll need to figure out which (if either) you qualify for and which will give you the greater tax savings.

If paying for education is a problem, it may be helpful to know that money can be taken out of a traditional IRA without penalty if it is used to pay for qualified higher education expenses for you, your spouse, or your dependents. The money withdrawn, however, is taxable.

# Other Deductible Business Expenses

# 30

As explained in Chapter 20, all ordinary and necessary business expenses are deductible. Some common deductible expenses are listed on page 123. It is not an exhaustive list and no one business will have all of the expenses. You are the person who is most familiar with the expenses of your business and can best decide how to categorize your expenses.

Most of the expenses are self-explanatory, but a few need further clarification.

- *Bank service charges and credit card fees* are 100% deductible if you have a separate business account, but these must be prorated if you have only one account.
- *Client consultation and supervision fees* are expenses that psychotherapists and some other health professionals have in meeting with supervisors and consultants to discuss and review their work.
- *Contract labor or subcontractor expenses* are less likely to be audited if listed on your tax return under the type of work provided (*e.g.*, computer consultant or landscaping services) rather than on the line on Schedule C labeled "contract labor." (Reread Chapter 15 to ensure that you're correctly classifying these people as independent contractors rather than employees.)
- *Dues* for professional organizations are deductible. Dues for health clubs or country clubs are not, even if that is where you sometimes meet or entertain clients.
- *Gifts* are deductible up to a maximum of $25 per person per year. You can spend more on the gift but can deduct only $25 of the total cost. For purposes of this expense, a *person* also refers to a married couple, meaning that a gift given to either spouse is considered given to both.

- *Interest* is 100% deductible if it is paid on business loans or on credit cards used solely for business purchases. With the exception of home mortgages and home equity loans, interest paid on personal loans and credit cards is not at all deductible. Make sure that money you borrow to pay for business expenses—whether it is actually called a business loan or not—is used only for that purpose. If you use some of the money for personal living expenses, you will lose the interest deduction on that portion of the loan.

  A loan or credit card doesn't need to be in the name of your business in order to be deductible. How the loan is used or what expenses are paid by the credit card determines whether the interest is considered business or personal.

  Auto loan interest is deductible only for the percentage that you use the car in your business. School loan interest is deductible as a business expense only if the education was a deductible expense. (See Chapter 29 for information about deductible education.) School loan interest that doesn't qualify as a business expense can, under certain conditions, be deducted as an adjustment to income on the front of Form 1040. (see page 141.)

  Interest on money borrowed to pay income taxes or set up a retirement plan is not deductible as these are considered personal expenses. If a home equity loan is used to pay these costs, the interest is claimed as a personal deduction on Schedule A.

- *Legal and professional fees* (including accounting and tax preparation) that involve the preparation of your business tax return are deductible. Usually, it's clear what portion of the bill is for preparing a corporate or partnership tax return. Schedule C, however, is done as part of your total personal return, so you'll need to ask your preparer how to allocate the costs.

- *Magazines and books* are deductible if they are expenses you wouldn't have incurred if you hadn't been in business. In other words, if you've always sub-scribed to the daily paper, you cannot deduct the cost for your business. Other general circulation papers and magazines—such as *Newsweek®*, *Money®*, or *the New York Times®*—are generally nondeductible unless purchased for your client waiting room. More specialized magazines and journals are deductible.

- *Maintenance and repairs* are the costs involved in keeping an asset in good working order and are deductible. For example, a roof repair is a deductible repair expense (assuming the roof is on a building used in your business). An *improvement*, unlike a repair, increases the value or prolongs the life of an asset. A new roof is an improvement and must be depreciated rather than deducted all in one year.

- *Online costs* are the fees for Internet services. This includes ISPs (such as AOL), as well as DSL or cable modem services. If you use the service for both business and personal purposes, you should prorate the expense accordingly.
- *Payroll tax expense* is the portion of taxes you pay on behalf of your employees. This includes the employer's share of Social Security and Medicare taxes. Depending on the state, payroll tax expense may also include unemployment or disability insurance paid for employees. Any tax you withhold from an employee's paycheck (*i.e.*, federal or state income tax) is not a payroll tax expense, as it is money withheld from the employee, not paid by you.
- *Sales or excise* tax paid should be deducted only if the amount you have collected is also included in your gross income figure on *Line 1* of Schedule C. As an aside, if your business is located in an Enterprise Zone (see page 65), you may be entitled to a tax credit for sales tax you paid on equipment used at your business location.

  Estimated tax payments and the balance paid (if any) with your tax return are not deductible as business expenses if you're a sole proprietor, S corporation, or partnership. Only C corporations can deduct the income taxes paid for the business.
- *Small equipment and furnishings* are items that either are very low in price or will last for less than a year. These items can be deducted. Any assets that will last for more than a year need to be depreciated. (see Chapter 22.)
- *Wages* are deductible and refer to the amount you pay your employees, not the amount you pay yourself, unless you're incorporated (and, therefore, you are an employee of your corporation). Fees paid to independent contractors are not wages.

To shift income among partners or to ensure that a partner will be paid for services performed, sometimes partnerships will pay *guaranteed payments to partners* instead of—or in addition to—draws. A guaranteed payment means that no matter how much or how little the partnership makes, the partner will receive a guaranteed amount. Because partners cannot be employees of the partnership, this payment is not salary and no taxes are withheld from it. Unlike draws, however, guaranteed payments are subtracted from the partnership's income to determine the net profit for the business. Also unlike draws, guaranteed payments are reported on the partner's tax return and are subject to self-employment tax. Whether or not a partnership will make guaranteed payments to partners is a tax-planning issue.

A generally nondeductible expense is clothes. Even though you might normally wear jeans to work, you cannot deduct the cost of a new suit you bought for a business event because anything that is commonly worn on the street or could be worn on the street is not deductible. However, a costume worn for work, uniforms, and special clothes (such as steel-toed boots or lab coats) are deductible. Jackets or t-shirts with the name of your company are also deductible, but as advertising.

Charitable contributions are not a business deduction for sole proprietors, S corporations, or partnerships. Any money given from your business to charitable organizations is a personal and not a business expense. If you itemize your personal deductions, you can deduct charitable contributions on Schedule A. C corporations are the only entities that can deduct charitable contributions as a business expense.

The value of the time you donate to a charitable organization is never deductible. This means you cannot deduct the value of donating an hour of your services to a charity's raffle.

Don't spend too much time worrying about the category in which to put an expense. For example, if you have business brochures printed, don't worry over whether to list the expense as advertising or printing. It really doesn't matter—neither printing nor advertising is a highly audited expense category. When appropriate, choose the category least likely to be audited (*e.g.*, put hotel telephone calls under "telephone" rather than "travel") and break down expenses into smaller categories to avoid large amounts in any one expense category.

## Casualty and Theft Losses

One other *expense* should be mentioned here, although it is not deducted on Schedule C. That is *casualty and theft losses*. The IRS defines a casualty loss as one that is caused by an identifiable event that is sudden, unexpected, and unusual. This would include hurricanes, fires, vandalism, heavy storms, and automobile accidents.

Thefts and casualty losses that involve business property or the business portion of mixed-use property are calculated on Part B of IRS Form 4684. The deduction is calculated by comparing the value of the item after the theft or casualty loss (in the event of a theft, the value will be zero) to the adjusted basis of the item. The adjusted basis is the original cost of the asset plus any improvements and minus any depreciation claimed. The allowable casualty or theft deduction is the lesser of the adjusted basis or the decline in fair market value due to the incident. Any insurance or other reimbursements received will affect this calculation.

## Common Business Expenses

Advertising

Accounting/bookkeeping fees

Bank service charges

Car and truck expenses

Client consultation and supervision fees (for therapists)

Contract labor (outside services, subcontractors, etc.)

Credit card fees

Depreciation on assets used in the business

Dues

Education

Entertainment/business meals

Freight

Gifts

Insurance

Interest on business credit cards and loans

Inventory/merchandise purchases (items the business has available
for sale to others)

Legal and professional fees

Magazines and books

Maintenance and repairs

Office supplies

Online fees

Payroll taxes (only for businesses with employees and only the
employer's share of taxes—not the taxes withheld from the
employee's paycheck)

Postage

Printing and copying

Rent/office-in-home expense

Sales or excise tax (only for businesses that collect this tax)

Small furnishings and equipment

Telephone (including pager, answering service, and cell phone)

Travel (outside normal business location)

Utilities

Wages (this refers to what is paid to employees, not to yourself or to
independent contractors)

Website hosting, creation, or maintenance fees

4

# Child Care Expenses | 31

Child care, although not a business expense, can be taken as a credit by self-employed people, as well as employees, when the following conditions are met.

- Care is for a dependent under age 13, a disabled spouse, or a dependent of any age who is unable to care for him- or herself.
- You and your dependent or disabled spouse live in the same home.
- The services were provided so you and your spouse (if married) could work or look for work. The expenses are also deductible if one spouse (when filing a joint return) is a full-time student, while the other spouse works.
- The person who provided the care was not your spouse or your dependent.
- You include Form 2441 with your tax return and on it you list the name, address, and Social Security or federal ID number of the persons or organizations that provided the care.

4

You cannot deduct child care expenses if you are filing as single or head of household and had no earned income (*i.e.*, wages or net profit from self-employment). If you're married and filing jointly, you cannot deduct the child care expense if either you or your spouse had no earned income (unless one of you is a full-time student). The child care deduction for a married couple is limited to the amount of income earned during the year by the lower-earning spouse.

If you qualify to deduct child care expenses, you can include after-school and summer programs. You cannot include school tuition for a child in the first grade or older. You cannot include overnight camp expenses for any child.

The credit is limited to child care expenses of $3,000 per child per year for a maximum of two children. Either $3,000 per child or the full amount spent on child or dependent care (whichever is less) is multiplied by a figure between 20% and 30% to determine your credit. The lower your income, the higher the percentage you can take.

<table>
<tr><td>E X A M P L E</td><td>Sara is single and provides all the support for her 5-year-old daughter, Frannie, whom she claims as a dependent. Sara's sole source of income is her business. It showed a net profit of $55,000 this year. Sara paid $4,300 for Frannie's child care this year. The applicable child care percentage for a parent with $55,000 income is 20%. Sara calculates her child care credit by multiplying $3,000 (the lesser of $4,300 or $3,000) by 20% for a total credit of $600.</td></tr>
</table>

A credit is not the same as a deduction. A deduction is subtracted from your income before the tax is calculated. A credit, on the other hand, is subtracted from your income tax after it is calculated. As a result, a credit saves you more money than a deduction of the same amount would. The child care credit is a nonrefundable credit, which means that if the credit is more than your total income tax liability, you won't get a refund of the excess credit. The credit cannot be used to reduce your self-employment tax—only your income tax.

Some companies offer their employees *dependent care programs (DCP)* or flexible spending accounts. If you or your spouse works for one of these companies, this is a benefit definitely worth looking into. With a DCP or flexible spending account, you can set aside a specific amount of your wages each year to be used for child care expenses. The amount set aside is not taxed. For example, if instead of being self-employed Sara worked as an employee in a company with a DCP, she would ask the company to set aside $4,300 for her daughter's child care. If Sara's salary is $55,000, her W-2 would show that she earned $50,700 ($55,000 salary minus $4,300 DCP). She would avoid paying tax on the $4,300, and since she's in the 25% federal tax bracket, that would save her $1,075 in federal tax ($4,300 x 25%).

Sara saves more by using the DCP than by taking the child care credit. You cannot do both. If you have the option of a DCP, determine which is best for you. Generally, the higher your (and your spouse's) income, the more tax you'll save by participating in the DCP rather than taking the child care credit. One caution to participating in a DCP is that once you've asked to have a certain amount set aside from your pay-check, if you don't use the full amount, you lose it.

For example, if Sara moved Frannie to less expensive child care that cost only $3,800 for the year, she would lose the remainder of the $4,300 that had been set aside for child care but wasn't used.

As a sole proprietorship or partnership, you can set up a DCP for your employees. Since you're not an employee of your business, however, you don't qualify for the benefits. If your spouse works in your business, he is eligible for a DCP offered by your company, but the benefit must be offered to all your other employees as well.

## Child Care Deduction Chart

| If your adjusted gross income is over | but not over | Deductible % is |
|---|---|---|
| $0– | $15,000 | 35% |
| 15,000– | 17,000 | 34% |
| 17,000– | 19,000 | 33% |
| 19,000– | 21,000 | 32% |
| 21,000– | 23,000 | 31% |
| 23,000– | 25,000 | 30% |
| 25,000– | 27,000 | 29% |
| 27,000– | 29,000 | 28% |
| 29,000– | 31,000 | 27% |
| 31,000– | 33,000 | 26% |
| 33,000– | 35,000 | 25% |
| 35,000– | 37,000 | 24% |
| 37,000– | 39,000 | 23% |
| 39,000– | 41,000 | 22% |
| 41,000– | 43,000 | 21% |
| 43,000– | and over | 20% |

Check with your state taxing agency to see whether there are state child care credits for which you are eligible. In California, for example, an employer who pays for an employee's child care costs receives a credit of up to $360 for each dependent covered. California law currently considers self-employed people to be both employee and employer for purposes of this credit. This means that a self-employed person who pays for child care for her own child can receive up to $360 per child in state tax credit for providing child care for an employee's dependent.

# Retirement Plans | 32

Tax-deferred retirement plans are valuable because, while saving for your retirement, you delay paying taxes on money you earn and contribute to one of these plans. Additionally, the interest and dividends earned on the money in the retirement plan is also tax-deferred. *Tax-deferred* means no taxes are paid on the money until it's taken out of the retirement account.

Theoretically, when you take the money out of the account, you'll be retired or working part-time. This will put you in a lower tax bracket than you were in when you invested the money. As a result, the money you contributed and the earned interest or dividends will be taxed at a lower rate than they would have been if you hadn't put the money in a tax-deferred account and instead had paid tax on it when it was earned.

Due to compounding, the earlier in life you begin contributing to a retirement plan, the less total amount you'll need to put in to accumulate a substantial amount of retirement money. The money you contribute to a retirement plan, however, should be money that you don't expect to need until you're at least 59½ years old. When you take a distribution from your retirement account, you are taxed on that money in the same way as you're taxed on other income. With few exceptions, the IRS also assesses a 10% penalty if money is taken out before you're age 59½. Your state may have a similar penalty, which means that if you take the money out prior to reaching the minimum age, you may lose nearly 50% to federal and state taxes and penalties.

4

## Tax-Sheltered or Tax-Deferred Annuities

If you're working as an employee in addition to being self-employed, you may have a 401(k) or 403(b) tax-sheltered annuity (TSA) or tax-deferred annuity (TDA) retirement plan available to you. There are a number of reasons why it's a good idea to take advantage of these plans if you have one.

- Your W-2 will show that the amount you earned is your wage amount minus the amount contributed to the tax-deferred plan. As a result, you pay tax on a lower amount of wage income.
- You may not be eligible to deduct an IRA contribution (explained later).
- Your employer may match your contributions to the retirement account. (If this is the case and you're not participating in the retirement plan, you're throwing money away.)
- Your plan may allow you to borrow against it in the event of emergency or to buy a house.
- It is relatively painless to have a deduction taken from your paycheck and put into your retirement account.

If you do not work as an employee or your employee job doesn't offer a tax-deferred retirement plan, you will want to consider one of the other types of retirement plans available to you.

## Traditional IRAs

Traditional *Individual Retirement Arrangements* (IRAs) are available to anyone with earned income (*i.e.*, wages or self-employment income). The 2004 maximum allowable contribution to an IRA account is the lesser of your earned income or $3,000 per year ($3,500 if you're age 50 or older). These amounts increase to $4,000/$4,500 for 2005 and $4,000/$5,000 for 2006. If you are single and have a loss from your business and no other earned income for the year, your compensation amount is less than zero—so you're not eligible for an IRA. A married couple can put up to $3,000 per spouse ($3,500 for each spouse age 50 or older) into an IRA, even if one spouse has no earnings. The couple's combined earned income must be at least as much as the total IRA contribution.

The ability to put money into an IRA doesn't necessarily mean that you'll be able to deduct the contribution. There are limits to its deductibility explained as follows.

- If your adjusted gross income is more than $40,000 ($60,000 if married) and you have a retirement plan at work, your IRA will be only partially deductible.

- If your adjusted gross income is over $50,000 ($70,000 if married) and you have a retirement plan at work, your IRA contribution won't be deductible at all.
- If you are married and your spouse has a retirement plan at work but you don't, you can deduct your IRA contribution as long as your joint income is under $150,000. If it's between $150,000 and $160,000, your IRA is partially deductible. If your joint income is more than $160,000, your IRA contribution isn't deductible.

Having a retirement plan at work refers to any type of retirement plan for which you are eligible at your employee workplace at any time during the year, whether you choose to participate in it or not. Having a retirement plan at work also refers to having a SEP IRA, SIMPLE, solo 401(k), or Keogh. These self-employed retirement accounts are discussed later in this chapter. If you had no retirement plan at work at anytime during the year, you can fully deduct your IRA contribution if you're single.

> **EXAMPLE**
>
> *Liz is single and has income in excess of $50,000. For part of this year she worked as an employee and had a 401(k) retirement plan at work. She cannot deduct her IRA contribution, even though she no longer works as an employee.*

As already mentioned, money taken out of an IRA before age 59½ is subject to an early withdrawal penalty. There are three situations in which the penalty is not assessed even though tax is still due on the distribution. The first situation occurs when money taken out is used to pay medical insurance premiums for someone who has received unemployment compensation during twelve consecutive weeks in the preceding year, or the year in which the withdrawal takes place. This also applies to self-employed people who would have received unemployment compensation but weren't eligible because they were self-employed.

The second instance in which the penalty isn't assessed is when the money is used to pay higher education expenses for the taxpayer, her spouse, her children, or her grandchildren.

There is also no penalty when up to $10,000 is taken out to be used in buying a first home for the IRA holder or an eligible relative.

## Roth IRAs

Up to $3,000 per year ($3,500 if age 50 or older) can be contributed to a Roth IRA. As with the traditional IRA, these amounts will increase for 2005 and 2006. The amount that can be contributed is reduced for single people with income over $95,000 ($150,000 if married). No contribution is allowed for single people with income over $110,000 or married couples with income over $160,000. A Roth IRA contribution is never deductible. The advantage of these IRAs is that no matter how much the account increases in value, no tax is ever owed on qualified distributions. The amount contributed can be taken out at any time without penalty or tax. The earnings on the account (*e.g.*, interest or dividends) can also be removed without tax being owed as long as:

■ the Roth IRA was opened at least five years prior and

■ the account holder is over 59½ or disabled; or,

■ the money is spent to buy a first home for the IRA owner or an eligible family member.

You can have a Roth IRA in addition to a retirement plan at your employee job or a self-employed retirement plan such as an SEP IRA or SIMPLE.

The total that can be contributed to any combination of traditional IRA or Roth IRA for 2004 is $3,000 per person ($3,500 for those age 50 or older).

## SEP IRA Accounts

The simplest retirement plan available specifically for small business owners is the SEP IRA. SEP stands for *Simplified Employee Pension*, but don't let the name confuse you—this plan is for sole proprietors, as well as partnerships, LLCs, and corporations. An SEP IRA can be set up at the same bank, brokerage house, mutual fund company, or other financial institution where you would open a traditional or Roth IRA.

Depending on your business income, you may be able to contribute substantially more to an SEP IRA than the $3,000 allowed for an IRA. The contribution to an SEP IRA is based on a percentage of your net self-employment income. Calculating the amount that can be contributed to an SEP IRA is described by the following.

Net self-employment income *(after expenses have been deducted)* –
½ of self-employment tax  x  20% maximum contribution percentage  =
Amount that can be contributed to an SEP IRA

This calculation is based on a contribution percentage of 20%. When you open your account, you will be told that the maximum contribution you can make is 25%. This is because a complex computation is done to calculate the allowable contribution amount. If you're interested in the details, review the IRS publication on retirement plans. (see Appendix D.) For expediency, know that the end result is an allowable contribution of 20% (to a maximum of $41,000). You do not, however, have to contribute the maximum to your SEP IRA each year. You can change your contribution percentage with each year's return and can also choose not to make a contribution at all.

As with the traditional IRA, contributions to an SEP IRA are intended for retirement, so a 10% penalty on top of the tax owed is assessed if there is a distribution before age 59½. You cannot borrow against an SEP IRA.

Contributions to an SEP IRA are not a business expense. The contribution amount is deducted at the bottom of page 1 of the 1040 Form in the adjustments section. (see page 141.) Because this is not a business deduction, it does not reduce self-employment tax. However, a taxpayer in the 25% federal tax bracket who contributes $1,000 to her retirement plan (whether traditional IRA, SEP IRA, or any of the other plans mentioned later in this chapter), will save $250 in income tax (more if she also pays a state income tax).

In addition to the higher contribution level of the SEP IRA, this plan has another advantage over the traditional IRA. Not only can it be opened as late as April 15, but if you need more time to come up with the money for your SEP IRA contribution, you can file an extension for your tax return. (see page 179.) This gives you until August 15 to fund your self-employed retirement plan. If that's still not enough time, you can apply for a second extension, which gives you until October 15 to come up with money that will save you tax on the previous year's return.

If you have employees and an SEP IRA, you must make a contribution on behalf of anyone who is over age 20, if she has worked for you any part of three of the last five years and earned at least $450 each year.

## Keogh Plans

Similar rules about covering employees, due dates, and maximum contribution amounts apply to another type of retirement plan available to business owners—the Keogh (pronounced *key oh*) defined contribution plan.

There actually are two kinds of Keogh plans. In addition to the defined contribution plan, there is a defined benefit plan. Contributions to a defined benefit Keogh plan are based on a calculation of how much needs to be contributed each year for the individual to be able to receive a predetermined amount at retirement. You need to use an actuarial table to determine the contribution amount, and typically will do this with the help of a financial professional. Therefore, the focus here will be only on the Keogh defined contribution plan.

It used to be that a larger contribution could be made to a Keogh plan than could be made to an SEP IRA, so self-employed people chose this type of plan in order to be able to contribute the maximum possible to a retirement plan. However, in the last few years the tax law changed and the same amount can now be contributed to an SEP IRA as to a Keogh.

The Keogh must be set up by December 31 and an annual report must be filed for accounts with balances over $100,000. The main advantage of a Keogh over an SEP IRA is that employees don't have to be covered until they've worked at least 1,000 hours during two twelve month periods. Otherwise, there is really no reason to select a Keogh plan over an SEP IRA, and many people are rolling over their existing plans into a different type of retirement account.

## SIMPLE Accounts

The SIMPLE (Savings Incentive Match Plan for Employees) is particularly designed for small businesses with employees, but it can also be used effectively by one-person businesses. In addition to sole proprietors, SIMPLEs can also be set up by partnerships, LLCs, and corporations.

While Keoghs and SEP IRAs must, under certain conditions, cover employees, only the employer may make contributions to those plans. A SIMPLE enables employees to contribute to a tax deferred retirement plan without subjecting the employer to the expense and complex administration of a traditional 401(k) type of retirement plan. Employers with SIMPLEs must either match employee contributions dollar-for-dollar up to 3% of pay or contribute 2% a year to the account of any employee who earns $5,000 or more during the year and who has received at least this much in any two preceding years. The maximum contribution required of the employer is $4,100 per employee.

The employer with a SIMPLE is limited to a yearly contribution of $10,000 for herself (plus an additional $2,000 *catch up contribution* if she's at least 50 years old). Since SIMPLEs can be set up only when there is no other business retirement plan, the employer cannot also make contributions to an SEP IRA or Keogh.

The SIMPLE can be an especially good choice for someone who has only a small net profit from self-employment. For purposes of the SIMPLE, the self-employed person is considered both employer and employee. As the employee, she can make a tax deferred contribution to a SIMPLE of up to 100% of her net profit (not to exceed $10,000, or $12,000 if 50 or older). As the employer, she matches her employee's contributions, including her own.

*Jennifer is employed as the manager of a construction company. She has a part-time business making gift baskets, and wants to save as much as possible for retirement. Her net income from self-employment is $5,500 for the year. If she opens an SEP IRA, she can put aside $1,022 ($5500 minus $389, which is ½ her self-employment tax, times the SEP IRA percentage of 20%). If she opens a SIMPLE, she can contribute $5,500 (100% of her net profit), plus match that amount with 3% of her net profit ($165), for a total retirement contribution of $5,665 ($7,665 if she's 50 or older).*

The SIMPLE must be opened by October 1 of the year for which you want to make contributions, and the administration of a SIMPLE is (despite the name) slightly more complex than an SEP IRA.

## Self-Employed 401(k) Plans

Within the last couple of years, a new type of retirement plan became available for self-employed people. This 401(k) plan, designed especially for sole proprietors and one-person corporations, is referred to by a number of names, including solo 401(k), solo(k), self-employed 401(k), individual(k), personal(k), one-person (k), and owner-only 401(k). This retirement plan is very similar to the tax-deferred retirement plans mentioned earlier in this chapter and offered by many employers. However, the difference is that this plan is easier and less expensive to set up and is available only to the owner of a sole proprietorship (and her spouse, if he works in the business). If you have employees who work for you more than 1000 hours a year, you cannot have this particular type of 401(k) plan.

The advantage of the solo 401(k) plan is that it allows the largest retirement plan contribution of any mentioned in this chapter. The owner is treated as both employer and employee. As employee, she is able to contribute 100% of her net profit up to $14,000 ($18,000 if age 50 or older). These amounts increase to $15,000/$20,000 in 2006. As the employer, she is able to contribute to the plan using the same calculation as used for an SEP IRA contribution (net profit minus ½ self-employment tax, times 20%).

*Amma is a 57-year-old sole proprietor with net profit of $50,000. She would like to contribute as much as possible to a retirement account. If she contributes to an SEP IRA or a Keogh, her maximum contribution will be $9,293 ($50,000 minus ½ of her self-employment tax, which is $3,533 times 20%). If she opens a SIMPLE,*

*continued...*

4

> her maximum contribution will be $13,500 ($10,000 plus $2,000 catch up plus employer contribution of 3%). If Amma chooses a solo 401(k), her maximum contribution will be $27,293 ($18,000 plus the employer contribution of $9,293).

To have a similar calculation done for your individual situation, go to **www.401khelpcenter.com** and choose the "Small Business Channel." From there, select "Solo(k) calculator." Enter the information asked for and you'll learn the maximum you can contribute to an SEP IRA, a SIMPLE, and a solo 401(k).

In addition to the larger contribution allowed, the self-employed 401(k) plan can be set up so that you can borrow against it, in the same way that many employer plans allow this. A reporting form must be filed annually once the balance in your solo 401(k) account reaches $100,000.

One caution about contributions to a SIMPLE or self-employed 401(k)—if, in addition to being self-employed, you also are an employee in a company that offers a tax-deferred retirement plan, you must take into consideration the amount you've already contributed to that plan when you calculate the maximum you can contribute to your self-employed plan. For example, if you're over age 50 and have had the $18,000 maximum withheld from your paycheck and put into your employer's 401(k) plan, you cannot contribute another $18,000 via your solo 401(k) plan. You can, however, make the *employer* contribution to your self-employed plan.

None of the retirement plans mentioned in this chapter have a minimum contribution requirement. However, it may be hard to find a financial institution willing to open a SIMPLE with less than $1,000. Some financial institutions will let you open an account with a small amount if you make automatic deposits on a monthly basis through the remainder of the year. No matter how little you're able to contribute, it's important to get into the habit of making an annual contribution to your retirement account.

## The Saver's Tax Credit

As an incentive to encourage people to save for retirement, there is a tax credit for lower income people who put money in their employee retirement account, an IRA, or a self-employed retirement plan. This credit can be as much as 50% of the first $2,000 contributed to a retirement account. A couple filing jointly can get up to $1,000 credit for each person, if each puts money away. Unlike a deduction, a credit does not get subtracted from your income. A credit is subtracted directly from your income tax liability, so is therefore more valuable than a deduction. If you qualify for the Saver's Tax Credit, Uncle Sam is actually paying for part of your retirement contribution. The credit is only scheduled to be available until 2006, so now is the time to take advantage of it. The table below shows the credit rate for different incomes and filing statuses.

| Credit Rate | Married and filing jointly | Single |
|---|---|---|
| 50% | Up to $30,000 | Up to $15,000 |
| 20% | $30,001–$32,500 | $15,001–$16,250 |
| 10% | $32,501–$50,000 | $16,251–$25,000 |

Although your income may be too high to qualify for the individual Saver's Tax Credit, you might be eligible for another retirement plan credit. The credit for small employer pension plan start-up costs is equal to 50% of the administrative expenses incurred in setting up a new retirement plan for employees. This credit applies to the first $1,000 in expenses for each of the first three plan years. Remember, the SIMPLE and solo 401(k) plans treat the business owner as both employee and employer, meaning that if you established one of these plans after December 31, 2001, you could be eligible for the credit. However, according to the rules for the credit, the employer, in the three previous years, cannot have maintained an employer plan in which it contributed for the same employees that are covered by the new plan.

**EXAMPLE**

Amma is a 57-year-old sole proprietor with a net profit of $50,000. She would like to put as much away as possible for retirement so she calculates the allowable maximum contribution for each of the self-employed retirement plans available to her.

  To calculate the amount she can contribute to an SEP IRA or a Keogh, Amma subtracts ½ of her self-employment tax ($3,533) from her $50,000 net profit. The result is $46,467. She multiplies that figure by the SEP IRA and Keogh deduction allowance of 20% and learns that she could put up to $9,293 in one of those accounts.

  If, instead, Amma were to open a SIMPLE retirement account, her maximum contribution would be $13,500. A SIMPLE account treats self-employed people as both employee and employer. The $13,500 amount is made up of the $10,000 Amma can contribute as employee, the $2,000 catch-up amount allowed because she's over 50, and the 3% of net profit ($1500) employer contribution. If Amma chooses a solo 401(k) as her retirement plan, her maximum contribution will be $27,293. As with the SIMPLE, the solo 401(k) treats Amma

continued...

4

*as both employee and employer. As employee, her contribution amount is $14,000, and she can make a $4,000 catch-up contribution. As employer, Amma can contribute the same amount she could have put into an SEP IRA or Keogh ($9293). Obviously, the solo 401(k) plan allows Amma to make the largest retirement plan contribution.*

# Tax Forms Used by Self-Employed People

# 33

As an independent contractor or self-employed person, you need to file specific tax forms to tell the IRS and state taxing agency about your business income and expenses. A sole proprietor includes these forms on her individual tax return, along with information about any other sources of income she might have. Business entities other than sole proprietorships must file a business tax return and, in addition, each partner or shareholder must file a separate individual return.

Tax returns are due on April 15 for sole proprietors and most partnerships. S corporations have a filing deadline of March 15. The forms are due for C corporations on the 15th day of the 3rd month following the end of the corporation's tax year. Generally, the tax returns submitted by all entities cover business activity for a twelve-month period.

Individuals, including sole proprietors, use a calendar year. Their tax returns include business and nonbusiness activity during the period January 1 to December 31. Usually, S corporations use a calendar year also, unless there is a business purpose for using a different year. C corporations can choose the beginning month of their tax year. Partnerships use the same tax year as the majority of their partners.

Because of the complexity of partnership and corporate tax returns, this book focuses only on the forms filed by sole proprietors (and single member LLCs). The business expenses discussed in Chapters 20 through 32 will be similar on the tax returns for each of the different entities (with some exceptions). However, the information requested on the partnership and corporation returns is more comprehensive than that on the sole proprietor's Schedule C. For more information about partnership tax returns, get a copy of IRS Form 1065 and instructions. Look at Form 1120 for C corporations, 1120-S for S corporations, or 1120-A for small corporations (those

5

with total income and total assets under $500,000). While single-member LLCs file Schedule C, limited liability companies with more than one member are generally treated as partnerships for federal income tax purposes, and file Form 1065.

# The 1040 Form

As a sole proprietor, you and your business are one and the same, so you report the information about your business income and expenses on your individual tax return. You are required to file your taxes on a the 1040 form. If you're used to filing one of the short forms—a 1040-EZ or 1040-A—owning a business will mean a change in forms. As a self-employed person, you can no longer use a short form, because a sole proprietor must attach a Schedule C to her tax return to show business income and expenses. You are not allowed to attach any forms to the 1040-A or 1040-EZ forms, so the 1040 form must be used.

The 1040 form acts as a cover sheet. It provides the IRS with a summary of your income and expense figures for the past year. The details supporting those summary figures are contained on the schedules that are filled out and attached behind the form.

A copy of the front of a 1040 form is found on page 141. Those parts of the form that are relevant to self-employed people are discussed in this chapter.

*Line 7* is the first income line. It says, "Wages, salaries, tips, etc. Attach Form(s) W-2." This is where you report income from those jobs you had as an employee in which taxes were taken out of your paycheck. Only report on this line money you earned from employers who gave you a W-2 form. Don't include income reported on 1099 forms or income received as an independent contractor. If your business operates as a corporation, this is where your wages from the corporation will be reported.

The next lines are for reporting interest and dividends earned and state tax refunds and alimony received. Interest earned on a business bank account is included on the interest line. On *Line 12*, the form says, "Business income or loss. Attach Schedule C or C-EZ." As mentioned previously, Schedule C is the form on which you report the income and expenses of your sole proprietorship.

Form **1040**

Department of the Treasury—Internal Revenue Service

**U.S. Individual Income Tax Return** 2004

(99)  IRS Use Only—Do not write or staple in this space.

For the year Jan. 1–Dec. 31, 2004, or other tax year beginning _____ , 2004, ending _____ , 20 ___

OMB No. 1545-0074

**Label**

(See instructions on page 19.)

**Use the IRS label.** Otherwise, please print or type.

L A B E L   H E R E

Your first name and initial | Last name | Your social security number

If a joint return, spouse's first name and initial | Last name | Spouse's social security number

Home address (number and street). If you have a P.O. box, see page 19. | Apt. no.

City, town or post office, state, and ZIP code. If you have a foreign address, see page 19.

▲ **Important!** ▲
You **must** enter your SSN(s) above.

**Presidential Election Campaign**
(See page 19.)

**Note.** Checking "Yes" will not change your tax or reduce your refund.

Do you, or your spouse if filing a joint return, want $3 to go to this fund? ► 

You: ☐ Yes ☐ No   Spouse: ☐ Yes ☐ No

**Filing Status**

Check only one box.

1 ☐ Single

2 ☐ Married filing jointly (even if only one had income)

3 ☐ Married filing separately. Enter spouse's SSN above and full name here. ►

4 ☐ Head of household (with qualifying person). (See page 20.) If the qualifying person is a child but not your dependent, enter this child's name here. ►

5 ☐ Qualifying widow(er) with dependent child (see page 20)

**Exemptions**

6a ☐ **Yourself.** If someone can claim you as a dependent, **do not** check box 6a

b ☐ **Spouse**

c Dependents:

| (1) First name   Last name | (2) Dependent's social security number | (3) Dependent's relationship to you | (4) ✔ if qualifying child for child tax credit (see page 21) |
|---|---|---|---|
| | | | ☐ |
| | | | ☐ |
| | | | ☐ |
| | | | ☐ |

If more than four dependents, see page 21.

d Total number of exemptions claimed

Boxes checked on 6a and 6b _____
No. of children on 6c who:
• lived with you _____
• did not live with you due to divorce or separation (see page 21) _____
Dependents on 6c not entered above _____
Add numbers on lines above ► _____

**Income**

**Attach Forms W-2 here. Also attach Form(s) W-2G and 1099-R if tax was withheld.**

If you did not get a W-2, see page 22.

Enclose, but do not attach, any payment. Also, please use Form 1040-V.

7 Wages, salaries, tips, etc. Attach Form(s) W-2 | 7

8a **Taxable** interest. Attach Schedule B if required | 8a

b Tax-exempt interest. **Do not** include on line 8a | 8b

9a Ordinary dividends. Attach Schedule B if required | 9a

b Qualified dividends (see page 23) | 9b

10 Taxable refunds, credits, or offsets of state and local income taxes (see page 23) | 10

11 Alimony received | 11

12 Business income or (loss). Attach Schedule C or C-EZ | 12

13 Capital gain or (loss). Attach Schedule D if required. If not required, check here ► ☐ | 13

14 Other gains or (losses). Attach Form 4797 | 14

15a IRA distributions | 15a | b Taxable amount (see page 25) | 15b

16a Pensions and annuities | 16a | b Taxable amount (see page 25) | 16b

17 Rental real estate, royalties, partnerships, S corporations, trusts, etc. Attach Schedule E | 17

18 Farm income or (loss). Attach Schedule F | 18

19 Unemployment compensation | 19

20a Social security benefits | 20a | b Taxable amount (see page 27) | 20b

21 Other income. List type and amount (see page 27) | 21

22 Add the amounts in the far right column for lines 7 through 21. This is your **total income** ► | 22

**Adjusted Gross Income**

23 Deduction for clean-fuel vehicles (see page 29) | 23

24 Certain business expenses of reservists, performing artists, and fee-basis government officials. Attach Form 2106 or 2106-EZ | 24

25 IRA deduction (see page 29) | 25

26 Student loan interest deduction (see page 31) | 26

27 Tuition and fees deduction (see page 32) | 27

28 Health savings account deduction. Attach Form 8889 | 28

29 Moving expenses. Attach Form 3903 | 29

30 One-half of self-employment tax. Attach Schedule SE | 30

31 Self-employed health insurance deduction (see page 33) | 31

32 Self-employed SEP, SIMPLE, and qualified plans | 32

33 Penalty on early withdrawal of savings | 33

34a Alimony paid  b Recipient's SSN ► _____ | 34a

35 Add lines 23 through 34a | 35

36 Subtract line 35 from line 22. This is your **adjusted gross income** ► | 36

**For Disclosure, Privacy Act, and Paperwork Reduction Act Notice, see page 77.**   Cat. No. 11320B   Form **1040** (2004)

5

# Schedule C

A copy of Schedule C is on page 145.

Notice that the title reads, "Schedule C, Profit or Loss From Business (Sole Proprietorship)." The form then reminds you that partnerships and other business entities must use a different form. Single-member LLCs, however, do file Schedule C. The form asks for your name, type of business, and the name of your business (if it's different from your own name). If you own several businesses and they are similar (*e.g.*, teaching and consulting), you can include them on the same Schedule C, identifying yourself, for example, as a teacher/consultant. However, if your businesses are not similar (*e.g.*, chiropractor and musician), you need to do a Schedule C for each business. If you are married and your spouse is also self-employed, you need to file a Schedule C for each of you. However, if you and your spouse are joint owners of this business, you file just one Schedule C for the business.

Next, Schedule C asks for your business address. This address should be the place where you conduct most of your business. In the top right corner is a space for you to record your Social Security number. Box B asks for your principal business code. The principal business codes are listed on pages 142–144. Many small businesses don't easily fit any of the existing business codes. Try to find a code that most closely matches your work. You may find it necessary to use a general code like 541990—*all other professional, scientific, and technical services*; or 453990—*all other miscellaneous store retailers* if you cannot find a more appropriate category.

After the business code, Schedule C asks for your employer ID number (EIN), if you have one. As discussed in Chapter 4, a sole proprietor is not required to have an employer ID number unless she has employees, a Keogh retirement plan, or self-employed 401(k). (see Chapter 32.)

## Principal Business or Professional Activity Codes

These codes for the Principal Business or Professional Activity classify sole proprietorships by the type of activity they are engaged in to facilitate the administration of the Internal Revenue Code. These six-digit codes are based on the North American Industry Classification System (NAICS).

Select the category that best describes your primary business activity (for example, Real Estate). Then select the activity that best identifies the principal source of your sales or receipts (for example, real estate agent). Now find the six-digit code assigned to this activity (for example, 531210, the code for offices of real estate agents and brokers) and **enter it on line B of Schedule C or C-EZ.**

**Note.** If your principal source of income is from farming activities, you should file **Schedule F**, Profit or Loss From Farming.

### Accommodation, Food Services, & Drinking Places
**Accommodation**
- 721310 Rooming & boarding houses
- 721210 RV (recreational vehicle) parks & recreational camps
- 721100 Travel accommodation (including hotels, motels, & bed & breakfast inns)

**Food Services & Drinking Places**
- 722410 Drinking places (alcoholic beverages)
- 722110 Full-service restaurants
- 722210 Limited-service eating places
- 722300 Special food services (including food service contractors & caterers)

### Administrative & Support and Waste Management & Remediation Services
**Administrative & Support Services**
- 561430 Business service centers (including private mail centers & copy shops)
- 561740 Carpet & upholstery cleaning services
- 561440 Collection agencies
- 561450 Credit bureaus
- 561410 Document preparation services
- 561300 Employment services
- 561710 Exterminating & pest control services
- 561210 Facilities support (management) services

- 561600 Investigation & security services
- 561720 Janitorial services
- 561730 Landscaping services
- 561110 Office administrative services
- 561420 Telephone call centers (including telephone answering services & telemarketing bureaus)
- 561500 Travel arrangement & reservation services
- 561490 Other business support services (including repossession services, court reporting, & stenotype services)
- 561790 Other services to buildings & dwellings

- 561900 Other support services (including packaging & labeling services, & convention & trade show organizers)

**Waste Management & Remediation Services**
- 562000 Waste management & remediation services

### Agriculture, Forestry, Hunting, & Fishing
- 112900 Animal production (including breeding of cats and dogs)
- 114110 Fishing
- 113000 Forestry & logging (including forest nurseries & timber tracts)
- 114210 Hunting & trapping

561720 Janitorial services

**Principal Business or Professional Activity Codes** *(continued)*

### Support Activities for Agriculture & Forestry

| | |
|---|---|
| 115210 | Support activities for animal production (including farriers) |
| 115110 | Support activities for crop production (including cotton ginning, soil preparation, planting, & cultivating) |
| 115310 | Support activities for forestry |

### Arts, Entertainment, & Recreation
#### Amusement, Gambling, & Recreation Industries

| | |
|---|---|
| 713100 | Amusement parks & arcades |
| 713200 | Gambling industries |
| 713900 | Other amusement & recreation services (including golf courses, skiing facilities, marinas, fitness centers, bowling centers, skating rinks, miniature golf courses) |

#### Museums, Historical Sites, & Similar Institutions

| | |
|---|---|
| 712100 | Museums, historical sites, & similar institutions |

#### Performing Arts, Spectator Sports, & Related Industries

| | |
|---|---|
| 711410 | Agents & managers for artists, athletes, entertainers, & other public figures |
| 711510 | Independent artists, writers, & performers |
| 711100 | Performing arts companies |
| 711300 | Promoters of performing arts, sports, & similar events |
| 711210 | Spectator sports (including professional sports clubs & racetrack operations) |

### Construction of Buildings

| | |
|---|---|
| 236200 | Nonresidential building construction |
| 236100 | Residential building construction |

#### Heavy and Civil Engineering Construction

| | |
|---|---|
| 237310 | Highway, street, & bridge construction |
| 237210 | Land subdivision |
| 237100 | Utility system construction |
| 237990 | Other heavy & civil engineering construction |

#### Specialty Trade Contractors

| | |
|---|---|
| 238310 | Drywall & insulation contractors |
| 238210 | Electrical contractors |
| 238350 | Finish carpentry contractors |
| 238330 | Flooring contractors |
| 238130 | Framing carpentry contractors |
| 238150 | Glass & glazing contractors |
| 238140 | Masonry contractors |
| 238320 | Painting & wall covering contractors |
| 238220 | Plumbing, heating & air-conditioning contractors |
| 238110 | Poured concrete foundation & structure contractors |
| 238160 | Roofing contractors |
| 238170 | Siding contractors |
| 238910 | Site preparation contractors |
| 238120 | Structural steel & precast concrete construction contractors |
| 238340 | Tile & terrazzo contractors |
| 238290 | Other building equipment contractors |
| 238390 | Other building finishing contractors |
| 238190 | Other foundation, structure, & building exterior contractors |
| 238990 | All other specialty trade contractors |

### Educational Services

| | |
|---|---|
| 611000 | Educational services (including schools, colleges, & universities) |

### Finance & Insurance
#### Credit Intermediation & Related Activities

| | |
|---|---|
| 522100 | Depository credit intermediation (including commercial banking, savings institutions, & credit unions) |
| 522200 | Nondepository credit intermediation (including sales financing & consumer lending) |
| 522300 | Activities related to credit intermediation (including loan brokers) |

#### Insurance Agents, Brokers, & Related Activities

| | |
|---|---|
| 524210 | Insurance agencies & brokerages |
| 524290 | Other insurance related activities |

#### Securities, Commodity Contracts, & Other Financial Investments & Related Activities

| | |
|---|---|
| 523140 | Commodity contracts brokers |
| 523130 | Commodity contracts dealers |
| 523110 | Investment bankers & securities dealers |
| 523210 | Securities & commodity exchanges |
| 523120 | Securities brokers |
| 523900 | Other financial investment activities (including investment advice) |

### Health Care & Social Assistance
#### Ambulatory Health Care Services

| | |
|---|---|
| 621610 | Home health care services |
| 621510 | Medical & diagnostic laboratories |
| 621310 | Offices of chiropractors |
| 621210 | Offices of dentists |
| 621330 | Offices of mental health practitioners (except physicians) |
| 621320 | Offices of optometrists |
| 621340 | Offices of physical, occupational & speech therapists, & audiologists |
| 621111 | Offices of physicians (except mental health specialists) |
| 621112 | Offices of physicians, mental health specialists |
| 621391 | Offices of podiatrists |
| 621399 | Offices of all other miscellaneous health practitioners |
| 621400 | Outpatient care centers |
| 621900 | Other ambulatory health care services (including ambulance services, blood, & organ banks) |

#### Hospitals

| | |
|---|---|
| 622000 | Hospitals |

#### Nursing & Residential Care Facilities

| | |
|---|---|
| 623000 | Nursing & residential care facilities |

#### Social Assistance

| | |
|---|---|
| 624410 | Child day care services |
| 624200 | Community food & housing, & emergency & other relief services |
| 624100 | Individual & family services |
| 624310 | Vocational rehabilitation services |

### Information

| | |
|---|---|
| 511000 | Publishing industries (except Internet) |

#### Broadcasting (except Internet) & Telecommunications

| | |
|---|---|
| 515000 | Broadcasting (except Internet) |
| 517000 | Telecommunications |

#### Internet Publishing & Broadcasting

| | |
|---|---|
| 516110 | Internet publishing & broadcasting |

#### Internet Service Providers, Web Search Portals, & Data Processing Services

| | |
|---|---|
| 518210 | Data processing, hosting, & related services |
| 518111 | Internet service providers |
| 518112 | Web search portals |
| 519100 | Other information services (including news syndicates and libraries) |

#### Motion Picture & Sound Recording

| | |
|---|---|
| 512100 | Motion picture & video industries (except video rental) |
| 512200 | Sound recording industries |

### Manufacturing

| | |
|---|---|
| 315000 | Apparel mfg. |
| 312000 | Beverage & tobacco product mfg. |
| 334000 | Computer & electronic product mfg. |
| 335000 | Electrical equipment, appliance, & component mfg. |
| 332000 | Fabricated metal product mfg. |
| 337000 | Furniture & related product mfg. |
| 333000 | Machinery mfg. |
| 339110 | Medical equipment & supplies mfg. |
| 322000 | Paper mfg. |
| 324100 | Petroleum & coal products mfg. |
| 326000 | Plastics & rubber products mfg. |
| 331000 | Primary metal mfg. |
| 323100 | Printing & related support activities |
| 313000 | Textile mills |
| 314000 | Textile product mills |
| 336000 | Transportation equipment mfg. |
| 321000 | Wood product mfg. |
| 339900 | Other miscellaneous mfg. |

#### Chemical Manufacturing

| | |
|---|---|
| 325100 | Basic chemical mfg. |
| 325500 | Paint, coating, & adhesive mfg. |
| 325300 | Pesticide, fertilizer, & other agricultural chemical mfg. |
| 325410 | Pharmaceutical & medicine mfg. |
| 325200 | Resin, synthetic rubber, & artificial & synthetic fibers & filaments mfg. |
| 325600 | Soap, cleaning compound, & toilet preparation mfg. |
| 325900 | Other chemical product & preparation mfg. |

#### Food Manufacturing

| | |
|---|---|
| 311110 | Animal food mfg. |
| 311800 | Bakeries & tortilla mfg. |
| 311500 | Dairy product mfg. |
| 311400 | Fruit & vegetable preserving & speciality food mfg. |
| 311200 | Grain & oilseed milling |
| 311610 | Animal slaughtering & processing |
| 311710 | Seafood product preparation & packaging |

| | |
|---|---|
| 311300 | Sugar & confectionery product mfg. |
| 311900 | Other food mfg. (including coffee, tea, flavorings, & seasonings) |

#### Leather & Allied Product Manufacturing

| | |
|---|---|
| 316210 | Footwear mfg. (including leather, rubber, & plastics) |
| 316110 | Leather & hide tanning & finishing |
| 316990 | Other leather & allied product mfg. |

#### Nonmetallic Mineral Product Manufacturing

| | |
|---|---|
| 327300 | Cement & concrete product mfg. |
| 327100 | Clay product & refractory mfg. |
| 327210 | Glass & glass product mfg. |
| 327400 | Lime & gypsum product mfg. |
| 327900 | Other nonmetallic mineral product mfg. |

### Mining

| | |
|---|---|
| 212110 | Coal mining |
| 212200 | Metal ore mining |
| 212300 | Nonmetallic mineral mining & quarrying |
| 211110 | Oil & gas extraction |
| 213110 | Support activities for mining |

### Other Services
#### Personal & Laundry Services

| | |
|---|---|
| 812111 | Barber shops |
| 812112 | Beauty salons |
| 812220 | Cemeteries & crematories |
| 812310 | Coin-operated laundries & drycleaners |
| 812320 | Drycleaning & laundry services (except coin-operated) (including laundry & drycleaning dropoff & pickup sites) |
| 812210 | Funeral homes & funeral services |
| 812330 | Linen & uniform supply |
| 812113 | Nail salons |
| 812930 | Parking lots & garages |
| 812910 | Pet care (except veterinary) services |
| 812920 | Photofinishing |
| 812190 | Other personal care services (including diet & weight reducing centers) |
| 812990 | All other personal services |

#### Repair & Maintenance

| | |
|---|---|
| 811120 | Automotive body, paint, interior, & glass repair |
| 811110 | Automotive mechanical & electrical repair & maintenance |
| 811190 | Other automotive repair & maintenance (including oil change & lubrication shops & car washes) |
| 811310 | Commercial & industrial machinery & equipment (except automotive & electronic) repair & maintenance |
| 811210 | Electronic & precision equipment repair & maintenance |
| 811430 | Footwear & leather goods repair |
| 811410 | Home & garden equipment & appliance repair & maintenance |
| 811420 | Reupholstery & furniture repair |
| 811490 | Other personal & household goods repair & maintenance |

5

## Principal Business or Professional Activity Codes *(continued)*

### Professional, Scientific, & Technical Services
541100 Legal services
541211 Offices of certified public accountants
541214 Payroll services
541213 Tax preparation services
541219 Other accounting services

### Architectural, Engineering, & Related Services
541310 Architectural services
541350 Building inspection services
541340 Drafting services
541330 Engineering services
541360 Geophysical surveying & mapping services
541320 Landscape architecture services
541370 Surveying & mapping (except geophysical) services
541380 Testing laboratories

### Computer Systems Design & Related Services
541510 Computer systems design & related services

### Specialized Design Services
541400 Specialized design services (including interior, industrial, graphic, & fashion design)

### Other Professional, Scientific, & Technical Services
541800 Advertising & related services
541600 Management, scientific, & technical consulting services
541910 Market research & public opinion polling
541920 Photographic services
541700 Scientific research & development services
541930 Translation & interpretation services
541940 Veterinary services
541990 All other professional, scientific, & technical services

### Real Estate & Rental & Leasing
#### Real Estate
531100 Lessors of real estate (including miniwarehouses & self-storage units)
531210 Offices of real estate agents & brokers
531320 Offices of real estate appraisers
531310 Real estate property managers
531390 Other activities related to real estate

#### Rental & Leasing Services
532100 Automotive equipment rental & leasing
532400 Commercial & industrial machinery & equipment rental & leasing
532210 Consumer electronics & appliances rental
532220 Formal wear & costume rental
532310 General rental centers
532230 Video tape & disc rental
532290 Other consumer goods rental

### Religious, Grantmaking, Civic, Professional, & Similar Organizations
813000 Religious, grantmaking, civic, professional, & similar organizations

### Retail Trade
#### Building Material & Garden Equipment & Supplies Dealers
444130 Hardware stores
444110 Home centers
444200 Lawn & garden equipment & supplies stores
444120 Paint & wallpaper stores
444190 Other building materials dealers

#### Clothing & Accessories Stores
448130 Children's & infants' clothing stores
448150 Clothing accessories stores
448140 Family clothing stores
448310 Jewelry stores
448320 Luggage & leather goods stores
448110 Men's clothing stores
448210 Shoe stores
448120 Women's clothing stores
448190 Other clothing stores

#### Electronic & Appliance Stores
443130 Camera & photographic supplies stores
443120 Computer & software stores
443111 Household appliance stores
443112 Radio, television, & other electronics stores

#### Food & Beverage Stores
445310 Beer, wine, & liquor stores
445220 Fish & seafood markets
445230 Fruit & vegetable markets
445100 Grocery stores (including supermarkets & convenience stores without gas)
445210 Meat markets
445290 Other specialty food stores

#### Furniture & Home Furnishing Stores
442110 Furniture stores
442200 Home furnishings stores

#### Gasoline Stations
447100 Gasoline stations (including convenience stores with gas)

#### General Merchandise Stores
452000 General merchandise stores

#### Health & Personal Care Stores
446120 Cosmetics, beauty supplies, & perfume stores
446130 Optical goods stores
446110 Pharmacies & drug stores
446190 Other health & personal care stores

#### Motor Vehicle & Parts Dealers
441300 Automotive parts, accessories, & tire stores
441222 Boat dealers
441221 Motorcycle dealers
441110 New car dealers
441210 Recreational vehicle dealers (including motor home & travel trailer dealers)

441120 Used car dealers
441229 All other motor vehicle dealers

#### Sporting Goods, Hobby, Book, & Music Stores
451211 Book stores
451120 Hobby, toy, & game stores
451140 Musical instrument & supplies stores
451212 News dealers & newsstands
451220 Prerecorded tape, compact disc, & record stores
451130 Sewing, needlework, & piece goods stores
451110 Sporting goods stores

#### Miscellaneous Store Retailers
453920 Art dealers
453110 Florists
453220 Gift, novelty, & souvenir stores
453930 Manufactured (mobile) home dealers
453210 Office supplies & stationery stores
453910 Pet & pet supplies stores
453310 Used merchandise stores
453990 All other miscellaneous store retailers (including tobacco, candle, & trophy shops)

#### Nonstore Retailers
454112 Electronic auctions
454111 Electronic shopping
454310 Fuel dealers
454113 Mail-order houses
454210 Vending machine operators
454390 Other direct selling establishments (including door-to-door retailing, frozen food plan providers, party plan merchandisers, & coffee-break service providers)

### Transportation & Warehousing
481000 Air transportation
485510 Charter bus industry
484110 General freight trucking, local
484120 General freight trucking, long distance
485210 Interurban & rural bus transportation
486000 Pipeline transportation
482110 Rail transportation
487000 Scenic & sightseeing transportation
485410 School & employee bus transportation
484200 Specialized freight trucking (including household moving vans)
485300 Taxi & limousine service
485110 Urban transit systems
483000 Water transportation
485990 Other transit & ground passenger transportation
488000 Support activities for transportation (including motor vehicle towing)

### Couriers & Messengers
492000 Couriers & messengers

### Warehousing & Storage Facilities
493100 Warehousing & storage (except leases of miniwarehouses & self-storage units)

### Utilities
221000 Utilities

### Wholesale Trade
#### Merchant Wholesalers, Durable Goods
423600 Electrical & electronic goods
423200 Furniture & home furnishing
423700 Hardware, & plumbing & heating equipment & supplies
423940 Jewelry, watch, precious stone, & precious metals
423300 Lumber & other construction materials
423800 Machinery, equipment, & supplies
423500 Metal & mineral (except petroleum)
423100 Motor vehicle & motor vehicle parts & supplies
423400 Professional & commercial equipment & supplies
423930 Recyclable materials
423910 Sporting & recreational goods & supplies
423920 Toy & hobby goods & supplies
423990 Other miscellaneous durable goods

#### Merchant Wholesalers, Nondurable Goods
424300 Apparel, piece goods, & notions
424800 Beer, wine, & distilled alcoholic beverage
424920 Books, periodicals, & newspapers
424600 Chemical & allied products
424210 Drugs & druggists' sundries
424500 Farm product raw materials
424910 Farm supplies
424930 Flower, nursery stock, & florists' supplies
424400 Grocery & related products
424950 Paint, varnish, & supplies
424100 Paper & paper products
424700 Petroleum & petroleum products
424940 Tobacco & tobacco products
424990 Other miscellaneous nondurable goods

#### Wholesale Electronic Markets and Agents & Brokers
425110 Business to business electronic markets
425120 Wholesale trade agents & brokers

999999 **Unclassified establishments (unable to classify)**

| SCHEDULE C<br>(Form 1040)<br><br>Department of the Treasury<br>Internal Revenue Service | **Profit or Loss From Business**<br>(Sole Proprietorship)<br>▶ **Partnerships, joint ventures, etc., must file Form 1065 or 1065-B.**<br>▶ **Attach to Form 1040 or 1041.** ▶ **See Instructions for Schedule C (Form 1040).** | OMB No. 1545-0074<br>20**04**<br>Attachment<br>Sequence No. **09** |
|---|---|---|

| Name of proprietor | Social security number (SSN) |
|---|---|

| **A** Principal business or profession, including product or service (see page C-2 of the instructions) | **B** Enter code from pages C-7, 8, & 9<br>▶ |
|---|---|

| **C** Business name. If no separate business name, leave blank. | **D** Employer ID number (EIN), if any |
|---|---|

**E** Business address (including suite or room no.) ▶ ................................................................
City, town or post office, state, and ZIP code

**F** Accounting method: **(1)** ☐ Cash **(2)** ☐ Accrual **(3)** ☐ Other (specify) ▶ ........................................

**G** Did you "materially participate" in the operation of this business during 2004? If "No," see page C-3 for limit on losses ☐ Yes ☐ No

**H** If you started or acquired this business during 2004, check here . . . . . . . . . . ▶ ☐

## Part I  Income

| | | | |
|---|---|---|---|
| 1 | Gross receipts or sales. **Caution.** If this income was reported to you on Form W-2 and the "Statutory employee" box on that form was checked, see page C-3 and check here . . . . . . . . ▶ ☐ | **1** | |
| 2 | Returns and allowances . . . . . . . . . . . . . . . . . . . . | **2** | |
| 3 | Subtract line 2 from line 1 . . . . . . . . . . . . . . . . . . | **3** | |
| 4 | Cost of goods sold (from line 42 on page 2) . . . . . . . . . . . . | **4** | |
| 5 | **Gross profit.** Subtract line 4 from line 3. . . . . . . . . . . . . . | **5** | |
| 6 | Other income, including Federal and state gasoline or fuel tax credit or refund (see page C-3) . . . | **6** | |
| 7 | **Gross income.** Add lines 5 and 6 . . . . . . . . . . . . . . ▶ | **7** | |

## Part II  Expenses. Enter expenses for business use of your home **only** on line 30.

| | | | | | | |
|---|---|---|---|---|---|---|
| 8 | Advertising . . . . . | **8** | | 19 Pension and profit-sharing plans | **19** | |
| 9 | Car and truck expenses (see page C-3) . . . . . . | **9** | | 20 Rent or lease (see page C-5): | | |
| 10 | Commissions and fees . . | **10** | | **a** Vehicles, machinery, and equipment . | **20a** | |
| 11 | Contract labor (see page C-4) | **11** | | **b** Other business property . . . | **20b** | |
| 12 | Depletion . . . . . | **12** | | 21 Repairs and maintenance . . . | **21** | |
| 13 | Depreciation and section 179 expense deduction (not included in Part III) (see page C-4) . . . . . | **13** | | 22 Supplies (not included in Part III) . | **22** | |
|  |  |  |  | 23 Taxes and licenses . . . . | **23** | |
|  |  |  |  | 24 Travel, meals, and entertainment: | | |
|  |  |  |  | **a** Travel . . . . . . . . | **24a** | |
| 14 | Employee benefit programs (other than on line 19). . | **14** | | **b** Meals and entertainment | | |
| 15 | Insurance (other than health) . | **15** | | **c** Enter nondeduct-ible amount in-cluded on line 24b (see page C-5) . | | |
| 16 | Interest: | | | | | |
| **a** | Mortgage (paid to banks, etc.) . | **16a** | | **d** Subtract line 24c from line 24b | **24d** | |
| **b** | Other . . . . . . . | **16b** | | 25 Utilities . . . . . . . | **25** | |
| 17 | Legal and professional services . . . . . . | **17** | | 26 Wages (less employment credits) . | **26** | |
| 18 | Office expense . . . . . | **18** | | 27 Other expenses (from line 48 on page 2) . . . . . . . | **27** | |

| 28 | **Total expenses** before expenses for business use of home. Add lines 8 through 27 in columns . ▶ | **28** | |
|---|---|---|---|
| 29 | Tentative profit (loss). Subtract line 28 from line 7 . . . . . . . . . . . | **29** | |
| 30 | Expenses for business use of your home. Attach **Form 8829** . . . . . . . . | **30** | |
| 31 | **Net profit or (loss).** Subtract line 30 from line 29.<br>● If a profit, enter on **Form 1040, line 12,** and **also** on **Schedule SE, line 2** (statutory employees, see page C-6). Estates and trusts, enter on Form 1041, line 3.<br>● If a loss, you **must** go to line 32. | **31** | |
| 32 | If you have a loss, check the box that describes your investment in this activity (see page C-6).<br>● If you checked 32a, enter the loss on **Form 1040, line 12,** and **also** on **Schedule SE, line 2** (statutory employees, see page C-6). Estates and trusts, enter on Form 1041, line 3.<br>● If you checked 32b, you **must** attach **Form 6198.** | **32a** ☐ All investment is at risk.<br>**32b** ☐ Some investment is not at risk. | |

**For Paperwork Reduction Act Notice, see Form 1040 instructions.**  Cat. No. 11334P  **Schedule C (Form 1040) 2004**

5

## ACCOUNTING METHODS

*Line F* of Schedule C asks which accounting method you use—cash, accrual, or other. If you use the cash method of accounting, you report on this tax return the income that you actually received between January 1 and December 31 of last year. You also report the expenses you paid during that period.

If you use the accrual method of accounting, you report your income not when you receive it, but when you earn it. You report your expenses when you accrue them or have them, rather than when you pay them. Some business owners choose to use the accrual method of accounting because they feel it gives them a more accurate picture of their business.

**EXAMPLE**

*Ramona, a graphic artist, has many expenses in doing work for her clients. Her clients generally pay her within sixty days of the date she bills them. Ramona did a large job in December and incurred many expenses. She paid some of those expenses in December and some in January. She received payment for the job in February. If Ramona uses the cash method of reporting her income and expenses, her records will look as though she didn't work in December (since no income was received), yet she had a great many expenses that month. If Ramona uses the accrual method, she lists in her December records the income she earned (even though she hasn't received it). She also lists the expenses she had (whether or not she's paid them). When looking at her financial records, Ramona can more easily match her income to the corresponding expenses. Using the accrual method provides her with more accurate picture of her business finances.*

The IRS requires certain businesses to use the accrual method of accounting, but since those rules apply to businesses with over $1,000,000 in sales, they will not be discussed. Most small business owners choose to use the cash method because it's the one they're most familiar with. Whichever method you choose the first year you start your business is generally the method you use for as long as you own the business. Any changes in accounting method must be approved by the IRS.

If you are using the cash method, you must include on this year's return any income you *constructively received* by December 31. This means if a client wrote you a check on December 28, 2005, but you didn't get around to picking it up until January 3, 2006, the income from that check belongs on your 2005 return. You could have had the money in 2005 had you chosen to pick up the check. Also, if you receive a check during the last week of December, you cannot delay paying taxes on the income by not depositing the check until January. If you received or could have received the money this year, it needs to be reported on this year's return.

Looking again at Schedule C, *Line G* asks whether you materially participated in the operation of your business during the year. This is simply asking if you were involved in operating the business on a regular and substantial basis. For example, if you had bought an ice cream parlor, hired a manager to run it, and gone to Tahiti to live, and if the ice cream parlor had more expenses than income, you would not be able to deduct the loss. You have to be involved in the operation of a business in order to deduct any loss.

*Line H* asks you to check the small box if you started or acquired the business during this year. In other words, the IRS wants to know if this is your first year in business. They claim that this information is used for statistical purposes in recording how many new businesses are started each year.

## THE INCOME SECTION OF SCHEDULE C

As you look further down Schedule C to Part I (the income section), you see that *Line 1* asks for the amount of your business's gross receipts or sales. *Line 2*, "Returns and allowances," is where you subtract refunds you've given or bounced checks you've received, unless those amounts have already been subtracted before the figure was entered on *Line 1*. If you have a service business and don't sell a product, the amount entered on *Line 3* will be the same as the amount entered on *Lines 5 and 7*.

If you sell a product, you need to fill out the "Cost of Goods Sold" section on the back of Schedule C. (see page 145.) You'll notice that this is similar to the example shown in Chapter 13. The back of Schedule C asks for the amount of inventory at the beginning of the year, purchases made during the year, and inventory left at the end of the year. When the ending inventory is subtracted from the combined total of beginning inventory plus purchases, the resulting figure is the cost of goods sold. That figure is entered on *Line 4* on the front of Schedule C and is subtracted from the gross receipts figure to calculate your gross profit. In most cases, gross income will be the same as gross profit.

## THE EXPENSE SECTION OF SCHEDULE C

Part II is the place to list business expenses. (See Chapters 20 through 32 for information about deductible expenses.) When you look at the categories listed in the "Expenses" section of Schedule C, you may find that a number of them are not applicable for your businesses. While you should use whichever categories apply to your business, you do not need to limit either your recordkeeping or your tax return to the

## Q & A

**Q: Should I leave the Schedule C lines totally blank and use only the other expenses lines?**

A: No, use the categories that are applicable to your business, but don't force your categories to match Schedule C. For example, there's an expense line labeled "Utilities," but no line called "Telephone" expenses. For many people, particularly those with a cell phone, telephone can be a big expense. If you include your telephone expense on the utilities expense line, along with your gas and electric expenses, you may end up with a large amount in the utilities category. You can reduce the amount in this category by recording your utilities on the utility line and adding another category on the back of the form labeled "Telephone" for those expenses.

expenses listed. On the back of Schedule C (see page 145) there's an area labeled "Other Expenses," which is where you can list your own expense categories. If there isn't enough room for all your expenses there, you can include as many extra pages of expense categories as needed. Just make sure that each sheet includes your name and Social Security number. The more you break down your expense categories, the more you're providing an explanation of your costs to the IRS. This should lessen your chance of being audited.

Between the "Cost of Goods Sold" and the "Other Expenses" sections on the back of Schedule C is an area labeled "Information on Your Vehicle." As explained in Chapter 25, there are two ways of deducting business use of a car or truck—the actual expense method and the standard or mileage rate method. If you use the standard method, you can use this section of Schedule C to provide all the required information on your vehicle. If you use the actual expense method, you'll need to fill out information similar to this on Form 4562, the depreciation form. (see page 89.)

Once you've listed all your expenses on Schedule C, add up the amounts and enter the total on *Line 28*. Then subtract the total expenses from gross income. The result is your tentative profit or loss. It's called *tentative* because the one expense not yet deducted is your office-in-home. As explained in Chapter 23, the reason for that is that you cannot deduct an office-in-home if you have a loss from your business, nor can the office-in-home deduction create a loss. The IRS wants to see first if you have a profit from your business (*Line 29*). Once you determine there is a profit, then you can deduct expenses on *Line 30* for business use of your home. After subtracting *Line 30* from your tentative profit or loss (*Line 29*), the balance is your net profit or loss. If you're not deducting expenses for office-in-home, your tentative profit or loss is going to be the same as your net profit or loss.

Schedule C (Form 1040) 2004            Page **2**

## Part III   Cost of Goods Sold (see page C-6)

**33**   Method(s) used to value closing inventory:    **a** ☐ Cost     **b** ☐ Lower of cost or market     **c** ☐ Other (attach explanation)

**34**   Was there any change in determining quantities, costs, or valuations between opening and closing inventory? If "Yes," attach explanation . . . . . . . . . . . . . . . . . . . . . ☐ **Yes**     ☐ **No**

**35**   Inventory at beginning of year. If different from last year's closing inventory, attach explanation . . | **35** |

**36**   Purchases less cost of items withdrawn for personal use . . . . . . . . | **36** |

**37**   Cost of labor. Do not include any amounts paid to yourself . . . . . . . . | **37** |

**38**   Materials and supplies . . . . . . . . . . . . . . . | **38** |

**39**   Other costs . . . . . . . . . . . . . . . . . | **39** |

**40**   Add lines 35 through 39 . . . . . . . . . . . . . . | **40** |

**41**   Inventory at end of year . . . . . . . . . . . . . | **41** |

**42**   **Cost of goods sold.** Subtract line 41 from line 40. Enter the result here and on page 1, line 4 . . | **42** |

## Part IV   Information on Your Vehicle. Complete this part **only** if you are claiming car or truck expenses on line 9 and are not required to file Form 4562 for this business. See the instructions for line 13 on page C-4 to find out if you must file Form 4562.

**43**   When did you place your vehicle in service for business purposes? (month, day, year) ▶ ......../......../........ .

**44**   Of the total number of miles you drove your vehicle during 2004, enter the number of miles you used your vehicle for:

**a** Business ...........................   **b** Commuting ...........................   **c** Other ...........................

**45**   Do you (or your spouse) have another vehicle available for personal use?. . . . . . . . . . . ☐ **Yes**     ☐ **No**

**46**   Was your vehicle available for personal use during off-duty hours? . . . . . . . . . . . ☐ **Yes**     ☐ **No**

**47a**   Do you have evidence to support your deduction? . . . . . . . . . . . . . . ☐ **Yes**     ☐ **No**

    **b**   If "Yes," is the evidence written? . . . . . . . . . . . . . . . . . . . . . ☐ **Yes**     ☐ **No**

## Part V   Other Expenses. List below business expenses not included on lines 8–26 or line 30.

| | |
|---|---|
| | |
| | |
| | |
| | |
| | |
| | |
| | |
| | |

**48**   **Total other expenses.** Enter here and on page 1, line 27 . . . . . . . . . . . . . | **48** |

Schedule C (Form 1040) 2004

5

## REPORTING LOSSES ON SCHEDULE C

If you have a loss, be sure to enter the amount in parentheses. A loss means that you have more expenses than income.

Even if you haven't shown a profit in a number of years, you can prove that you are really a business (have a *profit motive*) by keeping good records, advertising, having the appropriate knowledge and skills to operate your business, spending adequate time on the business, and so forth. In determining whether something is a hobby or a business, the IRS also looks at the personal pleasure involved. They are particularly apt to look carefully at photographers, artists, writers, and others whose work could be considered a pleasurable activity. You need to be able to show that you've done everything you could to be successful and it's not your fault if you have continued losses. Items such as rejection slips, receipts of crafts fair entry fees, or copies of ads you've placed can be important backup materials is the event of an audit.

---

### Q & A

**Q: Isn't there a limit on the number of years I can have a loss?**

A: You may have heard that you can show a loss only for a certain number of years. What the law actually says is that if you show a profit in three out of five years, you will be presumed to be a business rather than a hobby. Usually it's desirable to avoid being classified as a hobby. Hobby expenses are deductible only to the extent of hobby income, and then can be taken as an expense only if you can itemize your personal deductions and if your hobby expenses exceed 2% of your adjusted gross income.

The IRS is saying that if you show a profit in three out of five years, you won't have to prove that you're really a business and not a hobby. The law doesn't say that if you don't show a profit in three out of five years, you'll be presumed to be a hobby.

---

You may be surprised to learn that there is no place on Schedule C (or on any other tax form) to report income earned, but never received. It's a common but erroneous misconception that you can deduct the value of services you provided but didn't get paid for. When you are using the cash method of accounting—that is, you report your income only when you receive it—you cannot have a deductible bad debt. As far as the IRS is concerned, your time has no value. Since you're using the cash method, if you don't get paid for work you did, you don't have to report it as income. You can, however, deduct any expenses you had in doing the work. Generally, you can have a deductible bad debt only if you use the accrual method of accounting.

> **EXAMPLE**
>
> *On last year's tax return, Sandy, who uses the accrual method, reported money she earned but hadn't yet received. This year, she learned that the company she did the work for had declared bankruptcy and she would never be paid. Sandy has a deductible bad debt on this year's tax return. This year, she's deducting the income she reported last year but never received.*

## Schedule C-EZ

If you have a very small business, you may want to consider filing the EZ version of Schedule C. (see page 152.) There are restrictions about who is eligible to file Schedule C-EZ. You can use it instead of Schedule C if:

- your business expenses are less than $5,000;
- you have no inventory;
- you don't have a loss;
- you have only one business;
- you haven't bought any equipment or anything else that needs depreciating;
- you haven't had any employees during the year; and,
- you don't deduct expenses for business use of your home.

## More About Form 1040

Whether you use Schedule C or Schedule C-EZ, once you know what your net profit or loss is (*Line 31* of Schedule C or *Line 3* of Schedule C-EZ), that figure is carried to *Line 12* of the 1040 form. (see page 141.) Remember, if you show a loss on Schedule C, put parentheses around the amount as you note it on *Line 12*.

Looking again at the 1040 form, you'll notice that there are other lines on which to note capital gains, unemployment insurance, pensions, and other sources of income. *Line 17*, in addition to being used to report rental income, is used by partners and S corporation shareholders to report their share of the net profit or loss from their businesses. Partnership and S corporation tax returns include a page called a K-1 form, which is given to each partner or shareholder. It tells them the amount of their share of the profit or loss from the business. The partner or shareholder transfers that information to the back of Schedule E. The information from Schedule E is then entered on *Line 17* of the partner's or shareholder's individual tax return. (Remember, if you have a loss from your share of the business, be sure to record it in parentheses.)

All the income figures on Form 1040 are added together and the total is noted on *Line 22*. Self-employment income is just one part of your total income. If you have a loss from self-employment, it will offset some of your income from other sources. For

5

| SCHEDULE C-EZ<br>(Form 1040)<br><br>Department of the Treasury<br>Internal Revenue Service | **Net Profit From Business**<br>(Sole Proprietorship)<br>▶ **Partnerships, joint ventures, etc., must file Form 1065 or 1065-B.**<br>▶ **Attach to Form 1040 or 1041.** ▶ **See instructions on back.** | OMB No. 1545-0074<br>20**04**<br>Attachment<br>Sequence No. **09A** |
|---|---|---|
| Name of proprietor | | Social security number (SSN) |

**Part I**    General Information

| You May Use<br>Schedule C-EZ<br>Instead of<br>Schedule C<br>Only If You: | ▶ | • Had business expenses of $5,000 or less.<br>• Use the cash method of accounting.<br>• Did not have an inventory at any time during the year.<br>• Did not have a net loss from your business.<br>• Had only one business as a sole proprietor. | ▶ | And You: | • Had no employees during the year.<br>• Are not required to file **Form 4562,** Depreciation and Amortization, for this business. See the instructions for Schedule C, line 13, on page C-4 to find out if you must file.<br>• Do not deduct expenses for business use of your home.<br>• Do not have prior year unallowed passive activity losses from this business. |
|---|---|---|---|---|---|

| A | Principal business or profession, including product or service | | | B | Enter code from pages C-7, 8, & 9<br>▶ |
|---|---|---|---|---|---|
| C | Business name. If no separate business name, leave blank. | | | D | Employer ID number (EIN), if any |
| E | Business address (including suite or room no.). Address not required if same as on Form 1040, page 1. | | | | |
| | City, town or post office, state, and ZIP code | | | | |

**Part II**    Figure Your Net Profit

| 1 | **Gross receipts. Caution.** If this income was reported to you on Form W-2 and the "Statutory employee" box on that form was checked, see **Statutory Employees** in the instructions for Schedule C, line 1, on page C-3 and check here . . . . . . . . . . . ▶ ☐ | 1 | |
|---|---|---|---|
| 2 | **Total expenses** (see instructions). If more than $5,000, you **must** use Schedule C. . . . . | 2 | |
| 3 | **Net profit.** Subtract line 2 from line 1. If less than zero, you **must** use Schedule C. Enter on **Form 1040, line 12,** and **also** on **Schedule SE, line 2.** (Statutory employees **do not** report this amount on Schedule SE, line 2. Estates and trusts, enter on Form 1041, line 3.) . . . . . | 3 | |

**Part III**    Information on Your Vehicle. Complete this part **only** if you are claiming car or truck expenses on line 2.

4    When did you place your vehicle in service for business purposes? (month, day, year) ▶ ....../....../...... .

5    Of the total number of miles you drove your vehicle during 2004, enter the number of miles you used your vehicle for:

a  Business ................... b  Commuting .................... c  Other ...................

| 6 | Do you (or your spouse) have another vehicle available for personal use? . . . . . . . . . . | ☐ Yes | ☐ No |
|---|---|---|---|
| 7 | Was your vehicle available for personal use during off-duty hours? . . . . . . . . . . . . | ☐ Yes | ☐ No |
| 8a | Do you have evidence to support your deduction? . . . . . . . . . . . . . . | ☐ Yes | ☐ No |
| b | If "Yes," is the evidence written? . . . . . . . . . . . . . . . . . . | ☐ Yes | ☐ No |

For Paperwork Reduction Act Notice, see Form 1040 instructions.    Cat. No. 14374D    Schedule C-EZ (Form 1040) 2004

example, if you have a $2,000 loss from self-employment but also have $40,000 in wages, the $2,000 loss will offset $2,000 of the wages—making your total income figure $38,000. If you are married and filing a joint return, your spouse's income is also included in the total income figure.

Below the total income figure on Form 1040 are some lines on which to show adjustments (subtractions) to your income. Review the instructions to Form 1040 to see if any of the adjustments are applicable to your situation. *Line 26* is the place to list an IRA deduction if you contribute to a traditional IRA and qualify to deduct it. As you read in Chapter 32, this is dependent on your total income and whether you or your spouse is covered by a retirement plan at work. *Line 28* is where you deduct the amount con-

## Q & A

**Q: What if I total all my income and find that because of the loss from my business, my income is less than zero?**

A: In this case, you have what's called a Net Operating Loss (NOL). NOLs require a complex tax calculation that is beyond the scope of this book. If you have an NOL (which generally happens only when the loss from your business exceeds your income from other sources), be sure to take advantage of it. The loss can be carried back two years, and those years' returns can be amended so that you receive a refund. The other option is to carry the loss forward, where it's used to offset income earned in the following year. The IRS assumes you'll choose to carry back the loss, so you must include a statement (called an election) on the return with the NOL if you choose to carry the loss forward instead.

tributed to your Health Savings Account. (see Chapter 28.) *Line 30* is the place you deduct one half of your self-employment tax (as discussed in Chapter 16). This isn't a business deduction, but it does reduce your taxable income and, thus, your income tax.

*Line 31* of Form 1040 is for the self-employed health insurance deduction. On this line, sole proprietors, partners, and S corporation shareholders can deduct the health insurance and long-term care premiums (not the medical expenses) they paid for themselves, their spouses (if married), and any dependents. (See Chapter 28 for more information about deductible premiums.)

Below the line for health insurance is the line on which self-employed people deduct contributions to a retirement plan. (See Chapter 32 for more information about Keogh, SEP IRA, SIMPLE, and solo 401(k) retirement plans.)

All of these adjustments are added together and then subtracted from your total income. The result is your *adjusted gross income*. That figure is listed on *Line 36* and is also carried over to the back of Form 1040. (see page 141.)

5

Form 1040 (2004) — Page **2**

| | | | | 37 | |
|---|---|---|---|---|---|
| **Tax and Credits** | 37 | Amount from line 36 (adjusted gross income) . . . . . . | | 37 | |
| | 38a | Check { ☐ **You** were born before January 2, 1940, ☐ Blind. } Total boxes<br>if: { ☐ **Spouse** was born before January 2, 1940, ☐ Blind. } checked ▶ 38a | | | |
| **Standard Deduction for—** | b | If you are married filing separately and your spouse itemizes deductions, or you were a dual-status alien, see page 34 and check here . . . . . . ▶ 38b ☐ | | | |
| • People who checked any box on line 38a or 38b **or** who can be claimed as a dependent, see page 34. | 39 | **Itemized deductions** (from Schedule A) **or** your **standard deduction** (see left margin) . . | | 39 | |
| | 40 | Subtract line 39 from line 37 . . . . . . . . . . . . . | | 40 | |
| | 41 | If line 37 is $107,025 or less, multiply $3,100 by the total number of **exemptions** claimed on line 6d. If line 37 is over $107,025, see the worksheet on page 35 . . . . . . | | 41 | |
| • All others: | 42 | **Taxable income.** Subtract line 41 from line 40. If line 41 is more than line 40, enter -0- | | 42 | |
| Single or Married filing separately, $4,850 | 43 | **Tax** (see page 36). Check if any tax is from: a ☐ Form(s) 8814 b ☐ Form 4972 . . . | | 43 | |
| | 44 | **Alternative minimum tax** (see page 38). Attach Form 6251 . . . . . . | | 44 | |
| Married filing jointly or Qualifying widow(er), $9,700 | 45 | Add lines 43 and 44 . . . . . . . . . . . . . . ▶ | | 45 | |
| | 46 | Credit for child and dependent care expenses. Attach Form 2441 | 46 | | |
| | 47 | Credit for the elderly or the disabled. Attach Schedule R . . | 47 | | |
| Head of household, $7,150 | 48 | Education credits. Attach Form 8863 . . . . . . . | 48 | | |
| | 49 | Credits from: a ☐ Form 8396 b ☐ Form 8859 . . . | 49 | | |
| | 50 | Foreign tax credit. Attach Form 1116 if required . . . . | 50 | | |
| | 51 | Child tax credit (see page 40) . . . . . . . . | 51 | | |
| | 52 | Retirement savings contributions credit. Attach Form 8880 . | 52 | | |
| | 53 | Adoption credit. Attach Form 8839 . . . . . . | 53 | | |
| | 54 | Other credits. Check applicable box(es): a ☐ Form 3800<br>b ☐ Form 8801 c ☐ Specify _____ | 54 | | |
| | 55 | Add lines 46 through 54. These are your **total credits** . . . . . . | | 55 | |
| | 56 | Subtract line 55 from line 45. If line 55 is more than line 45, enter -0- . . . . ▶ | | 56 | |
| **Other Taxes** | 57 | Self-employment tax. Attach Schedule SE . . . . . . . . . | | 57 | |
| | 58 | Social security and Medicare tax on tip income not reported to employer. Attach Form 4137 | | 58 | |
| | 59 | Additional tax on IRAs, other qualified retirement plans, etc. Attach Form 5329 if required . | | 59 | |
| | 60 | Advance earned income credit payments from Form(s) W-2 . . . . . . . | | 60 | |
| | 61 | Household employment taxes. Attach Schedule H . . . . . . . | | 61 | |
| | 62 | Add lines 56 through 61. This is your **total tax** . . . . . . . . ▶ | | 62 | |
| **Payments** | 63 | Federal income tax withheld from Forms W-2 and 1099 . . | 63 | | |
| | 64 | 2004 estimated tax payments and amount applied from 2003 return | 64 | | |
| If you have a qualifying child, attach Schedule EIC. | 65 | **Earned income credit (EIC)** . . . . . . . . . | 65 | | |
| | 66 | Excess social security and tier 1 RRTA tax withheld (see page 56) | 66 | | |
| | 67 | Additional child tax credit. Attach Form 8812 . . . . . | 67 | | |
| | 68 | Amount paid with request for extension to file (see page 56) | 68 | | |
| | 69 | Other payments from: a ☐ Form 2439 b ☐ Form 4136 c ☐ Form 8885 | 69 | | |
| | 70 | Add lines 63 through 69. These are your **total payments** . . . . . . . ▶ | | 70 | |
| **Refund**<br>Direct deposit? See page 56 and fill in 72b, 72c, and 72d. | 71 | If line 70 is more than line 62, subtract line 62 from line 70. This is the amount you **overpaid** | | 71 | |
| | 72a | Amount of line 71 you want **refunded to you** . . . . . . . . ▶ | | 72a | |
| | ▶ b | Routing number [ ] ▶ c Type: ☐ Checking ☐ Savings | | | |
| | ▶ d | Account number [ ] | | | |
| | 73 | Amount of line 71 you want **applied to your 2005 estimated tax** ▶ | 73 | | |
| **Amount You Owe** | 74 | **Amount you owe.** Subtract line 70 from line 62. For details on how to pay, see page 57 ▶ | | 74 | |
| | 75 | Estimated tax penalty (see page 58) . . . . . . . . | 75 | | |

| **Third Party Designee** | Do you want to allow another person to discuss this return with the IRS (see page 58)? ☐ **Yes.** Complete the following. ☐ **No** |
|---|---|
| | Designee's name ▶ _____ Phone no. ▶ ( ) _____ Personal identification number (PIN) ▶ [ ] |

| **Sign Here**<br>Joint return? See page 20.<br>Keep a copy for your records. | Under penalties of perjury, I declare that I have examined this return and accompanying schedules and statements, and to the best of my knowledge and belief, they are true, correct, and complete. Declaration of preparer (other than taxpayer) is based on all information of which preparer has any knowledge. | | | |
|---|---|---|---|---|
| | Your signature | Date | Your occupation | Daytime phone number<br>( ) |
| | Spouse's signature. If a joint return, **both** must sign. | Date | Spouse's occupation | |

| **Paid Preparer's Use Only** | Preparer's signature ▶ | | Date | | Check if self-employed ☐ | Preparer's SSN or PTIN |
|---|---|---|---|---|---|---|
| | Firm's name (or yours if self-employed), address, and ZIP code ▶ | | | | EIN :<br>Phone no. ( ) | |

Form **1040** (2004)

♺ Printed on recycled paper

# Other Itemized Deductions and Exemptions

Several other items can be deducted from your adjusted gross income. These deductions have nothing to do with your self-employment and are available to all taxpayers.

First are your *personal itemized deductions*. If you own your home, have large medical expenses, or made large charitable contributions, you will probably be able to itemize your personal deductions. Note that these are personal, not business, deductions. They include mortgage interest, real estate taxes, state income taxes paid or withheld, charitable contributions, medical expenses, and so on.

If you don't have enough of those expenses to be able to itemize, you'll take the *standard deduction*. For 2004, the standard deduction is $4,850 if single and $9,700 if married, filing jointly. On *Line 39* of the return, you subtract out either your personal itemized deductions or the standard deduction.

The other amount deducted from your adjusted gross income (on *Line 41*) is a personal exemption for yourself, your spouse, and each dependent. This also has nothing to do with being self-employed—you get this personal exemption just for being you. For 2004, the exemption amount is $3,100 for each person being claimed on your return.

One thing to be aware of is that the personal exemption and personal itemized deduction amounts are reduced when your adjusted gross income exceeds about $140,000 (less if married and filing separately, and more if head of household or married and filing jointly). The instructions for Form 1040 include a worksheet to calculate this *phaseout* if it applies to you.

After the personal deductions and exemptions are subtracted, what's left is your *taxable income* (*Line 42*). Using the taxable income figure, your federal income tax is calculated and entered on *Line 43*.

The next section of Form 1040 lists several credits, including the child care credit, discussed in Chapter 31.

# Self-Employment Tax

After your credits (if any) are subtracted from your income tax, there's a section on Form 1040 to report other taxes owed. The other tax that applies to sole proprietors and partners is self-employment tax. Earlier in this chapter, you saw that the net profit or loss figure from Schedule C is carried to *Line 12* of Form 1040, where business income or loss is reported. That same figure is also carried to Schedule SE, which is the third tax form that all sole proprietors will need to include as part of their individual tax returns. A copy of Schedule SE is on page 157.

Partners in a partnership that has a profit will also need to attach a Schedule SE to their individual tax returns. Schedule SE is used to calculate the amount of self-employment tax owed. Self-employment tax, you'll remember, is Social Security tax for self-employed people. (Self-employment tax is discussed more fully in Chapter 16.)

Most self-employed people will be able to use the short Schedule SE. Under certain circumstances related to your non-self-employment income, the long Schedule SE will need to be used. (see page 157.)

The short Schedule SE has only six lines. The first two are used to report your net profit from farming (*Line 1*) or from your Schedule C business (*Line 2*). As explained earlier, each business must have its own Schedule C. However, only one Schedule SE is filled out for each person. The net profit from all businesses owned by that person are combined on that one Schedule SE.

If a married couple runs a business together as a sole proprietorship, they will file only one Schedule C for the business, but each spouse will need to include a Schedule SE showing his or her share of the self-employment tax on the business income.

If a husband and wife each own a business, each must file a Schedule C and a Schedule SE. The income reported on Schedule SE becomes part of your Social Security account earnings.

*Line 3* of the short Schedule SE is the total of *Lines 1 and 2*. On *Line 4*, your net profit from self-employment is multiplied by 92.35%. (As discussed in Chapter 16, having self-employed people pay self-employment tax on only 92.35% of their net self-employment earnings was Congress's attempt to equalize the amount self-employed people pay into Social Security with that paid by employees.)

*Line 4* says if 92.35% of your net self-employment income is less than $400, you don't need to file Schedule SE, as no self-employment tax is owed.

*Line 5* is used to calculate the self-employment tax at the 15.3% self-employment tax rate.

*Line 6* is where you divide your self-employment tax figure in half. As explained earlier, half of the self-employment tax you pay is deductible on *Line 30* of Form 1040—not as a business expense, but as an adjustment to income.

Once you've filled out the self-employment tax form, go back to *Line 62* of Form 1040 and record your self-employment tax amount. Then add your income tax to your self-employment tax. The result on *Line 62* is your total tax liability.

**SCHEDULE SE**
**(Form 1040)**

Department of the Treasury
Internal Revenue Service

### Self-Employment Tax

▶ **Attach to Form 1040.** ▶ **See Instructions for Schedule SE (Form 1040).**

OMB No. 1545-0074

20**04**

Attachment
Sequence No. **17**

Name of person with **self-employment** income (as shown on Form 1040)

Social security number of person
with **self-employment** income ▶

### Who Must File Schedule SE

You must file Schedule SE if:

- You had net earnings from self-employment from **other than** church employee income (line 4 of Short Schedule SE or line 4c of Long Schedule SE) of $400 or more **or**
- You had church employee income of $108.28 or more. Income from services you performed as a minister or a member of a religious order **is not** church employee income (see page SE-1).

**Note.** Even if you had a loss or a small amount of income from self-employment, it may be to your benefit to file Schedule SE and use either "optional method" in Part II of Long Schedule SE (see page SE-3).

**Exception.** If your only self-employment income was from earnings as a minister, member of a religious order, or Christian Science practitioner **and** you filed Form 4361 and received IRS approval not to be taxed on those earnings, **do not** file Schedule SE. Instead, write "Exempt–Form 4361" on Form 1040, line 57.

### May I Use Short Schedule SE or Must I Use Long Schedule SE?

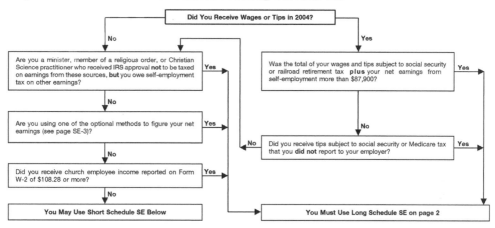

**Section A—Short Schedule SE. Caution.** Read above to see if you can use Short Schedule SE.

| | | |
|---|---|---|
| **1** Net farm profit or (loss) from Schedule F, line 36, and farm partnerships, Schedule K-1 (Form 1065), box 14, code A . . . . . . . . . . . . . . . . . . . | **1** | |
| **2** Net profit or (loss) from Schedule C, line 31; Schedule C-EZ, line 3; Schedule K-1 (Form 1065), box 14, code A (other than farming); and Schedule K-1 (Form 1065-B), box 9. Ministers and members of religious orders, see page SE-1 for amounts to report on this line. See page SE-2 for other income to report . . . . . . . . . . . . . . . . | **2** | |
| **3** Combine lines 1 and 2 . . . . . . . . . . . . . . . . . . . . | **3** | |
| **4** **Net earnings from self-employment.** Multiply line 3 by 92.35% (.9235). If less than $400, **do not** file this schedule; you do not owe self-employment tax . . . . . . . . . ▶ | **4** | |
| **5** **Self-employment tax.** If the amount on line 4 is: <br> • $87,900 or less, multiply line 4 by 15.3% (.153). Enter the result here and on **Form 1040, line 57.** <br> • More than $87,900, multiply line 4 by 2.9% (.029). Then, add $10,899.60 to the result. Enter the total here and on **Form 1040, line 57.** | **5** | |
| **6** **Deduction for one-half of self-employment tax.** Multiply line 5 by 50% (.5). Enter the result here and on **Form 1040, line 30** . . . . . | **6** | |

For Paperwork Reduction Act Notice, see Form 1040 instructions.   Cat. No. 11358Z   **Schedule SE (Form 1040) 2004**

5

Schedule SE (Form 1040) 2004      Attachment Sequence No. **17**      Page **2**

| Name of person with **self-employment** income (as shown on Form 1040) | Social security number of person with **self-employment** income ▶ | |
|---|---|---|

## Section B—Long Schedule SE

**Part I**    **Self-Employment Tax**

**Note.** If your only income subject to self-employment tax is **church employee income**, skip lines 1 through 4b. Enter -0- on line 4c and go to line 5a. Income from services you performed as a minister or a member of a religious order **is not** church employee income. See page SE-1.

**A**  If you are a minister, member of a religious order, or Christian Science practitioner **and** you filed Form 4361, but you had $400 or more of **other** net earnings from self-employment, check here and continue with Part I . . . . . . ▶ ☐

| | | | |
|---|---|---|---|
| **1** | Net farm profit or (loss) from Schedule F, line 36, and farm partnerships, Schedule K-1 (Form 1065), box 14, code A. **Note.** Skip this line if you use the farm optional method (see page SE-4) | **1** | |
| **2** | Net profit or (loss) from Schedule C, line 31; Schedule C-EZ, line 3; Schedule K-1 (Form 1065), box 14, code A (other than farming); and Schedule K-1 (Form 1065-B), box 9. Ministers and members of religious orders, see page SE-1 for amounts to report on this line. See page SE-2 for other income to report. **Note.** Skip this line if you use the nonfarm optional method (see page SE-4) | **2** | |
| **3** | Combine lines 1 and 2 . . . . . . . . | **3** | |
| **4a** | If line 3 is more than zero, multiply line 3 by 92.35% (.9235). Otherwise, enter amount from line 3 | **4a** | |
| **b** | If you elect one or both of the optional methods, enter the total of lines 15 and 17 here . . . | **4b** | |
| **c** | Combine lines 4a and 4b. If less than $400, **do not** file this schedule; you do not owe self-employment tax. **Exception.** If less than $400 and you had **church employee income,** enter -0- and continue ▶ | **4c** | |
| **5a** | Enter your **church employee income** from Form W-2. See page SE-1 for definition of church employee income . . . . . . . . . . **5a** | | |
| **b** | Multiply line 5a by 92.35% (.9235). If less than $100, enter -0- . . . . . . . | **5b** | |
| **6** | **Net earnings from self-employment.** Add lines 4c and 5b . . . . . | **6** | |
| **7** | Maximum amount of combined wages and self-employment earnings subject to social security tax or the 6.2% portion of the 7.65% railroad retirement (tier 1) tax for 2004 . . . . . . . | **7** | *87,900* | *00* |
| **8a** | Total social security wages and tips (total of boxes 3 and 7 on Form(s) W-2) and railroad retirement (tier 1) compensation. If $87,900 or more, skip lines 8b through 10, and go to line 11 . . . . . . . **8a** | | |
| **b** | Unreported tips subject to social security tax (from Form 4137, line 9) **8b** | | |
| **c** | Add lines 8a and 8b . . . . . . . . . . . . . . . | **8c** | |
| **9** | Subtract line 8c from line 7. If zero or less, enter -0- here and on line 10 and go to line 11 ▶ | **9** | |
| **10** | Multiply the **smaller** of line 6 or line 9 by 12.4% (.124) . . . . . . . | **10** | |
| **11** | Multiply line 6 by 2.9% (.029) . . . . . . . . . . . . . | **11** | |
| **12** | **Self-employment tax.** Add lines 10 and 11. Enter here and on **Form 1040, line 57** . . . . | **12** | |
| **13** | **Deduction for one-half of self-employment tax.** Multiply line 12 by 50% (.5). Enter the result here and on **Form 1040, line 30** . . . . **13** | | |

**Part II**    **Optional Methods To Figure Net Earnings** (see page SE-3)

**Farm Optional Method.** You may use this method only if **(a)** your gross farm income[1] was not more than $2,400 **or (b)** your net farm profits[2] were less than $1,733.

| | | | |
|---|---|---|---|
| **14** | Maximum income for optional methods . . . . . . . . . . . . . | **14** | *1,600* | *00* |
| **15** | Enter the **smaller** of: two-thirds (⅔) of gross farm income[1] (not less than zero) **or** $1,600. Also include this amount on line 4b above . . . . . . . . . . . . . . . | **15** | |

**Nonfarm Optional Method.** You may use this method only if **(a)** your net nonfarm profits[3] were less than $1,733 and also less than 72.189% of your gross nonfarm income[4] **and (b)** you had net earnings from self-employment of at least $400 in 2 of the prior 3 years.

**Caution.** You may use this method no more than five times.

| | | | |
|---|---|---|---|
| **16** | Subtract line 15 from line 14 . . . . . . . . . . . . . . | **16** | |
| **17** | Enter the **smaller** of: two-thirds (⅔) of gross nonfarm income[4] (not less than zero) **or** the amount on line 16. Also include this amount on line 4b above . . . . . . . . . . . . | **17** | |

[1] From Sch. F, line 11, and Sch. K-1 (Form 1065), box 14, code B.

[2] From Sch. F, line 36, and Sch. K-1 (Form 1065), box 14, code A.

[3] From Sch. C, line 31; Sch. C-EZ, line 3; Sch. K-1 (Form 1065), box 14, code A; and Sch. K-1 (Form 1065-B), box 9.

[4] From Sch. C, line 7; Sch. C-EZ, line 1; Sch. K-1 (Form 1065), box 14, code C; and Sch. K-1 (Form 1065-B), box 9.

Ⓐ *Printed on recycled paper*      **Schedule SE (Form 1040) 2004**

## The Tax Payments Section of Form 1040

After you've entered your total tax liability, the next section of the 1040 form is where you record the payments you've made. Add up how much you had withheld from your paycheck, how much you paid in estimated tax payments, and how much you paid with your extension—if you filed an extension. On *Line 70*, add up your total payments and compare that figure to your total tax amount on *Line 62*. Either you've overpaid—in which case you can have it refunded to you or applied to your next year's estimated taxes, or you've underpaid—in which case you owe the IRS.

There's a little space at the bottom of the 1040 form, labeled *Line 75*. This is where you calculate your estimated tax penalty if you haven't sent in enough taxes during the year. (Estimated taxes and related penalties are discussed in Chapter 35.)

### Q & A

**Q: If I realize that I made a lot of mistakes on last year's return, should I do something about that?**

A: Form 1040X (and a corresponding form for your state) is used to amend an individual tax return. On the 1040X, you show the figures as they were originally entered on your return. Then, you show the corrected figures. There is a section on the form to explain why you're amending the return. If you make extensive changes to a form such as Schedule C, also attach a revised version of the form. If the corrections are in your favor, you'll receive a refund plus interest. If the corrections are in the IRS's favor, you'll need to send an additional tax payment plus interest with the 1040X form. You have three years from the date the original return was filed, or two years from when you paid the tax (whichever is later) to amend a return.

5

# State Taxes | 34

Most states and the District of Columbia expect you to file a state return if your income is above the minimum requirement. If you live in one state and work in another, you may have to file a return in both states. Moving from one state to another in the course of a year means that you need to file a return in the state you left and in the state to which you moved, reporting the income earned in each state.

Seven states don't have a state income tax. Those states include: Alaska, Florida, Nevada, South Dakota, Texas, Washington, and Wyoming. Tennessee and New Hampshire assess income tax only on interest and dividends.

Generally, state tax returns are due the same date as federal returns—April 15. However, several states have different due dates for their returns. Hawaii returns are due April 20, Delaware and Iowa returns are due April 30, Virginia returns are due May 1, and Louisiana returns are due May 15.

Each state has its own way of handling taxes. Some follow the federal law and forms closely; others do not. Some state returns use your federal income in the calculation of your state taxes; other ignore totally the federal calculations. Some states allow you to deduct a portion of the federal taxes you pay, but most don't. Rhode Island and Vermont state taxes are calculated as a percentage of the federal tax paid.

In all states (except for the highest bracket in Montana), the state income tax rate is lower than federal rates. There also is no self-employment tax assessed at the state level. However, some states have special taxes for self-employed businesses. New Hampshire, for example, has a business profits tax of 8.5% on net profits over $50,000. Washington has a business and occupations tax for service businesses based on 1.5% of gross income.

5

Some cities also assess an income tax that is collected as part of the state return. New York City, for example, has a city income tax as well as an Unincorporated Business Tax (UBT) on income earned by a sole proprietor.

Detailing each state's tax requirements is beyond the scope of this book. Check with your own state taxing agency to find out what you need to know. A list of phone numbers and websites for each state tax agency can be found in Appendix D.

# Making Quarterly Estimated Tax Payments | 35

Our tax system is set up on a pay-as-you-go basis. Taxes are due at the end of the quarter in which money is earned. It is your tax return, not your taxes, that are due on April 15.

When you work as an employee, your employer withholds taxes from your paycheck. By the end of each quarter, your employer has remitted to the IRS and the state all the taxes that were withheld from paychecks during the quarter. As a self-employed person, you also are required to send in payments to the IRS and the state at the end of each quarter.

Corporations are required to make estimated tax payments throughout the year if the corporation's remaining tax liability will be $500 or more. Although the estimated tax information in this book is directed toward sole proprietors, the procedure is similar for corporations. Corporate estimated tax payments are submitted on Form 1120-W and are due on the 15th day of the 4th, 6th, 9th, and 12th months of the corporation's tax year.

Partnerships pay no tax as an entity, but each partner follows the same procedure used by sole proprietors to determine if estimated tax payments are needed. S corporations, like partnerships, do not pay taxes at the entity level. If there is a corporate profit after the employee-owners are paid, the shareholders must, like partners, calculate the individual income tax owed on their share of the profit. This tax may need to be paid quarterly.

6

## Determining Who Needs to Make Quarterly Payments

Any individual or couple (if married, filing jointly) who expects to have a *remaining tax liability* of $1,000 or more needs to make estimated tax payments. What does remaining tax liability mean? The following example helps to explain this term.

**EXAMPLE**

*Jack and Ellen are married and file jointly. Jack had wages of $40,000 this year. Ellen had self-employment net earnings of $30,000. (Remember, net is after business expenses have been deducted.) Jack and Ellen have a total income of $70,000 for the year. The full $70,000, minus personal itemized deductions and personal exemptions, is subject to federal income tax (which is approximately $7,400 on that amount of income). Only Ellen's self-employment income is subject to self-employment tax. The self-employment tax is calculated by multiplying her $30,000 net profit by 92.35%, then by 15.3%, resulting in a tax of $4,239. The total tax liability for Jack and Ellen is $11,639 ($7,400 income tax, plus $4,239 self-employment tax). Because Jack worked as an employee, he had $7,000 in federal income tax withheld from his paycheck. That means Jack and Ellen have a remaining tax liability of $4,639 ($11,639 minus the $7,000 withheld). In other words, if they do nothing, on April 15 they'll owe $4,639.*

Again, if you expect your remaining tax liability, after any withholding, to be $1,000 or more, you must make estimated tax payments. If you (or your spouse) worked part of the year as an employee and had some taxes withheld from your wages, take that amount into consideration in calculating your remaining tax liability. If neither you nor your spouse worked as an employee during the year, your remaining tax liability will be the same as your total tax liability. As explained in Jack and Ellen's example, total tax liability consists of your income tax plus your self-employment tax.

## Quarterly Payment Due Dates

If you do expect to have a remaining tax liability of $1,000 or more, estimated payments are due four times during the year. The due dates are April 15, June 15, September 15, and January 15. The payments are due *on* those dates, not sometime around the dates. The January 15 payment is not the first payment for the new year but rather the final payment for the prior year. For example, the payment made on January 15, 2006 is for the final quarter of 2005, not the first quarter of 2006.

# Estimated Tax Vouchers

Estimated tax payments are sent in with Form 1040-ES. Form 1040-ES is not a tax return, but instead serves the same purpose as a bank deposit slip. Examples of 1040-ES forms, which are also called estimated tax vouchers, are found on page 166. Note that the due date is indicated on each voucher. When you send in the voucher with your payment, you are making a deposit to your tax account. Until you file your tax return for the year, the IRS has no way of knowing why you're making the payments.

**Note:** *It's not only self-employed people who are required to send quarterly payments. Anyone who expects to owe $1,000 or more when she files her tax return must make these estimated payments.*

When the IRS receives your money, they don't know whether you've started a business, sold some stock at a gain, received a pension, or had some other source of taxable income. The IRS won't tell you that the payment arrived late, that it was too much, or that it wasn't enough. There will be no acknowledgment at all. The only thing you may get from the IRS, after you've sent in a payment for the first time, is a set of preprinted vouchers. The preprinted vouchers will have your name and Social Security number on them, but they won't indicate how much to send in because, again, the IRS has no way of knowing why you're making estimated payments nor the amount of your tax liability.

If you're married and file your tax return jointly with your spouse, be sure the names on the vouchers are consistent with your tax return. Whichever spouse is listed first on the tax return should also be listed first on the voucher, since the IRS uses the first name and Social Security number listed on the tax return as the tax account number for the couple. Even if your spouse isn't self-employed, be sure to list him on the estimated tax voucher so that the money gets credited to the correct tax account.

When calculating the amount to send (instructions are in Chapter 36), those who file a joint return need to look at the total income earned as a couple, not just the amount earned by the self-employed spouse. Similarly, if you have income from wages *and* from self-employment it will not be accurate to base your estimated payments solely on the self-employment income. The calculation must be based on the total picture, including the entire income you (and your spouse, if married and filing jointly) expect to have from all sources for the whole year. The reason estimated tax calculations cannot accurately be based solely on self-employment income—and only for the portion of the year that's already gone by—is because our tax system is a graduated one with a number of tax brackets, depending on income.

6

**Form 1040-ES**
Department of the Treasury
Internal Revenue Service

**2004** Payment Voucher **3**

OMB No. 1545-0087

**Calendar year- Due Sept. 15, 2004**

File only if you are making a payment of estimated tax by check or money order. Mail this voucher with your check or money order payable to the "**United States Treasury**." Write your social security number and "2004 Form 1040-ES" on your check or money order. Do not send cash. Enclose, but do not staple or attach, your payment with this voucher.

| Amount of estimated tax you are paying by check or money order. | | |
|---|---|---|
| | Dollars | Cents |

**Type or print**

| Your first name and initial | Your last name | Your social security number |
|---|---|---|
| If joint payment, complete for spouse | | |
| Spouse's first name and initial | Spouse's last name | Spouse's social security number |
| Address (number, street, and apt. no.) | | |
| City, state, and ZIP code. (If a foreign address, enter city, province or state, postal code, and country.) | | |

**For Privacy Act and Paperwork Reduction Act Notice, see instructions on page 5.**

------------------------------------------------------------
Tear off here
------------------------------------------------------------

**Form 1040-ES**
Department of the Treasury
Internal Revenue Service

**2004** Payment Voucher **2**

OMB No. 1545-0087

**Calendar year- Due June 15, 2004**

File only if you are making a payment of estimated tax by check or money order. Mail this voucher with your check or money order payable to the "**United States Treasury**." Write your social security number and "2004 Form 1040-ES" on your check or money order. Do not send cash. Enclose, but do not staple or attach, your payment with this voucher.

| Amount of estimated tax you are paying by check or money order. | | |
|---|---|---|
| | Dollars | Cents |

**Type or print**

| Your first name and initial | Your last name | Your social security number |
|---|---|---|
| If joint payment, complete for spouse | | |
| Spouse's first name and initial | Spouse's last name | Spouse's social security number |
| Address (number, street, and apt. no.) | | |
| City, state, and ZIP code. (If a foreign address, enter city, province or state, postal code, and country.) | | |

**For Privacy Act and Paperwork Reduction Act Notice, see instructions on page 5.**

------------------------------------------------------------
Tear off here
------------------------------------------------------------

**Form 1040-ES**
Department of the Treasury
Internal Revenue Service

**2004** Payment Voucher **1**

OMB No. 1545-0087

**Calendar year- Due April 15, 2004**

File only if you are making a payment of estimated tax by check or money order. Mail this voucher with your check or money order payable to the "**United States Treasury**." Write your social security number and "2004 Form 1040-ES" on your check or money order. Do not send cash. Enclose, but do not staple or attach, your payment with this voucher.

| Amount of estimated tax you are paying by check or money order. | | |
|---|---|---|
| | Dollars | Cents |

**Type or print**

| Your first name and initial | Your last name | Your social security number |
|---|---|---|
| If joint payment, complete for spouse | | |
| Spouse's first name and initial | Spouse's last name | Spouse's social security number |
| Address (number, street, and apt. no.) | | |
| City, state, and ZIP code. (If a foreign address, enter city, province or state, postal code, and country.) | | |

**For Privacy Act and Paperwork Reduction Act Notice, see instructions on page 5.**

# Federal Tax Rates

A copy of the 2004 federal tax rate schedule is shown below. The schedule changes slightly from year to year, so make sure you're working with the one that applies to the current year. The tax rate schedule is used to calculate your federal income tax liability, which is based on your taxable income. Taxable income is the figure arrived at after everything has been deducted, including your personal exemption and either your personal itemized deductions or the standard deduction.

The tax rate schedule for single people is read like this—if your taxable income is over zero but not over $7,150, your income tax is 10% of the amount over zero. That means a person with less than $7,150 taxable income is in the 10% tax bracket. If your taxable income is over $7,150, but not over $29,050, according to the tax rate schedule, your tax is 15% of the amount over $7,150, plus $715. That person is in the 15% tax bracket. This doesn't mean that all of her income is taxed at 15%. The first $7,150 of taxable income is taxed at 10%, and the next approximately $22,000 is taxed at 15%. The $715 figure is 10% of $7,150, since tax is paid at the rate of 10% on the first $7,150 of taxable income.

## 2004 Tax Rate Schedules

**Caution.** Do not use these Tax Rate Schedules to figure your 2003 taxes. Use only to figure your 2004 estimated taxes.

### Single- Schedule X

| If line 5 is: Over— | But not over— | The tax is: | of the amount over— |
|---|---|---|---|
| $0 | $7,150 | 10% | $0 |
| 7,150 | 29,050 | $715.00 + 15% | 7,150 |
| 29,050 | 70,350 | 4,000.00 + 25% | 29,050 |
| 70,350 | 146,750 | 14,325.00 + 28% | 70,350 |
| 146,750 | 319,100 | 35,717.00 + 33% | 146,750 |
| 319,100 | | 92,592.50 + 35% | 319,100 |

### Head of household- Schedule Z

| If line 5 is: Over— | But not over— | The tax is: | of the amount over— |
|---|---|---|---|
| $0 | $10,200 | 10% | $0 |
| 10,200 | 38,900 | $1,020.00 + 15% | 10,200 |
| 38,900 | 100,500 | 5,325.00 + 25% | 38,900 |
| 100,500 | 162,700 | 20,725.00 + 28% | 100,500 |
| 162,700 | 319,100 | 38,141.00 + 33% | 162,700 |
| 319,100 | | 89,753.00 + 35% | 319,100 |

### Married filing jointly or Qualifying widow(er)- Schedule Y-1

| If line 5 is: Over— | But not over— | The tax is: | of the amount over— |
|---|---|---|---|
| $0 | $14,300 | 10% | $0 |
| 14,300 | 58,100 | $1,430.00 + 15% | 14,300 |
| 58,100 | 117,250 | 8,000.00 + 25% | 58,100 |
| 117,250 | 178,650 | 22,787.50 + 28% | 117,250 |
| 178,650 | 319,100 | 39,979.50 + 33% | 178,650 |
| 319,100 | | 86,328.00 + 35% | 319,100 |

### Married filing separately- Schedule Y-2

| If line 5 is: Over— | But not over— | The tax is: | of the amount over— |
|---|---|---|---|
| $0 | $7,150 | 10% | $0 |
| 7,150 | 29,050 | $715.00 + 15% | 7,150 |
| 29,050 | 58,625 | 4,000.00 + 25% | 29,050 |
| 58,625 | 89,325 | 11,393.75 + 28% | 58,625 |
| 89,325 | 159,550 | 19,989.75 + 33% | 89,325 |
| 159,550 | | 43,164.00 + 35% | 159,550 |

6

In calculating the amount of estimated tax due, if you look only at the amount you earned this quarter or only at the self-employed spouse's income, without considering income from all sources for the entire year, the calculations will probably be incorrect.

*Juanita is a single woman who makes the mistake of calculating her estimated payments based solely on her self-employment income. She earns $7,000 net income from self-employment during the first quarter of the year. She looks at the tax rate schedule and, seeing that $7,000 is less than $7,150, she sends in 10% of $7,000 to cover her income tax. The next quarter she again has $7,000 net self-employment income. She sends in the same amount as she sent the first quarter. She earns the same amount in the third and fourth quarters, and sends in the same payment as in the first and second quarters. Each quarter she has sent in 10% of $7,000. By the end of the year, she has $28,000 of self-employment income and $30,000 in wages, for a total income of $58,000. Not only is she not in the 10% tax bracket, she's not even in the 15% tax bracket, but rather the 25% tax bracket. By considering each quarter of self-employment income by itself and not looking at her total income for the year, Juanita has not been sending in nearly enough money.*

## Q & A

Q: Does the IRS always penalize people who do not do their estimated payments correctly?

A: Every once in a while someone's underpayment is overlooked, but in general you will be penalized if you don't make a payment, send it late, or don't send enough. Because the IRS isn't aware of your tax situation during the year, the penalty won't be assessed until you file your tax return for the year.

To avoid Juanita's situation, you need to make an educated guess about the entire year's income from all sources. These are called *estimated tax payments*, because you're estimating what you think your income and taxes are going to be for the year. This is especially hard to do the first year you're in business. If you have no idea what you're going to earn that year, the only thing you can do is calculate your income and tax liability at the end of each quarter and project what the remainder of the year will be like. If you had been in business for ten years and could see that your income and expenses are about the same each year, you would know that if you send in the same amount this year as you did last year, most likely you will cover this year's taxes. But when you are just starting out in business, you don't have those prior year figures to use as a projection for the current year. You have to estimate what you think the year is going to look like, which can be a very difficult thing to do.

## Penalties

Incorrect estimated tax calculations can lead to penalties. If you don't send in enough during the year or if you send your payment in late, you will have a penalty. As of the end of 2004, the penalty is 4% a year on the amount that should have been sent in but was not. Since it's actually interest, the rate goes up and down quarterly as interest rates fluctuate. The penalty is calculated on a daily basis, so if you cannot send what you owe on the due date, you should send as much as you can as soon as possible rather than waiting until the next due date. If a payment was due April 15 and you send it on April 30, you'll have much less penalty than if you include the amount with your June 15 payment.

Remember, federal tax withheld from your (or your spouse's) paycheck as an employee has also been deposited to your tax account. While you may have neglected to send a quarterly estimated tax payment, your withholding for that quarter (if you had any) may be sufficient to protect you from penalties.

## Avoiding penalties

By using one of these three payment methods, you can avoid penalties.

1. Owe less than $1,000 when you file your tax return. If that's your situation, no estimated tax payments are necessary.
2. Each quarter, send one-quarter of what your total tax liability was last year.
3. Each quarter, send 90% of the amount you're really going to owe for that quarter.

The first method is self-explanatory. The second and third methods are not as straightforward. As explained earlier, when you add together your income tax and your self-employment tax on Form 1040, you get a figure called your *total tax liability*. Look at the back side of your Form 1040 from last year. Find the line that says "your total tax." The exact line number varies from year to year, but it will be somewhere between *Lines 60 and 65*. Note that this line has nothing to do with how much you owed or how much refund you received when you filed last year's return. If you divide your last year's total tax liability amount by the four quarters in a year, and every quarter send a payment equal to that amount, you will have no penalty when you file your return this year, no matter how much more you owe on April 15. This is the

6

second method of avoiding estimated tax penalties. You don't have to have been self-employed last year in order to use this method of paying the current year's estimated tax payments.

*Ali started her own business last year. She didn't make very much money, so her total tax liability for last year (income tax plus self-employment tax) was only $1,000. In order to avoid penalties this year, Ali must send estimated tax payments of at least $250 per quarter (¼ of $1,000). That amount bears no relation to the actual amount she's earning this year. To avoid penalties, she needs to send at least that amount each quarter—whether or not she has self-employment income during that quarter. She cannot wait until January and send the whole amount in then—equal payments must be sent throughout the year in order to use this method of avoiding penalties. By sending $250 each quarter, Ali is protected from penalties no matter how much she earns this year. As it turns out, Ali makes a lot of money this year, and her total tax liability is $10,000. She'll owe $9,000 ($10,000 minus the amount she's already sent in) when she files her return in April, but she'll have no penalties.*

The way Ali pays her quarterlies is the method used by many self-employed people to make their estimated tax payments. If your business gets to a very stable point and you earn a similar amount each year, basing the current year's payments on the prior year's tax amount means that you'll be sending in approximately enough to cover this year's tax. In any case, so long as you send in an amount equal to or more than 100% of the prior year's total tax liability, you'll at least be protected from penalties.

**Note:** *If you expect your adjusted gross income to be more than $150,000 ($75,000 if married, filing separately), your four payments must equal 110%—rather than 100%—of the prior year's total tax liability.*

The negative side of choosing this way of making your estimated payments is that you're only protecting yourself from penalties. It doesn't mean you won't owe any additional tax. You might end up owing a lot more when you file your tax return.

Using the prior year's tax liability as the method for determining how much to send for the current year's estimated payments won't make sense if you earned a lot more last year than you're going to earn this year. In that case, you wouldn't want to send in one-quarter of what your tax was last year in order to avoid penalties this year. The appropriate method to use in this situation is the next method.

This third method of avoiding penalties is done by estimating your real tax liability for the current year and sending in 90% of it on a quarterly basis. The advantage of sending in estimates based on current income figures is that when you prepare your tax return, you should owe very little, if any, additional tax. (The next chapter will explain how to calculate the tax liability on your current year earnings.)

Assuming that you earned less last year than you're going to earn this year, the ideal way to make estimated tax payments is to look at last year's total tax liability and send in a quarter of that amount each quarter, while saving the actual amount you are going to owe for this year. That money can be set aside in an interest-bearing savings account so that it's available to pay on April 15 with your tax return. Most people do not have enough discipline to do their estimated payments in this way. They may start out with good intentions of setting aside the money, but something comes up and they end up paying for it with what should be their tax money.

The crucial thing is to not be in denial about the taxes you'll owe. If you're not sending in the full amount you owe for each quarter, know that eventually (and no later than April 15 of the following year) you'll have to come up with that money.

If you're using a tax professional to prepare your quarterly estimates, make sure she asks whether you want to base your estimates on the prior year's tax liability or on what you're actually going to earn this year. If you don't specify, some preparers assume you want to base your payments on the prior year's tax. It's up to you. Remember, if you base it on the prior year's tax, that amount may or may not cover your total tax liability for this year. However, in any case, if all payments are made on time there will be no penalty.

# Form 2210

If you will have penalties for late or insufficient estimated tax payments, *Form 2210* is used to calculate those penalties. Form 2210 has another important function for those taxpayers who didn't send four equal estimated tax payments because they didn't have an equal amount of income in each of the four quarters.

If you're basing your payments on this year's true income, the IRS assumes that your income is the same each quarter, so they expect you to make four equal quarterly payments. Although you won't be contacted during the year, when you file your tax return, the IRS will be prepared to penalize you if you didn't make identical payments all four quarters.

6

Form 2210 can be used to show the IRS that varying amounts were earned each quarter and that the amount sent was based on the true amount earned in that quarter. If you didn't start your business until after March 31 (the end of the first quarter), you had a large amount of income one quarter but not another, or you had a seasonal business (such as selling Christmas trees), the only way to let the IRS know that you shouldn't be penalized for uneven payments is to file Form 2210 with your tax return. Be sure to show your actual quarterly income by filling out the Annualized Income Installment Method on page 4 of Form 2210. (see page 174.)

*Form 2210 is filed only once a year with your tax return in April. Don't send it with your quarterly payments. Attach it to your return to show the IRS why you shouldn't be penalized or to calculate the penalties for not having sent enough or having sent late payments during the year.*

---

**Q & A**

Q: **Should I send in Form 2210 with my tax return even if I don't have an excuse for not making an estimated tax payment? In other words, should I calculate my own estimated tax penalty?**

A: Form 2210 is a tedious form to fill out. If a preparer is doing your return or if you're using a computerized tax program, go ahead and fill out the form. Otherwise, unless there's a possibility you can get out of some of the penalty, let the IRS fill it out and bill you for penalties.

---

## State Estimated Tax Payments

The states that have an income tax (see Chapter 34) generally require people who will owe above a certain amount when they file their tax return to make estimated tax payments during the year. Some states require residents to make estimated payments whenever they're required by the IRS. For all states (except Hawaii), the estimated tax payments are due on the same dates as the federal payments. Hawaii's estimated tax payments are due on the 20th rather than the 15th day after the end of the quarter.

Form **2210**

Department of the Treasury
Internal Revenue Service

**Underpayment of
Estimated Tax by Individuals, Estates, and Trusts**
▶ See separate instructions.
▶ Attach to Form 1040, 1040A, 1040NR, 1040NR-EZ, or 1041.

OMB No. 1545-0140

20**04**

Attachment
Sequence No. **06**

| Name(s) shown on tax return | Identifying number |
|---|---|

## Do You Have To File Form 2210?

Complete lines 1 through 7 below. Is line 7 less than $1,000? → **Yes** → **Do not file Form 2210.** You do not owe a penalty.

↓ **No**

Complete lines 8 and 9 below. Is line 6 equal to or more than line 9? → **Yes** → You do not owe a penalty. **Do not file Form 2210** (but if box **E** below applies, you must file page 1 of Form 2210 below).

↓ **No**

You may owe a penalty. Does any box in Part II below apply? → **Yes** → You **must** file Form 2210. Does box **B, C,** or **D** apply?

↓ **No**

**No** | **Yes** → You must figure your penalty.

**Do not file Form 2210.** You are not required to figure your penalty because the IRS will figure it and send you a bill for any unpaid amount. If you want to figure it, you may use Part III or Part IV as a worksheet and enter your penalty amount on your tax return (see page 2 of the instructions), but **do not file Form 2210.**

You are **not** required to figure your penalty because the IRS will figure it and send you a bill for any unpaid amount. If you want to figure it, you may use Part III or Part IV as a worksheet and enter your penalty amount on your tax return (see page 2 of the instructions), but **file only page 1 of Form 2210.**

| **Part I** | **Required Annual Payment** | (see page 2 of the instructions) | | |
|---|---|---|---|---|
| 1 | Enter your 2004 tax after credits from Form 1040, line 56 (or comparable line of your return) | **1** | | |
| 2 | Other taxes, including self-employment tax (see page 2 of the instructions) . . . . . . . | **2** | | |
| 3 | Refundable credits. Enter the total of your earned income credit, additional child tax credit, credit for federal tax paid on fuels, and health coverage tax credit for eligible individuals . . . . | **3** | ( | ) |
| 4 | Current year tax. Combine lines 1, 2, and 3 . . . . . . . . . . . . . | **4** | | |
| 5 | Multiply line 4 by 90% (.90) . . . . . . . . . . . . . **5** | | | |
| 6 | Withholding taxes. **Do not** include estimated tax payments. See page 2 of the instructions . . | **6** | | |
| 7 | Subtract line 6 from line 4. If less than $1,000, you do not owe a penalty; **do not file Form 2210** . . . . . . . . . . . . . . . . . . . . . . . . . . | **7** | | |
| 8 | Maximum required annual payment based on prior year's tax (see page 2 of the instructions) | **8** | | |
| 9 | **Required annual payment.** Enter the **smaller** of line 5 or line 8 . . . . . . . . . . | **9** | | |

**Next:** Is line 9 more than line 6?

☐ **No.** You **do not** owe a penalty. **Do not file Form 2210** unless box **E** below applies.

☐ **Yes.** You may owe a penalty, but **do not file Form 2210** unless one or more boxes in Part II below applies.
   • If box **B, C,** or **D** applies, you must figure your penalty and file Form 2210.
   • If only box **A** or **E** (or both) applies, file only page 1 of Form 2210. You are **not** required to figure your penalty; the IRS will figure it and send you a bill for any unpaid amount. If you want to figure your penalty, you may use Part III or IV as a worksheet and enter your penalty on your tax return (see page 2 of the instructions), but **file only page 1 of Form 2210.**

| **Part II** | **Reasons for Filing.** Check applicable boxes. If none apply, **do not file Form 2210.** |
|---|---|

**A** ☐ You request a **waiver** (see page 1 of the instructions) of your entire penalty. You must check this box and file page 1 of Form 2210, but you are not required to figure your penalty.

**B** ☐ You request a waiver (see page 1 of the instructions) of part of your penalty. You must figure your penalty and waiver amount and file Form 2210.

**C** ☐ Your income varied during the year and your penalty is reduced or eliminated when figured using the **annualized income installment method.** You must figure the penalty using Schedule AI and file Form 2210.

**D** ☐ Your penalty is lower when figured by treating the federal income tax withheld from your wages as paid on the dates it was actually withheld, instead of in equal amounts on the payment due dates. You must figure your penalty and file Form 2210.

**E** ☐ You filed or are filing a joint return for either 2003 or 2004, but not for both years, and line 8 above is smaller than line 5 above. You must file page 1 of Form 2210, but you are **not** required to figure your penalty (unless box **B, C,** or **D** applies).

**For Paperwork Reduction Act Notice, see page 5 of separate instructions.**     Cat. No. 11744P     Form **2210** (2004)

6

Form 2210 (2004)  Page **4**

## Schedule AI—Annualized Income Installment Method (See pages 4 and 5 of the instructions.)

Estates and trusts, **do not** use the period ending dates shown to the right. Instead, use the following: 2/29/04, 4/30/04, 7/31/04, and 11/30/04.

| | | (a) 1/1/04–3/31/04 | (b) 1/1/04–5/31/04 | (c) 1/1/04–8/31/04 | (d) 1/1/04–12/31/04 |
|---|---|---|---|---|---|
| **Part I** | **Annualized Income Installments** | | | | |
| 1 | Enter your adjusted gross income for each period (see instructions). (Estates and trusts, enter your taxable income without your exemption for each period) . . . . . . . . . . . **1** | | | | |
| 2 | Annualization amounts. (Estates and trusts, see instructions.) . . . **2** | 4 | 2.4 | 1.5 | 1 |
| 3 | Annualized income. Multiply line 1 by line 2 . . . . . . . **3** | | | | |
| 4 | Enter your itemized deductions for the period shown in each column. If you do not itemize, enter -0- and skip to line 7. (Estates and trusts, enter -0-, skip to line 9, and enter the amount from line 3 on line 9.) **4** | | | | |
| 5 | Annualization amounts . . . . . . . . . . . . . . **5** | 4 | 2.4 | 1.5 | 1 |
| 6 | Multiply line 4 by line 5 (see instructions if line 3 is more than $71,350) **6** | | | | |
| 7 | In each column, enter the full amount of your standard deduction from Form 1040, line 39, or Form 1040A, line 24 (Form 1040NR or 1040NR-EZ filers, enter -0-. **Exception:** Indian students and business apprentices, enter standard deduction from Form 1040NR, line 36, or Form 1040NR-EZ, line 11.) . . . . . . . . . **7** | | | | |
| 8 | Enter the **larger** of line 6 or line 7 . . . . . . . . . **8** | | | | |
| 9 | Subtract line 8 from line 3 . . . . . . . . . . . . **9** | | | | |
| 10 | In each column, multiply $3,100 by the total number of exemptions claimed (see instructions if line 3 is more than $107,025). (Estates and trusts and Form 1040NR or 1040NR-EZ filers, enter the exemption amount shown on your tax return.) . . . . . . **10** | | | | |
| 11 | Subtract line 10 from line 9 . . . . . . . . . . . . **11** | | | | |
| 12 | Figure your tax on the amount on line 11 (see instructions) . . . . **12** | | | | |
| 13 | Self-employment tax from line 34 below (complete Part II) . . . . **13** | | | | |
| 14 | Enter other taxes for each payment period (see instructions) . . . **14** | | | | |
| 15 | Total tax. Add lines 12, 13, and 14 . . . . . . . . . . **15** | | | | |
| 16 | For each period, enter the same type of credits as allowed on Form 2210, lines 1 and 3 (see instructions) . . . . . . . . . **16** | | | | |
| 17 | Subtract line 16 from line 15. If zero or less, enter -0- . . . . **17** | | | | |
| 18 | Applicable percentage . . . . . . . . . . . . . . **18** | 22.5% | 45% | 67.5% | 90% |
| 19 | Multiply line 17 by line 18 . . . . . . . . . . . . **19** | | | | |
| | **Complete lines 20–25 of one column before going to the next column.** | | | | |
| 20 | Add the amounts in all previous columns of line 25 . . . . . **20** | | | | |
| 21 | Subtract line 20 from line 19. If zero or less, enter -0- . . . . **21** | | | | |
| 22 | Enter 25% (.25) of line 9 on page 1 of Form 2210 in each column **22** | | | | |
| 23 | Subtract line 25 of the previous column from line 24 of that column . . . . . . . . . . . . . . . . . . . **23** | | | | |
| 24 | Add lines 22 and 23 . . . . . . . . . . . . . . **24** | | | | |
| 25 | Enter the **smaller** of line 21 or line 24 here and on Form 2210, line 18 . . . . . . . . . . . . . . . . . ▶ **25** | | | | |
| **Part II** | **Annualized Self-Employment Tax (Form 1040 filers only)** | | | | |
| 26 | Net earnings from self-employment for the period (see instructions) **26** | | | | |
| 27 | Prorated social security tax limit . . . . . . . . . . . **27** | $21,975 | $36,625 | $58,600 | $87,900 |
| 28 | Enter actual wages for the period subject to social security tax or the 6.2% portion of the 7.65% railroad retirement (tier 1) tax . . . **28** | | | | |
| 29 | Subtract line 28 from line 27. If zero or less, enter -0-. . . . . **29** | | | | |
| 30 | Annualization amounts . . . . . . . . . . . . . . **30** | 0.496 | 0.2976 | 0.186 | 0.124 |
| 31 | Multiply line 30 by the **smaller** of line 26 or line 29 . . . . **31** | | | | |
| 32 | Annualization amounts . . . . . . . . . . . . . . **32** | 0.116 | 0.0696 | 0.0435 | 0.029 |
| 33 | Multiply line 26 by line 32 . . . . . . . . . . . . **33** | | | | |
| 34 | Add lines 31 and 33. Enter here and on line 13 above . . . ▶ **34** | | | | |

Form **2210** (2004)

♲ Printed on recycled paper

# Calculating the Amount to Send Quarterly

# 36

This chapter describes in detail how to calculate the amount of money to send in or set aside each quarter, based on this year's true tax liability. Whether you choose to actually send it in or to send in only the minimum amount necessary to avoid penalties, this calculation will help avoid the surprise of learning that you owe a great deal more on April 15.

An overview of the process for doing the estimated tax calculation is shown on the Summary of the Steps in Computing Estimated Tax Payments on page 177. This chapter will explain the process. For even more detailed explanation, Appendix B includes a step-by-step example of an estimated tax calculation, along with a worksheet for your use. The 2005 personal exemption, standard deduction, and tax rate amounts were not available when this book went to press. They will be slightly different than the 2004 amounts used here.

In calculating the amount to send with your estimated tax vouchers, first add together all income you expect to receive from all sources this year. This is your projected income. It includes your net self-employment income—net is after business expenses have been deducted—any wages, any other miscellaneous income, and your spouse's income, if you're married and filing jointly.

Then, calculate the self-employment tax on the portion of your total income that is from self-employment. Do this by multiplying your projected net self-employment income first by 92.35%, and then by 15.3%.

Next, using the figure in step 1—your projected total income—subtract the following things:

- half of your projected self-employment tax;
- the $3,100 personal exemption for you, your spouse, and each dependent; and,

6

## Q & A

**Q: I'm working as an employee and I'm not going to have that much income as a self-employed person. Can I just change my withholding at work and claim zero, or even have my employer withhold extra, so I don't have to make estimated payments?**

A: Yes, but you still need to calculate what you think you're going to owe for the year to ensure that your withholding covers the amount due on your self-employment income as well as your wages. Having extra tax withheld from your paycheck won't work if you have a lot of self-employment income and not a lot of wages.

However, this is one way to reduce or eliminate penalties. If you haven't made the estimated payments that you should have made, you can increase your withholding for the remainder of the year. Since the IRS assumes that your income was earned equally throughout the year, they also assume your withholding was done equally throughout the year. You can take advantage of that assumption to have more of your tax payment credited to the earlier quarters.

- your personal itemized deductions, if you itemize your personal deductions, or the standard deduction, which for 2004 is $4,850 if single and $9,700 if married and filing jointly.

The remaining figure is your projected taxable income for the year.

Then, using the tax rate schedule (see page 167) determine how much income tax there is on your projected taxable income. From that amount subtract out whatever amount you (or your spouse, if married) expect to have withheld from your paychecks, if any. If you earned money as an employee during part of the year or are continuing to earn money as an employee, look at your paystub to see how much federal income tax will be withheld from each check.

After you have subtracted the projected withholding amount (if any), the remainder is the amount you'll owe for federal income tax.

Add that figure to your projected self-employment tax in Step 2. The total is your remaining tax liability for the year. This is the balance you'll owe on April 15 with your tax return, unless you send it in earlier via estimated tax payments or additional withholding.

This is only a projected or estimated amount. If you have no idea what your income will be this year, you must redo this calculation each quarter before sending in your estimated tax voucher. However, once you understand how to compute this, it won't be difficult to redo each quarter.

If you're still feeling a little lost about how this calculation is done, take a look at the example in Appendix B.

## A Summary of the Steps in Computing Estimated Tax Payments

### Step 1
Add together all income you expect to receive from all sources this year. This includes your net self-employment income, any wages, other miscellaneous income, and your spouse's income (if married and filing jointly).

### Step 2
Calculate the self-employment tax on your projected self-employment income by multiplying the projected net self-employment income included in Step 1 by 92.35%, and then by 15.3%.

### Step 3
Starting with the figure in Step 1 (projected total income), subtract out:

- ½ of your projected self-employment tax (Step 2 result ÷ 2);
- $3,100 for yourself, your spouse, and each dependent; and,
- your personal itemized deductions or the $4,850 standard deduction ($9,700 if married).

What's left is your projected taxable income for the year.

### Step 4
Look on the tax rate schedule to find what the income tax is on your projected taxable income. Subtract out the amount of federal income tax that will be withheld from your and your spouse's wages (if any). The figure that's left is the remainder that you'll owe for federal income tax.

### Step 5
Take the income tax figure from Step 4. Add the projected self-employment tax figure from Step 2. The total of these figures equals your remaining tax liability. This figure is then divided by the number of quarters remaining in the year.

6

# Paying Your Taxes | 37

One crucial thing to remember about your taxes is that even if you don't have the money to pay them, your return should be filed on time. The penalty for not filing your tax return on time is 5% per month, whereas the penalty for not paying your taxes on time is only of 1% per month. Never delay filing your return because you don't have enough money to pay your taxes.

The late filing and late payment penalties are in addition to any penalties you might have for not making your estimated tax payments on time or not sending in enough each quarter. For more information on those penalties, see Chapter 35.

Each year, more than eight million taxpayers file Form 4868, asking the IRS for an *extension*. This is an extension of time to file your tax return, not an extension of time to pay any taxes due. As long as you send it in by April 15, Form 4868 is an automatic extension, giving you until August 15 to file your tax return. Anyone can ask for an extension—you do not need to supply a reason for waiting to send in your return.

| Form **4868** <br> Department of the Treasury <br> Internal Revenue Service | **Application for Automatic Extension of Time** <br> **To File U.S. Individual Income Tax Return** <br> For calendar year 2004, or other tax year beginning , 2004, ending , . | OMB No. 1545-0188 <br> 20**04** |
|---|---|---|
| **Part I** Identification | **Part II** Individual Income Tax | |

**Part I** Identification

1 Your name(s) (see instructions)

Address (see instructions)

City, town or post office, state, and ZIP code

2 Your social security number | 3 Spouse's social security number

**Part II** Individual Income Tax

4 Estimate of total tax liability for 2004 $ _____
5 Total 2004 payments . . . . . . _____
6 **Balance due.** Subtract 5 from 4 . . _____
7 Amount you are paying. . . . . ▶ _____

**Confirmation Number**

If you file electronically, you will receive a confirmation number telling you that your Form 4868 has been accepted. Enter the confirmation number here and keep it for your records . . . . . . . ▶

For Privacy Act and Paperwork Reduction Act Notice, see page 4.    Cat. No. 13141W    Form **4868** (2004)

7

If you need even more time to prepare your return, file Form 2688 by August 15. This is an application for an additional extension of time to file your return. Form 2688 is not an automatic extension. The IRS will give you an additional two months to file only if you have a good reason for the delay but, in reality, most excuses are accepted.

Until recently, the IRS required that any taxes due be paid with your extension form on April 15. If you file an extension on April 15, the IRS asks that you give a good faith estimate of the amount you expect to owe and pay whatever you can at that time. Interest and late payment penalties will be added to any additional amount due.

As emphasized in the chapters on estimated tax payments, you should send as much as you can as soon as you can to avoid or lessen penalties. Nevertheless, at some point you may find yourself unable to pay the remaining tax you owe.

In recent years the IRS has made it easier to pay your taxes by allowing *installment payments*. Form 9465 should be filled out and included when you file your federal return. (see page 181.) On this form you'll indicate how much you can afford to send each month. There is a $43 charge to set up the installment plan.

If you're on an installment plan and you're late making any of your monthly payments, the total amount you owe will immediately become due. Even with an installment agreement, interest and penalties (for not paying on time) will continue to accrue until you've paid off your tax liability. The interest amount changes each quarter and is currently 4% per year. The late payment penalty is ¼% rather than the regular ½% per month for people with installment plans.

If you owe so much that you cannot possibly ever pay it off, the IRS may accept an *Offer In Compromise*. This is an offer to pay a lesser amount than you owe in order to settle the bill immediately. You need to fill out a complete financial statement and present it with the appropriate paperwork. Your offer will be accepted only if the IRS believes it will not be able to collect the full amount due from you within the near future. Discussion of an Offer In Compromise is beyond the scope of this book. A tax professional will be able to provide you with more information.

Form **9465**
(Rev. December 2003)
Department of the Treasury
Internal Revenue Service

## Installment Agreement Request

▶ **If you are filing this form with your tax return, attach it to the front of the return. Otherwise, see instructions.**

OMB No. 1545-1350

**Caution:** *Do not file this form if you are currently making payments on an installment agreement. Instead, call 1-800-829-1040. If you are in bankruptcy or we have accepted your offer-in-compromise, see **Bankruptcy or Offer-in-Compromise** below.*

| 1 | Your first name and initial | Last name | Your social security number |
| | If a joint return, spouse's first name and initial | Last name | Spouse's social security number |

Your current address (number and street). If you have a P.O. box and no home delivery, enter your box number. | Apt. number

City, town or post office, state, and ZIP code. If a foreign address, enter city, province or state, and country. Follow the country's practice for entering the postal code.

**2** If this address is new since you filed your last tax return, check here . . . . . . . . . . . . . ▶ ☐

**3** ( ) _____ _____ | **4** ( ) _____ _____ _____
Your home phone number / Best time for us to call | Your work phone number / Ext. / Best time for us to call

**5** Name of your bank or other financial institution: | **6** Your employer's name:

Address | Address

City, state, and ZIP code | City, state, and ZIP code

**7** Enter the tax return for which you are making this request (for example, Form 1040) . . . . . . ▶ _____

**8** Enter the tax year for which you are making this request (for example, 2003) . . . . . . . . ▶ _____

**9** Enter the total amount you owe as shown on your tax return . . . . . . . . . . . **9**

**10** Enter the amount of any payment you are making with your tax return (or notice). See instructions **10**

**11** Enter the amount you can pay each month. **Make your payments as large as possible to limit interest and penalty charges.** The charges will continue until you pay in full . . . . . . . **11**

**12** Enter the date you want to make your payment each month. **Do not** enter a date later than the 28th. . ▶

**13** If you want to make your payments by electronic funds withdrawal from your checking account, see the instructions and fill in lines 13a and 13b.

▶ **a** Routing number
▶ **b** Account number

I authorize the U.S. Treasury and its designated Financial Agent to initiate a monthly ACH electronic funds withdrawal entry to the financial institution account indicated for payments of my Federal taxes owed, and the financial institution to debit the entry to this account. This authorization is to remain in full force and effect until I notify the U.S. Treasury Financial Agent to terminate the authorization. To revoke payment, I must contact the U.S. Treasury Financial Agent at **1-800-829-1040** no later than 7 business days prior to the payment (settlement) date. I also authorize the financial institutions involved in the processing of the electronic payments of taxes to receive confidential information necessary to answer inquiries and resolve issues related to the payments.

Your signature | Date | Spouse's signature. If a joint return, **both** must sign. | Date

7

# Getting Help with Recordkeeping and Tax Returns | 38

After reading this book, you may feel a bit overwhelmed and wonder if it's time to consider getting some help. There are many individuals that can provide that help.

## Bookkeepers

If you feel comfortable with the recordkeeping system you've set up for your business and you seem to have enough time to keep track of your income and expenses, it's probably not necessary for you to hire a bookkeeper. However, if you find that you're spending more time doing your recordkeeping than you want or you're spending time on that when you could be spending the time making money, it may be appropriate to consider hiring a part-time bookkeeper.

Talk to colleagues about possible bookkeeper recommendations. When talking to the prospective bookkeeper, ask her in what form she'll want information from you.

- Will she work from your checkbook and piles of receipts or will she expect you to have entered some information onto a spreadsheet?
- Will she be providing you with regular profit and loss reports?
- Is she willing to train you to do some of the work if you want to be more involved?
- If you'll be entering some of your financial information into a computer program, does the bookkeeper use the same program?
- Do you need to have a minimum number of hours of work for her to do before she's willing to work with you?
- Does she prepare tax returns?

# Tax Preparers

Similar guidelines regarding when to hire a bookkeeper are used in deciding when to enlist the services of a tax preparer. If you're spending time working on your tax return when you could be using that time more profitably by working on your business, it's time to think about using a tax preparer. Also, if you're not sure you're handling things correctly on your return, it may cost you less to use a preparer than pay penalties on an incorrectly prepared return. A preparer may also save you money by taking deductions you've forgotten to claim.

If you want to be more involved with your tax return preparation, one possibility is to prepare your own return and then have a tax preparer look it over. The preparer won't sign the return since it was prepared by you, but she should catch any blatant errors or answer questions you have. Not all preparers are willing to do this, but if you look around, you will find one who is.

Having a tax professional review your return is also important if you prepare the return on a computer. The tax preparation programs seem like a good idea and are marketed as containing all the help you need to do your own return. Yet many returns prepared using one of these programs contain problems or mistakes. Accidentally responding incorrectly to a question asked by the program can result in a return being calculated incorrectly. The most common problem area is depreciation. The programs don't seem to give enough information about what depreciation is, who should take it, and how to calculate it.

Also, people are surprised at the amount of time involved in learning and using a tax preparation program. The programs seem to be most useful for those who easily learn computer programs and who already understand what information goes into the tax return and which schedules to use. The programs can also be helpful for those who want to do *what if* scenarios (*e.g.*, *What would happen if we got married by December 31 rather than after January 1?*).

If you decide you want to hand your tax work over to someone else, find a qualified tax professional. There are different types of tax preparers, and you will need to decide what level of help you need. Searching for a tax preparer is best started by asking for recommendations from friends and colleagues. Try to get referral names from someone who has a business or tax situation similar to yours. It's best to look for a tax preparer as early as possible, rather than beginning your search in March or April.

You're probably most familiar with the chain operations. Generally, they are conveniently located and relatively inexpensive. The knowledge, experience, and skill level vary greatly among the personnel who work in these offices. Many of the chain operations pay their workers on commission, which means the preparers are anxious to complete your return quickly and move onto the next customer. Typically, you won't find preparers in this setting who will talk with you extensively about your business or help with planning for the future. However, the fee for an individual return with a Schedule C may be among the lowest you'll find. If you use a chain service, you may work with a different preparer each year—so if continuity is important to you, this choice may not be your best bet.

Some states require tax preparers to be licensed. A license may indicate a skill or knowledge level, or simply that a minimum number of hours of education have been completed. If your state requires preparers to be licensed, be sure to ask the preparers you interview if they have a current license.

The types of preparers discussed in the remainder of this section generally don't fall under state tax preparer licensing regulations because they have their own professional licensing requirements. Attorneys and certified public accountants (CPAs) are licensed by their respective states, whereas enrolled agents (EAs) are licensed by the IRS.

CPAs, enrolled agents, and tax attorneys can attend an IRS audit without you and can argue on your behalf. They can also represent you in other IRS-related matters. Other types of tax preparers can represent a taxpayer without her being present, but only for those tax returns they prepared.

*Enrolled agents* are either former IRS employees or tax preparers who have passed an exhaustive two-day exam on tax theory and practice given by the IRS. All enrolled agents specialize in tax return preparation and taxpayer representation. Some also do bookkeeping and accounting.

*CPAs* may or may not prepare individual and small business tax returns. Instead, their focus may be on large corporations, internal audits, or other types of financial services. Although many are, don't make the assumption that all CPAs are knowledgeable about or interested in working with small businesses or preparing individual tax returns.

*Tax attorneys* are tax specialists who provide the most expensive tax help you can get. Generally, it is not appropriate to have a tax attorney prepare your 1040 and Schedule C forms. However, if you are having difficult problems with the IRS or are considering a complicated transaction that has tax ramifications, a tax attorney's expertise may be well worth the cost.

Whichever category of preparer you select, you want to find someone who works regularly with and cares about very small (micro) businesses. Also, you want to make sure she's up to date on current tax law (ask when she took her last update class). You want someone who is available all year in case you get a letter from the IRS or want

7

to discuss changing your estimated tax payments in June or November. Ask for the names of several of her small business clients whom you can talk to as references.

When you talk to or meet with a potential preparer, listen to your intuition. You will want to know practical items, such as:

- how much she charges;
- whether she does tax planning;
- how she charges for your phone calls during the year;
- in what format she expects to receive tax information from you; and,
- whether she'll meet with you personally or hand your tax preparation over to someone else in the firm.

At the same time, pay attention to whether the preparer seems to care about you and your small business. Do you feel comfortable asking questions of this person, and does she answer them in a way that you understand? Are you two in synch as to how aggressive or cautious to be in the preparation of your tax return? Although tax laws appear to be black and white, there are many ways to interpret them. You want to work with someone who will prepare your return in the way that's most comfortable for you.

# Audits | 39

No one wants to be the recipient of the dreaded letter (or sometimes, phone call) saying, "Your return has been selected for review (audit)." In reality, only a small percentage of people are audited each year. Just 1.91% of all Schedule C filers were audited in 2003—but this was nearly triple the rate for other taxpayers. Those who believe their income is too small for the IRS to care about may be surprised to learn that in 2003, 3% of sole proprietors with gross receipts below $25,000 were examined.

Corporations and partnerships with less than $100,000 gross income are audited much less frequently than sole proprietors. For some taxpayers, this is a sufficient reason to choose to operate as one of those entities rather than as a sole proprietor.

The IRS sends out 100 million letters to taxpayers each year. Don't assume that a letter from the IRS means you're being audited. The majority of IRS correspondence is not related to audits. You may receive a bill with penalties for not making last year's estimated tax payments on time. Or you may receive a questionnaire asking whether you really qualify to claim your child as a dependent on your tax return. The IRS will contact you if the amounts received in estimated tax payments differ from the amount you listed on your tax return as having been paid. You'll also hear from the IRS if the math on your return is incorrect. None of these letters means that the IRS is auditing you or that it has reviewed your return other than in the specific area mentioned in the letter.

A true audit letter will tell you that your return has been selected for examination. If an appointment date is not indicated, you will be asked to schedule an appointment for the audit within ten days of the date of the letter. The letter will list the areas the IRS is questioning and there will be a list of items to bring (or have on hand, if it's a field audit). The list will include bank statements, invoices, receipts, and so on.

7

(Chapter 7 discusses more completely the items the IRS expects you to have.) The letter will also ask you to bring your tax return for the year before and year after the one being audited. That doesn't mean those years are being audited too. You're asked to bring those returns in case there are items being carried over from one year to another, and also so the auditor can see whether items have been handled similarly from year to year. As with everything else you bring to the audit, do not hand the returns to the auditor unless he or she asks for them.

Don't ever assume your income is too low for you to be audited. Since one major focus of IRS audits is unreported income, a small income may be exactly why you were chosen for an audit. While you may be supported by your family, your lover, or school scholarships, none of those sources are reported on your tax return, so the IRS may be wondering how you're managing to pay for food and rent. The auditor may ask you to list your monthly expenses and the sources of the money used to pay those expenses. The IRS is trying to determine if you could have lived on the amount of income you've reported on your tax return.

Currently, the IRS is not doing many random audits. That means there generally is a specific reason if you're chosen for an audit. For example, your expenses may exceed the average amount for similar businesses. Or maybe you listed a very large amount in one expense category and the IRS wants to make sure you are entitled to take the full deduction. The 1099 forms submitted to the IRS may indicate that your income was higher than the amount you reported. Sometimes just putting an item of income or expense on the wrong line of your tax return is enough to trigger an audit. Since the IRS only does an audit when they believe they will be able to assess enough additional tax to pay for the staff time involved, you can assume they're looking at something specific on your return.

In some IRS districts, soon after you receive your audit letter, you are sent a preliminary report of proposed changes. The report points out:
- which areas of the return the IRS is investigating;
- what unreported income they're aware of (if any); and,
- which expenses they're planning to disallow if you cannot prove your case.

The report will also indicate the additional taxes and penalties you can expect if you don't show up for the audit or don't win your case. You can choose to accept the report as it is and pay the additional amount due, or you can go to the audit (or have a representative go for you) and argue your case.

Generally, the worst thing that can happen in an audit is that an expense will be disallowed or unreported income will be added to your return. In either case, you are assessed penalties, as well as having to pay the additional tax due. The penalty for not reporting income you received is 50% of the additional tax due (75% for fraud). Only in cases where fraud is suspected or where there is a very large amount of unreported income will the Criminal Investigation Division of the IRS get involved. In general, you don't need to fear being sent to jail if a discrepancy is found during the audit. Although careless mistakes may have been responsible for you being audited in the first place, they are not considered to be fraud.

There are two types of audits—field audits and office audits. If you're scheduled for a field audit, the auditor will come to your place of work to do the audit. Business returns are often handled by field auditors. These auditors are usually more experienced and knowledgeable than office auditors. Often, they will spend several days or longer reviewing your records.

Office audits are held at the nearest IRS office. The auditor carefully writes down all information you provide. However, the initial meeting is likely to last a day or less. If there is additional information needed, you can send or bring it in.

The auditor will begin by asking you a number of questions. She'll ask whether you had income other than that shown on the return (*e.g.*, gifts or loans) and whether you participated in barter transactions. She'll want to know how long you've been in business and exactly how your business operates. Then she'll ask to see your bank statements and records of money deposited. If you invoice your clients or customers, she'll want to see copies of those invoices. Business owners who are required to collect a sales or excise tax will be asked to provide those tax returns for comparison with the income reported on their income tax return. Then, of course, the auditor will want to see the receipts for expenses claimed.

The auditor looks at your expense receipts not only to make sure you have them, but also to determine whether you were entitled to deduct the expenses. The following are some of the things an auditor is looking at in an audit.

- Did you report all money you earned?
- Did you write off personal expenses as business expenses?
- Does your reported income match your lifestyle?
- If you have employees, are you filing the appropriate payroll forms?
- If you have independent contractors, have they been misclassified?

You (or your representative) should go into the audit completely organized. If your business expenses are being investigated, bundle together all the receipts and canceled checks for each expense category shown on your return. If possible, attach to the top of the bundle an adding machine tape showing the total expenses for that category.

7

The auditor will be impressed with your thoroughness and you may be able to shorten the time spent in the audit. After adding up a few of the bundles and finding that her totals are the same as the totals on your tapes, the auditor may decide to accept your figures and forgo adding up all the receipts. If, in the course of preparing for the audit, you discover some expenses you didn't claim, be sure to take the receipts with you to the audit for use in offsetting any expenses that are disallowed.

The tendency for most taxpayers in an audit is to talk too much. People want to explain how they happened to have that expense and why their friend said it would be deductible. They reveal too much information and prolong the audit with unnecessary chatter. Don't fall into that trap. If you go to an audit, speak only when spoken to and answer concisely only the question you're asked. This is not the place to express hostility about the government or the amount of taxes you're required to pay.

## Deciding Who Goes to the Audit

Whether or not you need a tax professional to represent you at an audit depends on the issues involved. If they're straightforward and the audit appears to be focused on whether you have receipts to back up the expenses you claimed, you can probably represent yourself. On the other hand, if you deducted expenses that were in a gray area and you need to use previous court cases to back up the deductibility of the expense, you'll probably want a tax professional to go and argue your case for you. Even if you choose to represent yourself, a one-hour consultation with a tax professional prior to the audit will help you prepare correctly.

Generally, it's not a good idea for taxpayers to accompany their tax professional to the audit—either you should go or she should go. An unaccompanied taxpayer is given some leniency by the auditor because she's an amateur at preparing her return and representing herself. A tax preparer is given a certain respect because the auditor knows that she is a professional who is familiar with tax law. If the taxpayer and tax professional go together, the duo doesn't get the advantage that either would get if she went alone. Sometimes, however, the auditor will insist on meeting with the taxpayer before the audit can be wrapped up.

When shopping for a tax professional, make sure that person will be available to represent you in the event of an audit. Most preparers charge extra for audit representation. As discussed in Chapter 38, while anyone can accompany you to an audit and while the preparer of a tax return can represent that return, only attorneys, CPAs, and enrolled agents can represent all returns (whether or not prepared by them) without the taxpayer being there.

# At the End of the Audit

At the end of the audit, one of several things will happen. If expenses are disallowed, you (or your representative) will point out any expenses that weren't claimed on the original return. You'll try to negotiate with the auditor (*e.g., I understand why you need to disallow that, but I hope you agree with the appropriateness of accepting this*). The auditor may ask you to send additional information before concluding the audit. If possible, try to go to the audit with everything that might be asked for. When you provide missing information later, it can sometimes disappear in the bowels of the IRS (be sure to send copies, not originals, and send the information by certified mail with return receipt requested). Additionally, since you (or your representative) are not there to argue for its acceptance, the new information may be disregarded.

If everything necessary is at the audit, the auditor will generally conclude the audit before you leave. You will be given a final report showing the changes made. You can sign the report and pay any additional taxes and penalties assessed (or agree to the proposed refund) or you can appeal the audit decision to the auditor's supervisor, the appeals office, or tax court.

Not all audits result in you owing taxes. Sometimes the IRS owes you after the audit is completed. Other times neither of you owes the other because nothing significant was changed on the return. This is called a *no change* audit and is highly desirable. Not only do you not owe the IRS, but if you're called for an audit about identical issues for either of the two years following the audited year, you can tell the audit office that you had a *no change* for those items within the last two years. Sometimes the audit will be called off although cancellations due to a repetitive audit happens less frequently for Schedule C filers than for other types of returns.

7

# Holding on to Records | 40

Although most audits occur within twenty months of the time you file your return, the IRS actually has three years in which to examine your return. The statute of limitations increases to six years if the IRS believes that your return involves substantial understatement of income (that is, more than 25% of your income was not reported). If you didn't file a return, there is no statute of limitations protecting you from an IRS investigation.

Most audits occur at the federal level. The IRS then notifies the state of the results, which usually takes some time. Because the state also wants to be able to collect from you in cases in which, as a result of the audit, more income or fewer expenses are allowed, most states have a statute of limitations that exceeds that of the IRS. In California, for example, the tax department has four years in which to contact you about your return.

You'll want to hold on to all records (receipts, canceled checks, IRS correspondence, etc.) connected with your tax return until the statute of limitations runs out for all applicable taxing agencies. This will be between three and five years from the date you filed your return or paid the tax, whichever comes later. After that time, you can dispose of receipts, invoices, and canceled checks for most items related to a particular return.

The receipts for any assets you bought (e.g., computer, car, office furniture) that you're still using should be kept for as long as you own that asset, plus three to five years. Receipts related to a house you own (whether or not the home is used for business) should be kept for five years after it is sold.

Copies of your tax returns should be kept forever. They take up very little space and, if they serve no other purpose, the nostalgia element alone makes them worth holding onto. You never know when you may need something contained on a return from years ago.

**EXAMPLE**

*Marny, a self-employed house cleaner, was in an automobile accident last year and was unable to work for six months. The other party was at fault. When settling with the other driver's insurance company, Marny needed a way to show how her income had been reduced by not being able to work after the accident. Her tax returns from the previous five years provided her with the actual numbers she needed to present to the insurance company.*

**EXAMPLE**

*Each year for twenty years, Judy contributed money to an IRA account. Many of those years she had no other retirement account, but some years she was covered by an employer's pension plan. In the years she was part of another plan, Judy's IRA contribution wasn't deductible, so when she removes the money, there will be no tax due on those amounts. If Judy hasn't kept her tax returns for all the years she put money into an IRA, she won't know how many of the contributions were deductible, and therefore, how much of her distribution is taxable.*

Once you finish preparing a tax return, put all the receipts, canceled checks, and related materials into a box and label it with that year's date. Put it up on a closet shelf, in the basement, or in some other storage place. You don't need to pay any further attention to that box until four or five years later (when you'll throw most of it out)—but it's comforting to know the records are there if you need them.

# The End (Which is Really the Beginning)

41

If you've made it this far in this book, you should have most of the information you need to keep on track with your business finances. I know that sometimes it seems overwhelming. There may be times when you wonder if it's really worth being self-employed. Just remember, you've managed to become an expert in your field. Although you're capable of doing so, it may not be imperative that you also become an expert in the tax and recordkeeping field.

I recently met with Rosa to prepare her tax return. Since she was a new client, I asked about her computer consulting business. For almost half an hour, she talked with enthusiasm and answered my questions about the wireless networks she sets up and operating system problems she solves for clients. As an often frustrated computer user, I understood only a portion of what she was talking about, but her enthusiasm was contagious. Finally, I told Rosa we needed to talk about her taxes. I began asking her questions about various items to be included on her tax return. Little by little, I saw the enthusiasm leave Rosa's face as she realized she didn't know the answers to some of my questions. Perhaps she felt she should have a better knowledge of her finances. Maybe she thought I would think less of her abilities because she didn't understand what I was asking for.

What was apparent to me is that Rosa is an expert in her field and loves her work. I'm also an expert in my field and love my work (most of the time!). Eventually I hope to have a better understanding of how my computer works (and why it sometimes doesn't), and I know that one day Rosa will have a better understanding of her business taxes. For either of us to feel stupid for not being experts in each other's fields doesn't make sense.

Not understanding everything we'd like to know doesn't mean we're unable to learn. There is a lot of information in the world—most of us are still in the process of grasping what we think will be meaningful for us.

When it comes to recordkeeping and taxes, there may be a limit as to how much you want to learn before passing the work on to an expert in the field. You may decide that you want to learn enough to be comfortable in preparing your own tax returns. Having reached this point in the book, you're off to a great start.

However you use what you've learned here, may your business prosper!

# Glossary

## A

**actual expense method.** One of the ways of deducting vehicle expenses. All expenses are added together and then multiplied by the percentage the vehicle is used for business.

**accrual method of accounting.** Taxpayer reports all income earned during the year, whether or not it was received, and all expenses incurred during the year, whether or not they were paid.

**adjusted gross income (AGI).** Total income minus certain adjustments to income on Form 1040.

**asset.** Something of value, such as a computer, a house, or a car.

## B

**balance sheet.** The portion of a financial statement that reports what assets are owned and what debts (liabilities) are owed to others.

**basis.** The cost of an asset for tax purposes. In some cases, the basis will be the original cost of the item plus sales tax, shipping, and installation (if appropriate). Much of the time, the basis will be the original cost plus improvements made or minus depreciation claimed. The business basis of an item that's used both personally and for business is the basis times the percentage of business use.

**bonus first-year depreciation.** An accelerated depreciation method that allows an extra amount to be deducted the first year an asset is placed in service, with less than normal amounts deducted in later years.

# C

**cash flow projection.** A report that projects how much income will be received and what the expected expenses will be for a given time period.

**cash method of accounting.** Taxpayer reports all income received and all expenses paid during the year. Does not include income earned but not received.

**C corporation.** A regular corporation.

**columnar pad.** A pad of paper with a number of columns on each page. Frequently used for manual business recordkeeping.

**constructively received.** Money earned that is available to the business owner, even if she hasn't yet gotten it in her hands.

**cost of goods sold (COGS).** A figure that is arrived at by adding the current year's inventory purchases to the business' beginning year inventory figure and then subtracting the year-end inventory amount. This is the only inventory figure that can be deducted as a business expense.

# D

**deduction.** An expense that can be subtracted either from business income (if a business deduction) or from total income (if not business-related).

**dependent.** A person who can be claimed on someone else's tax return, generally because she is supported financially more than 50% by the person who is claiming her.

**depreciate.** Any business asset that is expected to last a year or more must be deducted (depreciated) over a period of years. There is also a method of depreciation that allows depreciation of the full cost in the year the item is purchased.

**disbursements.** Expenses that have been paid.

**draw.** Money taken out of a business account and used for personal purposes. Only sole proprietors and partners in a partnership can take a draw.

# E

**employee.** A worker who has taxes withheld from her paycheck.

**Enterprise Zone.** An economically disadvantaged area of a city. Tax programs provide benefits to businesses that operate in or hire from an Enterprise Zone.

**estimated taxes.** Quarterly payments based on the amount of tax the taxpayer estimates she will owe this year.

**exemption.** Deduction amount given to the filer of a tax return for herself, her spouse, and each dependent she claims on the return.

**extension.** An additional amount of time given for a tax return to be filed. This is not, however, an extension of time to pay.

# F

**federal employer identification number (FEIN).** Tax number assigned by the IRS to employers, corporations, partnerships, and those who have Keogh or self-employed 401(k) retirement plans.

**federal insurance contributions act (FICA) tax.** A combination of Social Security and Medicare tax. Employees have this tax withheld from their paycheck and their employer contributes an equal amount to the employee's Social Security account. Self-employed people pay FICA as part of the self-employment tax.

**fictitious name.** Business name that isn't the same name as that of the owner.

**Form K-1.** Annual form received by a partner in a partnership, a shareholder in an S corporation, or a beneficiary of an estate or trust. Form K-1 shows the recipient's portion of income and expenses, which are then reported on that person's individual tax return.

# H

**health savings account (HSA).** High deductible health insurance policy paired with a savings account.

# I

**income tax.** Federal, state, or city tax based on taxable income.

**independent contractor.** Worker who is not considered to be an employee and has no taxes withheld from the payment she receives.

**inventory.** The finished goods and raw materials a business has on hand to sell to others.

**individual retirement arrangement (IRA).** A retirement account available to (but not always deductible by) all taxpayers. Can be either a traditional IRA or a Roth IRA.

**itemized deductions.** *See personal deductions.*

# K

**Keogh.** Type of retirement plan available to self-employed people.

# L

**lease inclusion.** An amount specified by the IRS that decreases the allowable deduction for a leased car.

**liability.** An amount owed to others.

**limited liability company (LLC).** Form of doing business that combines the advantages of a partnership and an S corporation.

**listed property.** Assets that are not used exclusively at a business establishment or a qualified home office. Also applies to property used for entertainment or recreation. These assets must be listed separately on the depreciation form and have additional restrictions imposed on them.

# M

**Modified Accelerated Cost Recovery System (MACRS).** The method most commonly used to calculate depreciation on business assets.

**married and filing jointly (MFJ).** Tax return filing status that applies to a heterosexual couple who file a joint return and who were married as of the last day of the calendar year.

**Medicare tax.** A portion of the FICA and self-employment taxes. The tax is used primarily to provide medical assistance to the elderly.

**mileage rate method.** One of the ways of deducting vehicle expenses. The number of business miles driven is multiplied by a cents-per-mile figure provided by the IRS each year.

**mixed-use property.** Personal items that are sometimes used in the business, such as a car.

# N

**net operating loss (NOL).** Occurs when the loss from a business exceeds the income from all other sources on a tax return. Requires a complex calculation that allows the loss to be carried back to prior or ahead to future tax returns.

**net profit.** The resulting figure after business expenses are deducted from business income.

# P

**partnership.** An entity in which two or more people own the business together. Profit or loss from the partnership is reported on each partner's individual tax return.

**personal deductions.** Specific deductions that can be claimed by those who have enough of them to be able to itemize. They include medical expenses, state and real estate taxes, mortgage interest, charitable contributions, investment expenses, and employee work-related expenses.

**petty cash.** A small amount of cash kept on hand by a business to pay minor expenses.

**placed in service.** The date an asset was first used in a business.

**profit and loss statement.** A report that shows the income and expenses of the business during a given time period.

# Q

**quarterly taxes.** Estimated tax payments owed on income received during each quarter of the year.

# R

**remaining tax liability.** Remainder owed by a taxpayer after withheld taxes and/or estimated tax payments are subtracted from the total tax liability.

# S

**Section 179.** A section in the IRS code that allows assets to be depreciated (deducted) in full in the year they are purchased.

**Schedule C.** Tax form filed by sole proprietors and one-person limited liability companies.

**Schedule C filers.** Term used by the IRS to refer to people who file a Schedule C.

**Schedule SE.** Tax form used to calculate self-employment tax owed by sole proprietors, partners, and S corporation owners.

**S corporation.** A corporation that has made an election to pass through to the individual owners whatever business profit or loss there is.

**self-employed 401(k).** A special retirement plan just for sole proprietors who have no employees. Allows a higher retirement contribution than most other plans.

**self-employment tax.** What Social Security tax is called when it's paid by self-employed people.

**SEP IRA.** An easy to set up retirement plan for small business owners.

**SIMPLE.** A retirement plan for small business owners that accepts contributions from both the employer and employee.

**single filing status.** Filing status available to any person who is unmarried as of the last day of the year.

**sole proprietor.** One person who operates a nonincorporated business. This is the easiest business entity to set up.

**standard deduction.** Taxpayers who don't have a large amount of personal deductions (medical expenses, taxes paid, interest, and charitable contributions) take a standard amount. For 2004, this amount is $4,850 for single people and $9,700 if married.

# T

**tax credit.** An allowed amount that is subtracted on the tax return directly from total tax liability. Tax credits are available for child care, nonbusiness education, and various other expenses.

**taxable income.** The amount of income that remains after all sources of income have been added together and adjustments to income, personal itemized deductions, and exemption amounts have been subtracted out.

**tax liability.** The total tax on taxable income. For federal tax purposes, this is the income tax, minus any tax credits, plus the self-employment tax.

# W

**wages.** Compensation paid to an employee of a business. Social Security and income taxes are withheld from wages.

**withholding.** The amount taken out of an employee's paycheck to cover FICA and federal and state income tax.

# How to Reconcile a Bank Statement

A

Chapter 6 provides general information about balancing your checkbook and reconciling it to your bank statement. The instructions here take you through the process in detail.

The back of the bank statement usually has an area in which to do the reconciliation. The following steps can be done on the back of the statement or on a separate piece of paper.

1. Make a list of all outstanding checks, including the check number and amount. These are checks that you've written but that don't yet show on the bank statement as having been cashed.

2. Make a list of all outstanding deposits. These are deposits that you have made to your account but that don't yet show up on your bank statement.

3. Begin with the ending bank balance as shown on the bank statement. Subtract from that number the total of the outstanding checks and add to it the total of the outstanding deposits. This will give you an adjusted bank balance.

4. In your check register, enter all the transactions that show up on your bank statement but that have not yet been entered into your own records. These might include unrecorded bank service fees, automatic transfers between bank accounts, interest earned on the account, ATM withdrawals, and automatic bill payments. Be sure to add those that should be added (credits) and subtract those that should be subtracted (debits).

5. Having made the adjustments in your check register, calculate your new checkbook balance.

6. Compare your adjusted bank balance to your new checkbook balance.

If the two still don't match, try these steps.

- Check the addition and subtraction in your checkbook by going back to the last date in which the checkbook balance matched the bank balance. Redo the math on all transactions since that date. Be sure you didn't add a transaction when you should have subtracted it and vice versa.
- See whether the amount of the discrepancy matches a check or a deposit amount.
- Compare, one by one, the amounts of the checks and deposits on the bank statement with the amounts entered in your checkbook. If the difference between the checkbook balance and the bank statement balance can be divided by 9, there is likely a transposition error (the correct numerals are recorded, but they're entered in the wrong order). For example, if your bank statement balance is $101.92 and your checkbook balance is $101.29, the difference is $.63, which can be divided by 9. Most likely a check was entered in the checkbook for a different amount than was actually written on the check. Sometimes the numerical amount on a check is different from the written amount (a mistake was made when the check was written). Look at the bank statement to see which amount was used when the check was cashed.
- Review the bank statement for any entries you haven't picked up. Occasionally, an amount is subtracted without a check number being listed next to the amount. Make sure you haven't counted the corresponding check as outstanding.
- Compare the amount of the discrepancy to the outstanding checks and deposits on your prior month's bank statement to see whether it matches any of those.
- If you have carbon checks, the amounts on the duplicates are sometimes not very legible. Verify that you subtracted the correct amount from your checkbook balance.

Don't assume that the amount of the discrepancy between the bank statement and your checkbook balance is the amount you need to find. For example, if the balances differ by $204.34, it may be because you didn't record a deposit for one amount and a check for another, which together total $204.34.

If the discrepancy is large, that doesn't mean it will be harder to find. A discrepancy of $650.00 is usually no harder to locate than one of $6.50.

Banks rarely make mistakes that show up on the bank statement, but it is possible. With the use of computers, mistakes in calculations are unlikely. More likely, a bank error occurs when the bank cashes a check for an amount different from the one you wrote. This type of error is caught when you compare the check amounts on the bank statement to those noted in your check register.

If you still cannot get the two balances to match, take your bank statement and checkbook to the bank and ask someone to help you. Some banks now charge for this service.

Once you have a reconciled balance, draw a line in your check register and enter the new balance. Next month, if the bank statement and checkbook balances don't match, it will be helpful to know at what point you last had an accurate balance.

# How to Calculate Estimated Tax Payments: A Step-by-Step Example

# B

For general information about who needs to make estimated tax payments and how to calculate the amounts due, refer to Chapters 35 and 36. This example will provide you with specific instructions for performing each step in the estimated tax calculation. There is extra space on these pages for you to fill in your own numbers, and calculate your own estimated tax figures.

First, let's look at Erin's situation and her calculation. All the numbers in Erin's calculation have been rounded to the nearest dollar. Also, since 2005 tax rates were not yet available when this book went to press, 2004 personal exemption, standard deduction, and income tax amounts have been used.

It's April 13. Erin has an estimated tax payment due on April 15 to cover income she received during the period January 1 to March 31. This is her first year of self-employment, she is single, and she does not itemize her personal deductions but instead takes the standard deduction. Erin has no dependents (so is able to take a personal exemption only for herself) and this year she has no income other than self-employment income. Because she operates a hair salon, Erin receives all her income as she earns it. She does her bookkeeping and taxes on a cash basis. These factors make the following example as simple as possible. If your situation is different from Erin's (*e.g.*, you're married, you have some income from wages or another source, or you itemize your personal deductions), you will need to adjust your figures accordingly.

Erin has been keeping very good records of her income and expenses. When she reviews them, she discovers that she has had $4,000 net profit from her business for the first quarter. Remember, net profit is determined after business expenses have been deducted. Because she's never been self-employed before, Erin has no idea what she is going to earn this year. Using her first quarter profit as a guide, Erin guesses that she might have $4,000 profit in each of the following quarters. She multiplies this quarter's $4,000 by 4 quarters to calculate the amount she expects to earn for the year, thus projecting that her net self-employment income for the year will $16,000.

To begin figuring her tax liability, Erin first calculates the self-employment tax on her projected $16,000 net profit. To do this, she multiplies the $16,000 by 92.35%, and then by the 15.3% self-employment tax rate. The result is a projected self-employment tax of $2,261 for the year.

Next, from Erin's $16,000 projected income she subtracts her personal exemption of $3,100, her standard deduction of $4,850, and half of her projected self-employment tax ($1130). The result is a projected taxable income for the year of $6,920. If you've forgotten what the personal exemption and standard deduction are, review page 175. When Erin looks at the tax rate schedule, she sees that $6,920 falls within the 10% tax bracket, which covers taxable income from $0 to $7,150. To figure the income tax on her projected income, Erin multiplies $6,920 by 10%—for a total income tax of $692.

Adding Erin's projected federal income tax of $692 to her projected self-employment tax of $2,261 equals a total tax for the year of $2,953. Erin divides the $2,953 into 4 quarterly payments and sends in one quarter, or $738 on April 15.

*Here is the calculation Erin did for the 1ˢᵗ quarter:*          *Your calculations:*

| | | |
|---|---|---|
| $4,000 | Net profit from self-employment | - - - - - - - - - - - - - |
| x 4 | Number of quarters in a year | x 4 |
| $16,000 | Projected net profit for the year | - - - - - - - - - - - - - |
| x 92.35% | Self-employed people pay self-employment tax on this percentage of their net self-employment earnings | x 92.35% |
| $14,776 | | - - - - - - - - - - - - - |
| x 15.3% | This is the self-employment tax rate | x 15.3% |
| $2,261 | Projected self-employment tax for the year | - - - - - - - - - - - - - |
| $16,000 | Projected net profit for the year | - - - - - - - - - - - - - |
| - 3,100 | Personal exemption, available for each taxpayer, spouse, and dependent | - - - - - - - - - - - - - |
| - 4,850 | Standard deduction for single taxpayers ($9,700 for married taxpayers) | - - - - - - - - - - - - - |
| - 1,130 | ½ of the projected self-employment tax | _____ |
| $6,920 | Projected taxable income for the year | - - - - - - - - - - - - - |
| x 10% | Tax rate for this amount of income | X *(see tax rate schedule)* |
| $692 | Projected federal income tax for the year | - - - - - - - - - - - - - |
| $692 | Projected federal income tax for the year | - - - - - - - - - - - - - |
| + 2,261 | Projected self-employment tax for the year | _____ |
| $2,953 | Total tax liability for the year | - - - - - - - - - - - - - |
| ÷ 4 | The 4 quarters of the year | ÷ 4 |
| $738 | Amount Erin needs to send this quarter | - - - - - - - - - - - - - |

On June 15, Erin's second quarterly payment is due. This payment is for income earned during the period from April 1 through May 31. Notice that the second quarter is only a two-month quarter. The first and third quarters are three months each. The second quarter is two months, and the fourth quarter is four months.

In calculating the payment due for the second quarter, an extra step is needed because the payment covers two, rather than three, months. In the first quarter, Erin had $4,000 net profit from self-employment. In the second quarter, her profit was $14,000. Erin adds the two quarters together and sees that in five months she's had a net profit of $18,000. She divides the $18,000 income by the 5 months that have gone by, which equals $3,600 per month. Erin needs to project her income for the year based on what she's already earned, so she multiplies the $3,600 monthly net profit by 12 months. The result is projected income for the year of $43,200. This is almost three times as much as the $16,000 annual income she projected when she did this calculation last quarter.

The remaining steps for this quarter's calculation are similar to those done last quarter. Erin next computes her projected self-employment tax by multiplying the $43,200 by 92.35%, then by 15.3%. The result is a projected self-employment tax for the year of $6,104. She then subtracts her personal exemption, the standard deduction, and half of her projected self-employment tax from her $43,200 projected income. The result is $32,198 projected taxable income for the year.

As shown on the tax rate schedule, the 10% tax bracket for single people ends at $7,150. The 15% tax bracket is for taxable incomes between $7,151 and $29,050. Since Erin's projected taxable income is over $29,050, she needs to look at the line for the 25% tax bracket. The first $7,150 of her income will be taxed at 10%, the next approximately $22,000 will be taxed at 15%, and the remainder will be taxed at 25%. To calculate her projected income tax for the year, Erin subtracts $29,050 (the bottom of the 25% tax bracket) from her taxable income of $32,198. The result is $3,148 which she then multiplies by 25%. The result is $787 which Erin then adds to the $4,000 figure shown on the schedule. The $4,000 represents the tax on the amount of her income that falls in the 10% and 15% brackets. Erin sees that her projected income tax for the year is $4,787. She adds this amount to her $6,104 projected self-employment tax. It now appears that her total tax for the year will be $10,891.

Erin has two choices at this point. She can send in just one quarter's worth ($2,723) of the total amount she owes in order to cover the second quarter. Or she can catch up with the amount she really owes the IRS at this point. Since she thought she would be earning so much less this year, her payment last quarter doesn't equal one quarter of what it now appears her total tax liability will be. Erin decides that she doesn't want to have to come up with a large amount of money for taxes next April. She would rather send enough now so that the sum of her April and June payments equals two quarters' worth of the total taxes that will be due for this year. She divides the $10,891 total tax liability by 4 quarters, multiplies it by 2 (for the two quarters that have gone by), and the result is a total amount due for the two quarters of $5,446. Since Erin sent in $738 last quarter, she sends in the remaining $4,708 this quarter. This is a large amount to pay on her $14,000 earnings this quarter, but Erin is making up for the small amount sent in the first quarter.

When Erin files her tax return in April, the IRS will notice that Erin paid different amounts for the first and second quarters. The IRS will assume that Erin's income was the same both quarters and will think that Erin underpaid the amount owed for the first quarter. They will be ready to penalize Erin unless she sends Form 2210 with her tax return (see pages 173–174), to show the IRS her first-quarter income and why she paid only $738 for that quarter. This information will enable them to see that she sent in the correct amount based on her true quarterly income.

| *Here is the calculation Erin did this quarter:* | | *Your calculations:* |
|---|---|---|
| $4,000 | Net profit earned 1st quarter | - - - - - - - - - - - - - - - - |
| + 14,000 | Net profit earned 2nd quarter | _____ |
| $18,000 | Total profit for the first 5 months | - - - - - - - - - - - - - - - - |
| ÷ 5 | Number of months that have gone by | ÷ 5 |
| $3,600 | Average net profit per month | - - - - - - - - - - - - - - - - |
| x 12 | Number of months in the year | x 12 |
| $43,200 | Projected net profit for the year | - - - - - - - - - - - - - - - - |
| x 92.35% | Self-employed people pay self-employment tax on this percentage of their net profit from self-employment | x 92.35% |
| $39,895 | | - - - - - - - - - - - - - - - - |
| x 15.3% | This is the self-employment tax rate | x 15.3% |
| $6,104 | Projected self-employment tax for the year | |
| $43,200 | Projected net profit for the year | - - - - - - - - - - - - - - - - |
| - 3,100 | Personal exemption, available for each taxpayer, spouse, and dependent | - - - - - - - - - - - - - - - - |
| - 4,850 | Standard deduction for single taxpayers ($9,700 for married taxpayers) | - - - - - - - - - - - - - - - - |
| - 3,052 | ½ of the projected self-employment tax | _____ |
| $32,198 | Projected taxable income for the year | |
| - 29,050 | This is where the 25% bracket starts for single people | _____ |
| $3,148 | | - - - - - - - - - - - - - - - - |
| x 25% | Federal income tax rate for a single person's taxable income that exceeds $29,050 and is less than $70,350 | X *(see tax rate schedule)* |
| $787 | 25% tax on this portion of the income | - - - - - - - - - - - - - - - - |
| + 4,000 | 10% & 15% tax on the first $29,050 of taxable income | _____ |
| $4,787 | Projected federal income tax for the year | - - - - - - - - - - - - - - - - |
| $4,787 | Projected federal income tax for the year | - - - - - - - - - - - - - - - - |
| + 6,104 | Projected self-employment tax for the year | _____ |
| $10,891 | Total tax liability for the year | - - - - - - - - - - - - - - - - |
| ÷ 4 | The 4 quarters of the year | ÷ 4 |
| $2,723 | | - - - - - - - - - - - - - - - - |
| x 2 | Erin wants to, with this payment, have paid in 2 quarters' worth of the tax she'll owe | x 2 |
| $5,446 | | - - - - - - - - - - - - - - - - |
| - 738 | Amount Erin sent 1st quarter | _____ |
| $4,708 | Amount Erin sends this quarter | - - - - - - - - - - - - - - - - |

Just prior to the third-quarter payment due date, Erin again calculates the amount she needs to send to the IRS. Payment is due on September 15 for money received between June 1 and August 31. Erin estimates her income for the year by adding together the $4,000 she earned in the first quarter, the $14,000 from the second quarter, and the $9,000 she earned in the third quarter. After adding those figures together, Erin sees that her year-to-date income is $27,000. She divides that figure by the eight months that have gone by and gets an average income of $3,375 a month. She multiplies that figure by 12 months, which results in a yearly projected income of $40,500, not too different than the $43,200 she projected last quarter.

As in the previous quarters, Erin calculates the self-employment tax on $40,500. It is $5,722.

She then subtracts out her personal exemption, her standard deduction, and half of her projected self-employment tax from $40,500. The end result is projected taxable income for the year of $29,689. As was true in the second quarter, most of this amount is taxed in the 10% and 15% tax brackets, but a small portion of it will be taxed at the 25% rate because it's more than $29,050. The income tax on Erin's projected taxable income is $4,160. Because her estimated self-employment tax is $5,722, Erin's projected tax for the year is $9,882. Erin divides that figure by the 4 quarters of the year. By the time she makes this payment, Erin wants to have sent in three quarters' worth of tax, or $7,412. So far she's sent in $738 for the first quarter and $4,708 for the second quarter, leaving her $1,966 to send in this quarter.

## *Here is the calculation Erin did this quarter:*          *Your calculations:*

| Erin's calculation | Description | Your calculations |
|---|---|---|
| $4,000 | Profit earned 1st quarter | ---------------- |
| + 14,000 | Profit earned 2nd quarter | ---------------- |
| + 9,000 | Profit earned 3rd quarter | _____ |
| $27,000 | Total profit for first 8 months | ---------------- |
| ÷ 8 | Number of months year-to-date | ÷ 8 |
| $3,375 | Average net profit per month | ---------------- |
| x 12 | Number of months in the year | x 12 |
| $40,500 | Projected profit for the year | ---------------- |
| x 92.35% | Self-employed people pay self- employment tax on this percentage of their net profit from self-employment | x 92.35% |
| $37,402 | | ---------------- |
| x 15.3% | This is the self-employment tax rate | x 15.3% |
| $5,722 | Projected self-employment tax for the year | |
| $40,500 | Projected net profit for the year | ---------------- |
| - 3,100 | Personal exemption, available for each taxpayer, spouse, and dependent | ---------------- |
| - 4,850 | Standard deduction for single taxpayers ($9,700 for married taxpayers) | ---------------- |
| - 2,861 | ½ of the projected self-employment tax | _____ |
| $29,689 | Projected taxable income for the year | ---------------- |
| - 29,050 | This is where the 25% bracket starts for single people | _____ |
| $639 | Amount to be taxed at 25% | ---------------- |
| x 25% | **Federal income tax rate for a single** person withtaxable income over $29,050 and less than $70,350 | X *(see tax rate schedule)* |
| $160 | 25% tax on this portion of the income | ---------------- |
| + 4,000 | 10% & 15% tax on the first $29,050 of taxable income | _____ |
| $4,160 | Projected federal income tax for the year | ---------------- |
| $4,160 | Projected federal income tax for the year | ---------------- |
| + 5,722 | Projected self-employment tax for the year | _____ |
| $9,882 | Total federal tax liability for the year | ---------------- |
| ÷ 4 | The 4 quarters of the year | ÷ 4 |
| $2,471 | | ---------------- |
| x 3 | Erin wants, with this payment, to have paid in 3 quarters' worth of the tax she'll owe | x 3 |
| $7,412 | | |
| -738 | Amount Erin sent 1st quarter | ---------------- |
| - 4,708 | Amount Erin sent 2nd quarter | _____ |
| $1,966 | Amount Erin needs to send this quarter | ---------------- |

On January 15, Erin's final payment of the previous year's tax is due. Since the tax year ended December 31, theoretically by this time Erin knows what she earned during the previous year. It turns out that Erin's net profit for the year was $35,000. This is quite a bit more than the $16,000 she originally projected, but less than the $43,200 and $40,500 she estimated in the second and third quarters.

Again, Erin does the estimated tax calculation. The self-employment tax on her $35,000 net profit is $4,945. Erin subtracts her personal exemption, her standard deduction, and half her self-employment tax from the $35,000 profit. The result is taxable income for the year of $24,577. This means that Erin is in the 15% income tax bracket. The income tax on $24,577 is $3,329. Erin's total tax (income tax plus self-employment tax) for the year is $8,274. So far she's sent in $7,412 during the year, leaving her $862 to pay for this quarter. This is a relatively small amount to pay because Erin overpaid in the second and third quarters when she thought her taxable income for the year would be more. Erin pays the remainder of her estimated taxes on January 15 and files her tax return on April 15. No additional tax is due with her return.

| *Here is the calculation Erin did this quarter:* | | *Your calculations:* |
|---|---|---|
| $35,000 | Net profit for the year | - - - - - - - - - - - - - - - |
| x 92.35% | Self-employed people pay self-employmenttax on this percentage of their net profit from self-employment | x 92.35% |
| $32,323 | | - - - - - - - - - - - - - - - |
| x 15.3% | This is the self-employment tax rate | x 15.3% |
| $4,945 | Self-employment tax for the year | - - - - - - - - - - - - - - - |
| $35,000 | Net profit for the year | - - - - - - - - - - - - - - - |
| - 3,100 | Personal exemption, available for each taxpayer, spouse, and dependent | - - - - - - - - - - - - - - - |
| - 4,850 | Standard deduction for single taxpayers ($9,700 for married taxpayers) | - - - - - - - - - - - - - - - |
| - 2,473 | ½ of the self-employment tax | _____ |
| $24,577 | Taxable income for the year | - - - - - - - - - - - - - - - |
| - 7,150 | This is where the 15% bracket starts for single people | - - - - - - - - - - - - - - - |
| $17,427 | Amount to be taxed at 15% | - - - - - - - - - - - - - - - |
| x 15% | Federal income tax rate for a single person with taxable income over $7,150 and less than $29,050 | X *(see tax rate schedule)* |
| $2,614 | 15% tax on this portion of the income | - - - - - - - - - - - - - - - |
| + 715 | 10% tax on the first $7,150 of taxable income | _____ |
| $3,329 | Federal income tax for the year | - - - - - - - - - - - - - - - |
| $3,329 | Federal income tax for the year | - - - - - - - - - - - - - - - |
| + 4,945 | Self-employment tax for the year | _____ |
| $8,274 | Total federal tax liability for the year | - - - - - - - - - - - - - - - |
| - 738 | Amount Erin sent 1st quarter | - - - - - - - - - - - - - - - |
| - 4,708 | Amount Erin sent 2nd quarter | - - - - - - - - - - - - - - - |
| - 1,966 | Amount Erin sent 3rd quarter | _____ |
| $862 | Remaining tax liability to send this quarter | - - - - - - - - - - - - - - - |

And that's how you do the estimated tax calculation!

# Resources for Small Business Owners

# C

This Appendix contains lists of helpful resource for small business owners, including groups, websites, and publications of particular interest to female entrepreneurs.

## Internal Revenue Service

As you know, the *Internal Revenue Service* (IRS) is the federal agency that deals with your taxes—individual, business, and payroll. The IRS telephone number is 800-829-1040. The IRS offers telephone help with your tax questions. However, you may find that calling the IRS more than once with the same question will result in two or more dissimilar answers. If you prepare your tax return based on an answer you receive from the IRS, you are not protected from penalties if it turns out that you were given an incorrect answer. The IRS website at **www.irs.gov** has available for download all IRS forms and publications. In addition, there is a great deal of taxpayer information on the website.

The IRS also has a special section on the website for small business owners at **www.irs.gov/smallbiz** as well as a Business and Specialty Tax Line (telephone assistance) at 800-829-4933.

One particularly helpful IRS department is the *Taxpayer Advocate Service* (TAS). The TAS is an independent organization within the IRS that is designed to help taxpayers resolve problems with the IRS. If you've had ongoing correspondence with the IRS over an issue that hasn't been resolved, you can call the Taxpayer Advocate Service at 877-777-4778.

If you need one, the phone number for requesting a *Federal Employer Identification Number* (FEIN) from the IRS is 800-829-4933.

You may find it helpful to use the IRS' *Electronic Federal Tax Payment System* (EFTPS) to make your federal estimated tax payments. This program allows you to have money for your estimated tax payments automatically debited from your bank account. You can schedule in advance your estimated payments for the whole year, check the website to confirm what payments you've already made, and make estimated payments on a weekly or monthly basis if you prefer that to the quarterly due dates. For more information, call 800-945-8400 or go to **www.eftps.gov**.

Employers can also use EFTPS to make payroll tax deposits. Another helpful resource for employers is **www.socialsecurity.gov/employer**, W-2 forms for employees can be prepared free online with no charge. The employee copy of the form is printed out while an electronic copy is submitted to the Social Security Administration.

The IRS offers free small business tax seminars covering general information for entrepreneurs, as well as tax information for employers. Check with your local IRS office for upcoming programs. IRS tax classes are also offered online at **www.irs.gov/businesses/small** (click "online classroom").

The IRS has many publications of special interest to business owners. These can be downloaded from the IRS website, ordered from the IRS by phone, or picked up at an IRS office.

### Selected IRS Publications of Interest to Business Taxpayers

| | |
|---|---|
| 1 | Your Rights as a Taxpayer |
| 15 | Employer's Tax Guide |
| 17 | Your Federal Income Tax (for individuals) |
| 51 | Agricultural Employer's Tax Guide |
| 225 | Farmer's Tax Guide |
| 334 | Tax Guide for Small Business |
| 463 | Travel, Entertainment, Gift, and Car Expenses |
| 505 | Tax Withholding and Estimated Tax |
| 533 | Self-Employment Tax |
| 535 | Business Expenses |
| 536 | Net Operating Losses |
| 538 | Accounting Periods and Methods |
| 541 | Partnerships |
| 542 | Corporations |
| 544 | Sales and Other Dispositions of Assets |
| 547 | Casualties, Disasters, and Thefts |
| 551 | Basis of Assets |
| 553 | Highlights of Tax Changes |
| 556 | Examination of Returns, Appeal Rights, and Claims For Refund |
| 560 | Retirement Plans for Small Business |
| 583 | Starting a Business and Keeping Records |
| 587 | Business Use of Your Home |

| 595 | Tax Highlights for Commercial Fishermen |
|---|---|
| 910 | Guide to Free Tax Services |
| 911 | Direct Sellers |
| 946 | How to Depreciate Property |
| 954 | Tax Incentives for Distressed Communities |
| 966 | Electronic Federal Tax Payment System (EFTPS) |
| 969 | Medical Savings Accounts |
| 1518 | Tax Calendar for Small Businesses |
| 1542 | Per Diem Rates |
| 1635 | Understanding Your EIN (Employer Identification Number) |
| 3207 | Small Business Resource Guide (CD) |
| 3693 | Introduction to Federal Taxation (CD) |
| 3780 | Tax Information for Small Construction Businesses |
| 3998 | Choosing A Retirement Solution for Your Small Business |
| 4035 | Home-Based Business Tax Avoidance Schemes |
| 4222 | 401(k) Plans for Small Businesses |

# Small Business Administration

The *Small Business Administration* (SBA), a federal government agency, offers free and low-cost workshops for new and existing business owners on topics such as small business management and creating business websites. SBA centers may also include a *Business Information Center* (BIC) that provides books, magazines, software, and other valuable resources for small business owners. Check the government pages in your phone book to find the nearest SBA office or go to **www.sba.gov/ regions/states.html**. The SBA also offers free online classes in subjects of interest to entrepreneurs at **www.sba.gov/training/courses.html**.

The SBA also funds the *Service Corps of Retired Executives* (SCORE), a group that offers free business counseling. Business participants in this program are matched with a retired person who has operated a similar business and can provide guidance and support. In addition to in-person counseling, SCORE offers online help via e-mail. To find the location of the nearest SCORE program, look in the "United States Government" section of the phone book or go online to **www.score.org**.

Other very helpful resources are the *Small Business Development Centers* (SBDCs) located throughout the country. These organizations are funded jointly by the SBA and large corporations and are usually affiliated with local colleges. They offer free and low-cost workshops and individual counseling, specifically geared to small businesses. To locate your nearest SBDC, check with local colleges or go to **www.sbaonline.sba.gov/SBDC/sbdcnear.html**.

*Small Business Success* is a free magazine published twice a year. It has excellent articles and extensive resources. You can find a copy at your local SBA office or Small Business Development Center. The SBA also has a number of other free and low-cost publications helpful to small business owners. Many of the pub.lications can be downloaded at no charge from the SBA website at **ww.sba.gov/lib/library.html**.

Nationwide there are nearly one hundred SBA Women's Business Centers that provide training and individual counseling specifically for women entrepreneurs. The list of centers, as well as information about SBA loans and services designed for women can be found at **www.onlinewbc.gov**.

# Women Entrepreneur Organizations

These organizations have speaker and seminar programs where you can make invaluable contacts with other small business owners.

### American Business Women's Association (ABWA)

9100 Ward Parkway
P.O. Box 8728
Kansas City, MO 64114
800-228-0007
www.abwahq.org

*There are 2100 local chapters throughout the country. Seminars, magazine, and corporate discounts available to members.*

### National Association for Female Executives (NAFE)

P.O. Box 3052
Langhorne, PA 19047
800-927-NAFE
www.nafe.com

*Nearly 200,000 members in affiliated chapters throughout the country. Programs are geared to corporate employees as well as to self-employed women. Offers magazine and other benefits to members.*

### National Association of Women Business Owners (NAWBO)

8405 Greensboro Drive
Suite 800
McLean, VA 22102
800-55N-AWBO
www.nawbo.org

*Chapters throughout the U.S. Emphasis on building networks with other members. Speakers, conferences, and corporate discounts for members.*

# Online Support and Resources

There are many online areas of interest to small business owners. Do a search for "small business" or "small business taxes" in any search engine and you'll find more sites than you'll be able to look at in a lifetime. Following are some sites that are specifically for women entrepreneurs or are especially helpful to all small business owners.

**Note:** *Websites with tax information are not always updated regularly. Double check with the IRS website any figures that change each year such as the maximum allowable contribution to a retirement plan or the cents-per-mile allowance for business car usage.*

## TAX SITES

**www.irs.gov**

> *Federal tax forms and publications can be downloaded, and the answers to frequently asked questions are posted on this site. Links are available from this site to the fifty state sites.*

**www.fairmark.com**

> *Easy-to-understand site covering various tax topics. The focus is not self-employment, but there are articles on retirement plans, investing, and making estimated tax payments.*

**www.naea.org**

> *Website of the National Association of Enrolled Agents. Tax information, links to other tax sites, and nationwide directory for finding a tax advisor.*

**www.payroll-taxes.com**

> *If you're an employer, you'll find helpful answers about preparing employee payrolls here. This site also has a payroll calculator. Enter your employees' gross pay and all the appropriate deductions will be calculated for you. All you have to do is write the check.*

**www.quicken.com**

> *Lots of advertising for their products but click "taxes" or "small business" to find articles on various tax and business topics, including self-employment.*

**http://taxes.about.com**

> *Find answers to lots of tax questions and a place to ask your own.*

**www.taxmamma.com**

> *Easy-to-understand tax articles. Make sure to sign up for her informative free email tax newsletter.*

## SMALL BUSINESS SITES

**www.barbarabrabec.com**

> *Website for Barbara Brabec, author of* The Crafts Business Answer Book, Handmade for Profit, *and several other books about running a home-based business. Website has lots of helpful articles and Barbara also has a free newsletter.*

**www.buzgate.org**

> *Business Utility Zone Gateway website. Provide state-by-state links to small business organizations and sources of assistance.*

**www.entreworld.org**

> *Sponsored by the Kauffman Foundation Center for Entrepreneurial Leadership, this site includes all kinds of information for new and growing businesses. Be sure to check out the "women's channel."*

**www.gohome.com**

> *Website with helpful articles for people working from their homes.*

**www.isquare.com**

> *The Small Business Advisor site. Resources and articles for small business owners. Free email newsletter.*

**www.microenterpriseworks.org/nearyou**

> *State-by-state links to organizations working with micro-enterprises (very small businesses).*

**www.sbtv.com**

> *Website for Small Business TV. Archives of interviews with experts on small business topics. Also, TV coverage of the highlights of small business conferences.*

**www.smallbusinessadvocate.com**

*Website with hundreds of searchable audio archives from host Jim Blasingame's weekday radio/internet talk show. Business experts share valuable information and tips on how to be more successful in your small business.*

**www.workingsolo.com**

*Hosted by Terri Lonier, author of* Working Solo *and other small business books. Contains articles and information helpful to small business owners. Terri also writes a free email newsletter.*

## WOMEN IN BUSINESS SITES

**www.bizymoms.com**

*Hosted by Liz Folger, author of* The Stay-at-Home Mom's Guide to Making Money, *this is a site for moms with (or wanting to have) home businesses. One especially valuable part of the site is the section on business ideas. Women who own/have owned specific types of businesses have written short articles about what they like abut that business. Online classes about starting a business also offered.*

**www.count-me-in.org**

*Count Me In uses a women-friendly credit scoring system to make loans of $500-$10,000 available to women who need money to start or grow a business. Website also has lots of information about starting and operating a business.*

**www.digital-women.com**

*Email newsletter and lots of information for women already in business or considering starting a business. Has a section that answers the perennial question "Where is all the free money for women?"*

**www.enterprisingwomen.com**

*Website for Enterprising Women Magazine. Subscribe to their print edition or read articles from the current edition online.*

**www.fodreams.com**

*Website for the Field Of Dreams, a support site for women business owners. Free email newsletter.*

**www.hbwm.com**

*Website for Home Based Working Moms. Newsletter, articles, message boards, and Work at Home Kit for new business owners.*

**www.homeworkingmom.com**

*Website for Mothers' Home Business Network. An especially helpful part of the site is the reviews they do of home business opportunity sites—We Buy It and Try It So You Don't Have To.*

**www.ivillage.com**

*Among the many general topics of discussion on this website are home businesses (look under "work"). Message boards, articles, and free newsletter for work-from-home women.*

**www.momsbusinessmagazine.com**

*The Best of Mom's Business Magazine: A Behind-the-Scenes How-To for Mom Entrepreneurs by Nancy Cleary. This quarterly magazine consists of articles and products of interest to moms who are running a business.*

**www.mlmwoman.com**

*Bulletin boards, newsletter, and other tools for women involved in multi-level (network) marketing.*

**www.mydswa.org**

*Website for the Direct Selling Women's Alliance. Articles and resources for women involved in direct selling or network marketing ventures.*

**www.onlinewbc.gov/womens_business.html**

*Links to women's business organizations throughout the U.S.*

**www.wahm.com**

*Website for Work At Home Moms (WAHM). Online message boards, support, and information.*

**www.we-inc.org**

*Website for Women Entrepreneurs Inc. (WE Inc.), an organization that focuses on resources and advocacy for women entrepreneurs. Their "resources" section has lots of tax tips as well as other business management information.*

# Books

The following books are available in local and online bookstores, as well as libraries.

*About My Sister's Business: The Black Woman's Road Map to Successful Entrepreneurship*, by Fran Harris, includes ideas and advice for African American women starting a business.

*Business Mastery: A Business Planning Guide for Creating a Fulfilling, Thriving Business and Keeping it Successful*, by Cherie Sohnen-Moe, combines the practical and psychological aspects of owning a business. Originally written for healing arts professionals, this book is appropriate for business professionals in all fields. Available from Sohnen-Moe Associates at 800-786-4774. The Sohnen-Moe website at **www.sohnen-moe.com** also has other publications and courses for healing arts practitioners.

*Clearing the Hurdles: Women Building High-Growth Businesses* by Candida Brush et al is directed at women who have a vision for a high-potential business. The authors discuss how to get credible, fill the technical and management gaps in your expertise, link yourself to the right resources, and get over the funding hurdles.

*The Crafts Business Answer Book and Resource Guide*, *Handmade for Profit*, and *Homemade Money* are just three of the books by Barbara Brabec that give guidance to small business owners selling crafts. Check out her website **www.barbarabrabec.com** for more information.

*The Exhausted Woman's Guide to Starting Your Own Business: Run a Successful Business Without Running Yourself Ragged* by Kris Atkins provides a realistic picture of what it means to run a business. Her website at **www.krisatkins.com** has a number of helpful small business articles.

*Family Child Care Tax Workbook and Organizer*, *Family Child Care Recordkeeping Guide*, and *Family Child Care Audit Manual*, all by Tom Peopeland, are designed to familiarize owners of child care centers with tax regulations.

*422 Tax Deductions For Businesses and Self-Employed Individuals* by Bernard B. Kamoroff is an alphabetical encyclopedia of tax deductions.

*Girl Boss: Entrepreneurial Skills, Stories, and Encouragement for Modern Girls* by Stacy Kravetz is a fun guide to being an entrepreneur for the young woman who wants to get a business started.

*The Girl's Guide to Starting Your Own Business: Candid Advice, Frank Talk, and True Stories for the Successful Entrepreneur* by Caitlin Friedman and Kimberly Yorio is not, despite its title, geared to the under age 18 female.

*I Love My Life! A Mom's Guide to Working from Home* by Kristie Tamsevicius provides tips on running a business that doesn't run all over you, reducing stress, and balancing work with home life.

*Keeping the Books: Basic Recordkeeping and Accounting for the Small Business*, by Linda Pinson and Jerry Jinnett, provides very complete information on recordkeeping as well as using financial statements to measure the health of your business.

*Kitchen Table Entrepreneurs: How Eleven Women Escaped Poverty and Became Their Own Bosses* by Martha Shirk and Anna S. Wadia provides inspirational stories of eleven low-income women who are moving their families out of poverty by starting their own businesses.

*Mompreneurs: A Mother's Practical Step-By-Step Guide to Work-At-Home Success* and *Mompreneurs Online: Using the Internet to Build Work at Home Success*, are both by Ellen H. Parlapiano and Patricia Cobe. Each provides hints and resources for working at home and being a parent at the same time.

*The New Tax Guide for Artists of Every Persuasion* by Peter Jason Riley, CPA, is a comprehensive guide for visual artists, writers, actors, and musicians. Peter's websites at **www.artstaxinfo.com** and **www.cpa-services.com** have many easy-to-understand tax articles.

*101 Best Home-Based Businesses For Women, The Self-Employed Woman's Guide to Launching a Home-Based Business, 101 Best Home-Business Success Secrets for Women,* and *Herventure.com: Your Guide to Expanding Your Small or Home Business to the Internet* are just a few of the books Priscilla Y. Huff has written for potential women entrepreneurs. These resources provide ideas for the type of business to start and some hints in getting started.

*Our Wildest Dreams: Women Entrepreneurs Making Money, Having Fun, Doing Good,* by Joline Godfrey, is a look at how women can change the face of business. By talking about her own experiences in the corporate world and providing interviews with women entrepreneurs, Joline helps us consider a new definition of business success.

*Sister CEO: The Black Woman's Guide to Starting Your Own Business,* by Cheryl Broussard, is a look at the businesses operated by fifty women who were interviewed by the author. Their hardships, triumphs, and lessons are shared with the reader.

*Small Business Taxes Made Easy: How to Increase Your Deductions, Reduce What You Owe, and Boost Your Profits* by Eva Rosenberg. Eva is also known as "Tax Mamma" and provides a helpful newsletter at **www.taxmamma.com**.

*Small Time Operator: How to Start Your Own Small Business, Keep Your Books, Pay Your Taxes, and Stay Out of Trouble,* by Bernard Kamaroff, CPA, is an easy to understand book that's been around in revised editions for more than twenty years.

*The Small Business Money Guide, Smart Strategies for Growing Your Business,* and *Working Solo* are all books by Terri Lonier. She also has a website at **www.workingsolo.com** that contains helpful information for the small business owner.

*The Stay-at-Home Mom's Guide to Making Money: How to Choose the Business That's Right for You Using the Skills and Interests You Already Have* by Liz Folger provides ideas and tips for getting a business going at home.

*201 Great Ideas for Small Businesses* and *The Entrepreneur's Desk Reference* by Jane Applegate aren't specifically geared to women entrepreneurs, but both will be helpful in growing your business.

*What Business Should I Start: Seven Steps to Discovering the Ideal Business for You* by Rhonda Abrams and Scott Cook is for the person who wants to start a business but can't decide what kind. The book walks you through various business possibilities, making sure they meet your needs, suit your personality, fit your interests and goals, and have a realistic chance of success.

*The Women's Home-Based Business Book of Answers* by Maria Bailey provides good information about operating a business. Many of the answers are provided by the forty successful home-based businesswomen interviewed for the book.

*The Work-At-Home Mom's Guide to Home Business* and *It's a Jungle Out There and a Zoo in Here: Run Your Home Business without Letting It Overrun You* are two books by Cheryl Demas, the founder of Work at Home Moms (**www.WAHM.com**).

*Working from Home, Home Businesses You Can Buy, Making Money With Your Computer At Home, The Entrepreneurial Parent: How to Earn Your Living and Still Enjoy Your Family, Your Work and Your Life,* and *The Best Home Businesses For People 50+* all by Paul and Sarah Edwards. These gurus of self-employment have sold over one million books aimed at helping the small business owner. They also write small business columns for a number of publications and host a radio show for entrepreneurs.

# State-by-State Taxation Department Information

D

Unless you live in one of the states that doesn't have an income tax, your state has an agency that performs functions parallel to those of the IRS. For some states, this is the agency that handles your personal and business tax return while a different agency deals with payroll taxes if you have employees.

If your state has an excise or sales tax and your product or service is taxable, look in the white or blue government pages of your phone book, in the state section, to find the agency responsible for collecting this tax. Look in the same area of the phone book, in the city section, to find the business license division. Contact that office about requirements for operating your business within the city.

Some localities have *one-stop shops*, which are a collaboration between city and county agencies to provide all the needed information about licenses, permits, sales taxes, and so on, in one location.

Some cities publish booklets, with names such as *Starting a Business in* [Name of city] that tell you all the requirements for operating a business in your locale. Your city or state Chamber of Commerce may publish a business guide specific to your area. This appendix contains the telephone number and website address for each state's and the District of Columbia's taxing authority.

**Alabama Dept. of Revenue**
www.ador.state.al.us
334-242-1170

**Alaska Dept. of Revenue**
www.revenue.state.ak.us
800-733-8813

**Arizona Dept. of Revenue**
www.revenue.state.az.us
800-352-4090

**Arkansas Dept. of Finance
and Administration**
www.arkansas.gov/dfa
800-882-9275

**California Franchise Tax Board**
www.ftb.ca.gov
800-852-5711

**Colorado Dept. of Revenue**
www.colorado.gov/taxes.htm
303-238-7378

**Connecticut Dept. of Revenue**
www.ct.gov/drs
800-382-9463

**Delaware Dept. of Finance**
www.state.de.us/revenue
302-577-8200

**District of Columbia Office of Tax
and Revenue**
http://cfo.dc.gov/otr/site/default.asp
202-727-4TAX

**Florida Dept. of Revenue**
www.myflorida.com/dor
800-352-3671

**Georgia Dept. of Revenue**
www2.state.ga.us/Departments/DOR
404-417-4480

**Hawaii Dept. of Taxation**
www.state.hi.us/tax/tax.html
800-222-3229

**Idaho Dept. of Revenue and Taxation**
www.tax.idaho.gov/index.html
800-972-7660

**Illinois Dept. of Revenue**
www.revenue.state.il.us
800-732-8866

**Indiana Dept. of Revenue**
www.ai.org/dor/index.html
317-233-4018

**Iowa Dept. of Revenue**
www.state.ia.us/tax/index.html
800-367-3388

**Kansas Dept. of Revenue**
www.ksrevenue.org
785-368-8222

**Kentucky Revenue Cabinet**
www.revenue.ky.gov
502-564-4581

**Louisiana Dept. of Revenue**
www.rev.state.la.us
225-219-2448

**Maine Revenue Service**
www.state.me.us/revenue
207-626-8475

**Maryland Revenue Admin.**
www.comp.state.md.us
800-MD-TAXES

**Massachusetts Dept. of Revenue**
www.dor.state.ma.us
800-392-6089

**Michigan Dept. of the Treasury**
www.michigan.gov/treasury
800-367-6263

**Minnesota Dept. of Revenue**
www.taxes.state.mn.us
651-296-3781

**Mississippi State Tax Commission**
www.mstc.state.ms.us
601-923-7300

**Missouri Dept. of Revenue**
www.dor.state.mo.us
573-522-1578

**Montana Dept. of Revenue**
www.state.mt.us/revenue
406-444-6900

**Nebraska Dept. of Revenue**
www.revenue.state.ne.us
800-742-7474

**Nevada Dept. of Taxation**
www.tax.state.nv.us
775-684-2000

**New Hampshire Dept. of Revenue Administration**
www.state.nh.us/revenue
603-271-2191

**New Jersey Division of Taxation**
www.state.nj.us/treasury/taxation
609-292-6400

**New Mexico Taxation & Revenue**
www.state.nm.us/tax
505-827-0700

**New York State Dept. of Taxation and Finance**
www.tax.state.ny.us
800-225-5829

**North Carolina Dept. of Revenue**
www.dor.state.nc.us
877-252-3052

**North Dakota Office of State Tax Commissioner**
www.state.nd.us/taxdpt
701-328-2770

**Ohio Dept. of Taxation**
www.tax.ohio.gov
800-282-1780

**Oklahoma Tax Commission**
www.oktax.state.ok.us
405-521-3160

**Oregon Dept. of Revenue**
www.dor.state.or.us
800-356-4222

**Pennsylvania Dept. of Revenue**
www.revenue.state.pa.us
717-787-8201

**Rhode Island Division of Taxation**
www.tax.state.ri.us
401-222-1040

**South Carolina Dept. of Revenue**
www.sctax.org
843-852-3600

**South Dakota Dept. of Revenue**
www.taxesindepth.com/state-taxes-
South-Dakota.html
605-773-3311

**Tennessee Dept. of Revenue**
www.state.tn.us/revenue
800-342-1003

**Texas Comptroller of Public Accounts**
www.cpa.state.tx.us
877-662-8375

**Utah State Tax Commission**
www.tax.utah.gov
800-662-4335

**Vermont Department of Taxes**
www.state.vt.us/tax
802-828-2865

**Virginia Dept. of Taxation**
www.tax.state.va.us
804-367-8031

**Washington Dept. of Revenue**
www.dor.wa.gov
800-647-7706

**West Virginia State Tax Dept.**
www.state.wv.us/taxdiv
800-982-8297

**Wisconsin Dept. of Revenue**
www.dor.state.wi.us
608-266-2772

**Wyoming Dept. of Revenue**
http://revenue.state.wy.us
307-777-7961

# Index

# M

M.Y.O.B.®, 39
MACRS (Modified Accelerated Cost
  Recovery System), 84, 85, 86, 88
magazines, 120, 123
maintenance, 93, 120, 123
McBee®, 38
meals, 19, 109, 110, 123
  travel, 114
medical expenses, 116, 153, 155
Medicare, 60, 63
Microsoft Excel®, 39
Microsoft Money®, 39
mileage, 19, 93, 99
mileage method, 104, 148
money in, 37
mortgage interest, 93, 96, 155

# N

net operating loss, 153
net profit, 43
New Hire Reporting, 65
no change audit, 191
number-phobia, 1

# O

Offer In Compromise, 180
office supplies, 123
officers, 7
one-write systems, 38
ordinary and necessary, 77
outstanding deposits, 16

# P

partnerships, 4, 6, 9, 11, 12, 13, 22, 51,
  57, 121, 127, 132, 139, 151, 163
  with lovers or friends, 10
payroll records, 19
payroll taxes, 63, 64, 121, 123
Peachtree Accounting®, 39
Peachtree Complete Accounting®, 39
*per diem* rate, 110
permits, 11, 12

personal digital assistant (PDA), 19
personal exemption, 175
personal service corporations, 7, 9
petty cash, 27, 28
phaseout, 155
postage, 123
prices, 44
principal repayments, 26
profit and loss statement, 42, 43
profit motive, 150

# Q

qualified distributions, 132
QuickBooks®, 39
Quicken Home and Business®, 39
Quicken®, 39

# R

real estate taxes, 93, 96, 155
receipts, 18, 19, 31, 37, 109, 110
receipts sheets, 34, 35
recordkeeping, 17, 18, 19, 193
  on computer, 39
regularly and exclusively, 92, 94
reimbursements, 25, 27
remaining tax liability, 164
rent, 96, 123
renters insurance, 115
repairs, 120, 123
reporting losses, 150
retirement plans, 120, 129, 130, 131,
  132, 133, 134, 135, 136, 137, 142, 153
Roth IRAs, 131, 132

# S

S corporations, 7, 8, 9, 10, 139, 151, 163
safe harbor, 55
Safeguard®, 38
sales taxes, 121, 123
Saver's Tax Credit, 136
Schedule A, 94, 120, 122
Schedule C, 6, 23, 32, 94, 98, 99, 121,
  122, 139, 140, 142, 146, 147, 148,
  150, 151, 155, 156

# About the Author

**Jan Zobel** has her own tax preparation and consultation business in which, for 25 years, she has specialized in working with self-employed people. As an enrolled agent (a tax professional licensed by the IRS), Ms. Zobel has prepared over 8,000 tax returns for small business owners. In addition to preparing returns and doing individual tax consultations for nearly 500 clients each year, Jan teaches small business tax classes throughout the western United States.

Her tax articles have appeared on the *Microsoft* and *Charles Schwab* websites, as well as in many magazines and newspapers. She frequently is quoted as a tax expert by such publications as *Newsweek, WallStreetJournal.com, Entrepreneur Magazine, Working Mother,* and *Quicken.com.*

Citing her ability to make complex tax topics understandable by the average person, Jan was given the Small Business Administrations' Accountant Advocate of the Year Award. She also is listed in Who's Who of American Women and Who's Who of Finance and Industry.

Jan lives in the San Francisco Bay Area the majority of the year and in Kailua-Kona, Hawaii the remaining months. She can be reached via her website **www.JanZtax.com.**